CRYSTAL
CO·CREATORS

CHANNELED BY
DOROTHY ROEDER

CRYSTAL CO✦CREATORS

Channeled
by
Dorothy
Roeder

Cover art by
Tria (Trish) Schwartz

ISBN 0-929385-40-3
Published by
**Light Technology
Publishing**
P.O. Box 3540
Flagstaff, AZ 86003
1-800-450-0985
e-mail: sedonajo@sedonajo.com
www.lighttechnology.com

Printed by

Sedona Color Graphics
■ ■   ■ PRINTING SPECIALISTS
2020 Contractors Road
Sedona, AZ 86336

To the Crystal Kingdom
and to those who are using
crystals for their own
transformation

OTHER CHANNELED BOOKS
by DOROTHY ROEDER

REACH FOR US

Your cosmic teachers and friends are here for you! Who are they and what do they look like? Can you connect with them to learn your part in The Cosmic plan?

Dorothy Roeder channels messages from 37 Cosmic beings, Ascended Masters, Archangels and the Space Command. Their teachings and inspiring guidance are vital to understanding their roles and yours in bringing the New Age on Earth for humanity.

Focusing on love, they offer assistance that permits us to experience ourselves as Divine Beings in the Divine blueprint.

ISBN 0-929385-25-X $13.00

THE NEXT DIMENSION IS LOVE

Ranoash through Dorothy Roeder portrays beings from another dimension, parallel to ours yet far beyond it who give their views of what is happening on Earth now. They describe how our fear of change threatens our survival as a race and limits our ability to reach our full potential.

It is humanity's special capacity to love that is our contribution to the Cosmos.

Discover how we can help them help us and teach the rest of the universe about creating love. Explore their answers to the questions of our time – a time for healing and transformation.

ISBN 0-929385-50-0 $11.95

Table of Contents

Table of Color Photos

Notes from the Author

The information given in this book is not meant to replace what has been received by other channels or through experiment and experience. It is simply another viewpoint and it is hoped it will complement the information given through others and make your work with crystals more effective and enjoyable. The mineralogical data was taken from the references given, mostly from Simon & Schuster's *Guide to Rocks and Minerals* and *Guide to Gems and Precious Stones*. Both are beautifully illustrated with color photos for every entry. They are highly recommended. The reference, *Gems, Their Sources, Descriptions and Identification*, by R. Webster gives a good explanation of how crystals are classified by system.

Nobody, however great in their consciousness, has the whole answer to anything until they can use Source's perspective. It is possible that even Source perspective is incomplete or we would not be trying to expand it. While I have made some attempt to make this book as complete as possible, it cannot have the whole picture. It is the whole picture as seen through this channel at this stage of development. If everyone in the world contributed, it would be more complete. So, the teachers seemed more interested in giving out new information here than validating or redoing what already exists. I have tried to summarize what seemed appropriate from the already available material. This is included, where available, under the sections headed "Traditional and other sources." The information in these sections about elixirs comes from *Gem Elixirs and Vibrational Healing, Vol. I*, by Gurudas. If you are interested in doing healing work you will want to study the information there on enhancing elixirs with pyramids and colored light, and their use in oils. The dream symbols are from *Watch your Dreams*, by Ann Rae Colton. Other sources are listed with the references. The research by Kunz seems to be used by almost everyone who writes about crystal legends and lore.

The metaphysical properties are all channeled. I sit down at my computer, "tune in" to my channel, think about the particular crystal, or hold it, and write down what comes into my head. I do not go into trance. Some of the information I have felt and verified myself through working with them. Some of the information is new to me as I write it. The information comes from a group of individuals at spiritual levels who are interested in helping you understand yourself and your purpose. None have physical or astral bodies.

One, who particularly helps me focus the flow of information, is Vywamus, a very cosmic being who is working through our planetary Logos, to help us clear our misperceptions about ourselves so we can work from our hearts, in harmony with our divine souls. Another is Lenduce, Vywamus's teacher, a fully developed CoCreator. The only step remaining in his/her (English doesn't have a pronoun for someone who has combined and balanced perfectly the male and female energies, except "it," and that doesn't sound right) evolution is to return to Source Itself. At the Harmonic Convergence, in August 1987, he/she brought the energy of his/her heart into a special focus which surrounds Earth with a beautiful, joyous, all-encompassing love. Lenduce is serving as teacher to all the kingdoms of Earth, plant, animal, mineral, and human.

There is also Koryu, a "Crystal Master" from the Galactic Core. The interests of this being go beyond the crystals themselves into the structure of creation and its evolving perfection. There is Archangel Gabriel, whose substance serves as the whole of what is the astral level or plane of creative emotions for our universe. He/She is also involved in making clearer the crystalline structure of the Divine Plan and is working and coordinating efforts to shape the creative thoughts and feelings of Earth into a vehicle that will align with it. The whole angelic kingdom is constantly clearing as many negative thought forms from Earth as we are willing to let go of.

Some information came from the group soul of the crystals themselves. Boji Stones and Herkimer Diamonds, for instance, are highly individualized and have very clear ideas about their role in humanity's transformation process. Other ideas about using crystals come from various members of the Space Command who will be happy to teach any of you about using crystals. You can reach them through your own crystals and your own spiritual connection.

All of these wonderful teachers are available to all of you, if you are willing to accept that you are part of the whole and that at least part of yourself is in contact with the whole. You have only to release your sense of isolation and separateness and open to the infinite flow of knowledge and love that is always available to enrich and support your life.

We haven't tried to include every mineral or stone known. Each part of Earth has its own special energy and gifts. New mineral finds are occurring all the time. Some are big and some very limited. Once a mine is exhausted, the material is harder to find and you will possibly never find it. Use some of the general guides given here and your own intuition in learning to use them.

We all hope that this book will help you expand your awareness of the support that the universe is sending you through the Crystal Kingdom. You don't need crystals to evolve, but for those of you who love them and feel drawn to use them, they are a wonderful tool for understanding more of yourself.

Dorothy Roeder
Phoenix, AZ

CoCreating with Crystals

Crystals are not magic and will not do anything for you. They are wonderful tools that can assist you in your life to do your best to realize your full divine potential. They will help you express your abilities to the extent to whichplants and you are willing to go with them. They can be mirrors that teach you that you are light and show you the ideal you hold within yourself. They can become good friends and coworkers with whom you feel comfortable and familiar as you take more responsibility for making the world a better place. They can be a key to knowledge that the world needs now at this critical time of great changes. They can be a connection with Earth that helps you be a more effective cocreator with her.

If Earth is going to reach the full potential of these new times, we all, as part of Earth, must each do our share. Crystals are part of the consciousness of Earth, with humanity, plants and animals and we must learn to consciously work together with Earth to create a place where all can be free to realize their full creative potential. Humanity, as the most evolved part of Earth's consciousness at the physical level, bears the most responsibility for preserving and assisting its evolution. The Crystal Kingdom is willing to do its part to assist and is very eager to share love in as many ways as are possible here. Admiring and using crystals is one way of acquiring knowledge from many dimensions, past, present, and future, and a way of allowing crystals to help us.

Consciousness in Crystals

Crystals have fascinated people since the beginnings of life on Earth. Their beauty and durability have often given them great value. But we want to talk about their spiritual value, not their monetary value. In order to recognize the nature of their spiritual value, we must first recognize that they, as well as everything else on Earth and in the universe, have life or consciousness.

The consciousness of a crystal is not as fully developed as that of a person. It must be different, of course, because a crystal cannot see, feel, or hear as we do, nor can it express itself as we do. It can only express itself at the physical level through its color and shape and the way it reflects light. But at soul level, there are many more possiblities for creative expression. At this nonphysical level of consciousness there is wisdom, knowledge and even will. This will is expressed as a desire to be physical and to reflect the beauty of the Creator and the Divine Plan.

Contrary to what you might see or believe about life on Earth, there is a purpose to it which only the Creator can see perfectly. One purpose of life is to learn to understand who that Creator is, but It is so vast and has so many variations that it takes billions of lives to do this. No individual consciousness can do it alone. Each must learn to tap into universal consciousness, offering his or her learning and wisdom before he or she can share that of the whole. Life may be experienced in humanoid form or as an animal, plant, or mineral. Anything that has its own specific form can be thought of as reflecting some sort of guiding influence over its existence and having consciousness and the capability of evolving.

A crystal grows much more slowly than a person and is formed in the womb of Earth itself, in soil, rock, water. Somehow, guided by higher consciousness, the proper elements come together and precipitate out of their watery carrier, forming a wonderful array of beautiful and fascinating forms. Each place on Earth creates its own unique varieties, just as each set of human parents creates unique individuals in their own image. It is really more difficult to imagine how this could happen with such regularity by chance rather than by intention.

Each place produces individual mineral specimens that can be traced to their origins, but there are certain similarities among all minerals of a type that place them in the whole pattern of what Earth creates. Quartz has a basic six-sided crystalline form wherever it is found, but variations in that form exist which make Arkansas quartz look and feel different from that of Madagascar or Brazil.

The consciousness that guides the building of form is soul or spirit. It is a higher consciousness that has awareness of subtle energies and dimensions beyond what we see at the physical level. This higher consciousness can see and understand the Divine Plan more completely than we can. Earth is a sort of collection of many consciousnesses that have chosen to come together to work out the meaning and purpose of the Divine Plan. These many consciousnesses are divided into groups, sub-groups, sub-sub-groups, and so on. The smaller working units are groups of individual consciousnesses associated with a particular place on physical Earth.

Each of these small groups maintains a connection to that higher level of consciousness which is more aware of the whole picture of what is happening on Earth. For humanity, that is a group of divine beings called the Planetary Hierarchy, the White Brotherhood or sometimes the Brotherhood of Saints. (Planetary Hierarchy might be best because it is certainly not limited to males.) For crystals, the higher connection is an angel who serves as the consciousness of the mineral kingdom.

This angel, also called a deva, includes in its sphere of influence other angels who serve to ensoul specific kinds of crystals and, in turn, guide still others who make up the sub-groups down to the place-specific groups. Those crystals which are developed enough in their individuality have their own angel who is part of the crystal hierarchy. So quartz has its own angel who guides all quartz crystals.

There are many angels who work within its guidance as the guide for each specific place. For instance, unique quartz crystals are found near Herkimer, New York. Each one forms individually in its own "womb of clay." They are quite sparkling and are called Herkimer

Diamonds. As a group they are special, but each individual crystal is unique and has its own angelic consciousness. This makes them quite fun and useful to work with because they are able to focus on individual purposes. Quartzite, on the other hand, is a massive conglomeration of tiny Quartz crystals formed into one whole deposit in the Earth which could extend for miles. If you break off two pieces of a mountain made of Quartzite, they would probably not have individual angels but would remain under the guidance of the angel of the mountain.

When a crystal forms on a substrate that connects it to many other crystals, it shares the consciousness of the whole group. If it should be broken off from the group, it probably will develop a consciousness of its own and gain its own angel. When this occurs naturally underground, the crystal remains in the Earth and the broken area heals over, eventually forming another point on the broken end if it has enough time. These crystals become very secure in their own individuality, or you could say their individuality is very well expressed in their physical form. They become aware of existence separate from the group soul and develop individuality, "earning" an individual soul focus. They are especially useful for healing because they have had the opportunity to learn to be perfectly whole in their individuality. A crystal that is dynamited out of the Earth and its substrate, on the other hand, might need to receive healing for a time rather than be able to give it.

A crystal can be cut and enhanced by someone who tries to understand it, so that it is not damaged but is given new life through the love of the person working with it. So the individuality of a precious diamond is aided in its development by a consciousness who has abilities it does not. Its power is refined and focused as it is carefully and thoughtfully cut by someone who understands it. The best gem-cutters might not recognize that they have been guided by the angelic consciousness of the crystal as well as by their own knowledge and artistic sense, but they have learned to tune in at an intuitive level. They must develop this inner sense about the stones they work with or they will never be really successful at what they do. Their love of their work allows them to help the gem perfect its understanding of itself and that is, ultimately, the goal of any consciousness.

On the other hand, a crystal that is badly cut might be unable to express truth as it sees it, and this distortion of its energy makes it very difficult to use. It might bring "bad luck" to those who work with it rather than protection and love, not because it is full of evil, but because it cannot express itself as it needs to to bring out its true potential. It is like a child who never receives love and therefore does not know how to give love as it would like to. It might grow up to become a person who cannot contribute positively to society.

How Do Crystals Work?

To understand how crystals can help us, we need to look some more at what consciousness is. Let's say for now that the perfect understanding of the Creator is Its consciousness and this is expressed through love. This love is greater than anything we can understand and must support the purposes of everything that is experiencing life or consciousness at this time. It becomes light when consciousness directs it into a specific purpose. Then light becomes the substance from which the universe and everything in it is made. Each one of us is light and is created because of the desire of the Creator to expand Its use of love. The Creator is always maintaining everything by the love flowing throughout everything which It has created. This love is present everywhere as a connection into the whole. It is an infinite, everlasting continuum that puts everything into contact with everything else by being part of the whole.

Humanity, when it became physical, forgot that it was part of the whole, but crystals did not. Their physical bodies do not cut them off from the spiritual knowledge that they are still in the flow of universal love. They are a doorway into the wisdom and experience of the whole. Your mind may have learned to say that you are part of the Creator's love, but your bodies and your cells probably have not. You can connect into the flow of universal love without a crystal, certainly, but if you sometimes feel separated and even alienated from everything but your present experiencing, they can help you get reconnected. They do this by showing your subconscious, which runs your life and your body, how to connect with that universal flow at the physical and emotional level. When you hold a crystal to seek help, to communicate or simply to admire its form, you make a connection with it that is formed from love. Your subconscious focuses in on the crystal, sees how it is flowing with its universal connection and realizes that it can do the same thing.

If you work with the crystal intently and consistently enough it will show you how to heal your own separation from the whole. It can help you resolve your negative emotions into expressions of love. It can help you understand the meaning of who you are. It can help you restore the divine light connection into your physical body so it can move out of the patterns of separation from perfection and reflect the ideal. It can show you the crystal form of your own ideal and show you how to use it at the physical level. It will also reflect back to your own love so that you learn to appreciate and understand it more fully.

To summarize, creation begins with consciousness. Thought and knowledge are aspects of consciousness. The basic stuff of which the universe is made is love because the Creator is love. That love becomes light when it is transformed into objective purpose by will. Thought organizes this light which comprises creation into shapes that are, to us, crystalline. Crystals therefore mirror the shape of the Creator's thought and reflect the shape of creation. Quartz represents the ideal expression of love at the physical level on Earth.

What Do Crystals Do?

We have talked mostly about Quartz so far because it carries the basic pattern of the ideal for humanity and Earth. The shape of the light flow through its crystal matrix is similar to that through your DNA, so that it can serve as a template for the ideal flow. It doesn't distort the light flow with hate, fear, loneliness, and so forth, as some hidden parts of yourself might be doing, so it shows you how to use the patterns of life the Creator has given in the ideal way. Quartz, then, shows your subconscious, and therefore your body, how to use the ideal to create perfection in your body and in your life. It makes it available to you and literally shows you how to flow the ideal at all levels of self. This subconscious recognition of how to use the ideal at levels that might not have seen it before will support other work that you do at more conscious levels to understand life and your divine purpose.

Other types of crystals complement Quartz in showing you how to use light. Calcite is almost as common as Quartz and is a basic prototype for organizing the flow of light. It shows your body how to use the electrical components of light, whereas Quartz manifests the basic fact that light is electrical in nature. Calcite is important now because the Earth is moving into a new, higher-energy format. You see it as moving into an area of space that is more radioactive. This is part of Earth's evolution in learning to use light creatively, a sort of infusion of new material to keep things from getting stagnant. We can't learn anything new about ourselves if we just do the same things over and over, so the Creator keeps urging us along in expanding our potential by always giving us new things to work with.

Many minerals form microcrystalline masses of very tiny crystals compacted together. Actually, each of these tiny crystals has its own angel or consciousness, but they are embryonic at this point and cared for by the greater angel who ensouls the whole mass. When they are broken into smaller pieces and shaped into pebbles by nature or carved by man, they can begin the process of realizing their individuality and expanding their consciousness. If you have one that you use and enjoy, you are helping this process. Just as a child's perception of itself is enhanced by its parents' love, so a stone learns what it is by sharing its light with you.

Some stones like Onyx and Agate are often dyed to make the common pieces more interesting, but don't refuse to work with them for that reason. It won't necessarily ruin them to make them more beautiful. Agate is now being dyed a beautiful violet which actually energizes it and adds the energy of the violet ray which is bringing in the new age. See how a stone feels or looks to you and let that be your guide rather than someone else's beliefs. The dye is only on the outside, after all. It doesn't necessarily take anything away from it. They are all healing, energizing, balancing, and uplifting. They are complete in their ability to recognize the whole ideal, but each has its special uses for which it is particularly adapted.

How to Choose a Crystal

You are the best one to choose your own crystal. It is sort of like choosing a mate. Others might think they know best, and maybe they do, but you might not ever be really satisfied unless you yourself choose. If you are the sort of person who prefers to let others make your decisions, crystals can help you learn to rely on your own feelings and knowledge. We would suggest that Quartz is a good first choice because its uses are so basic, but if you feel drawn to something else, go with that.

If you find your own crystal in the Earth and dig it yourself, you become the crystal's mother in a sense, because you have brought it out of its womb. Such a crystal is special and can "bond" with you so that it understands you and your problems in a very personal way. Carving or shaping a stone for yourself can produce similar results if the stone agrees to the process. How do you know what a stone wants? Listen to it by paying attention to your feelings about it. Don't let your desires override other messages that may be coming to you. If the purpose for which you choose it flows well, it probably agrees with your decision.

Accepting that crystals do have consciousness and their own purpose or will is probably the first step in choosing the right one for yourself. By recognizing that its needs are as important as your own, you can form a working partnership that will help you both. Crystals, remember, are using love unconditionally, so they will usually do whatever they can to help you achieve your purpose. If you are choosing to align with the Divine Plan, it will be easy to work with them because they are flowing the light of that Plan as their consciousness and form.

If you don't have the opportunity to go out and dig for crystals, you might receive one as a gift or you will probably buy one. Let your intuition be your guide here. So often a person will look at what is available and immediately pick up one and hold it. Then he or she will start looking for the right one. The mind starts working on finding what is "right" and seeks out the advice of someone who is supposed to know which one is best. The person doesn't seem to realize that she or he already knows and is holding it.

Quartz that has "clouds" in it and is not completely transparent will tend to hold energy and a program better. Clear ones are the best transmitters. The huge "Earthkeeper" quartz crystals are not clear and are already programmed with vast amounts of knowledge about Earth's past, present, and future. They work by keying into specific aspects of the knowledge of the whole, the past or even the future, called the Akashic Records, for those who are ready for it. As you work with crystals, you will find that many have specific programs they are working on, but they will be willing to fit yours into what they are doing. You will find the right one because your soul and that of the crystal will work together to help you find each other.

Cleansing Your Crystal

Once you have found your crystal you need to make it part of yourself. If you dug it yourself, washing off the dirt will be sufficient cleansing. As you carry it in your pocket or hold it, you become acquainted and get used to each other. That is all that is necessary. If you bought it, it might need to be cleaned. There are various ways to do this. You primarily want to get rid of any energy that may be sticking to it that is not compatible with yours. One good way is just to hold the crystal in your right hand and imagine light flowing from you into the crystal, sweeping away anything that is not needed. You can also hold the crystal under running water while doing this. Salt water has traditionally been recommended, but it should be very dilute and is not often necessary. Too much salt distorts the crystal's energy. If you need soap or solvent to clean it, that's okay; follow with water and light. Clear Quartz is routinely soaked in acid (usually oxalic acid) to remove stains, but the crystals usually enjoy having their full beauty revealed.

Some crystals like time in the sunlight periodically to realign with its light. This is very energizing for Clear Quartz, but will cause Amethyst to fade. (Don't heat your Amethyst either or it will change color. That's how much Citrine is produced.) Other crystals like moonlight. If a crystal has been abused or misused it might benefit from being buried in Earth for a time, three days to a few weeks. Again, let your intuition be your guide. If you need energy from the Earth, burying your crystal for a time might help it bring you that energy. But crystals are already quite comfortable with being physical; after all they've been in the Earth for thousands, maybe millions of years already. They accept that they are part of Earth so all crystals are already "grounded." The burying process is usually more for you than the crystal.

Not much "sticks" to transparent crystals. They are clear transmitters. Dark or opaque ones might need to be cleaned periodically with light or water. If you have some sort of polarizing device, that would be very useful also. You can make your own polarizer by getting some copper wire and making it into a loop that is big enough to pass the crystal through. Or just move it over the crystal a few times. This will realign the crystal energy without damaging any patterns you might have set up to work with it. Black Obsidian is a good stone for removing negativity, but it tends to hold on to energy. If you let it sit for a time the negativity will dissipate, but if you use it intensively, it needs to be cleansed often and the copper coil is one good way to do that.

Using Crystals

The most important thing to do in using crystals is to let it know what you want to do with it. If you want it to help you heal yourself or someone else, tell it. If you want it to help you communicate with friends or teachers in other dimensions or levels of spiritual reality, it can do that if you ask. If you want it to help you focus your meditations, let it know. Choose your crystal with the purpose for it in mind, if possible. Some crystals can do many things, but most will be more effective if you do one thing at a time and give yourself and the crystal some time to work out the best relationship and procedure.

You need to be clear in your own mind about what you want to do. The crystal can help you do that. If you want it to do something that is inappropriate or impossible, it will let you know. Remember that it can't do anything for you. It is not magic in itself. It shows you, by its example, how to be a clear channel for light and Divine Will. The magic comes when you are able to use your full creative potential to achieve what you want or need to do. The crystal can help you learn to do that or help you connect with someone else who can.

Don't be too specific about exactly how you want to accomplish what you and the crystal are going to do, unless you are very experienced or have specific guidance from an expert. Once you have decided on what you want to do, let the method of doing it evolve on its own. You might use a technique you learned from someone else as a starting point. But don't be rigid in its use. If variations begin to occur to you, try them and see how they feel. What works best for someone else will not necessarily be best for you. Do try your best to observe how the process is working with all your senses, even your unconscious ones. This allows you to make necessary adjustments as you go. The more you are open to the flow of the process at all levels, the more you will learn about what is going on at all levels. Practice and being open to new ways of looking at things will create the vision and the wisdom you seek.

In meditating with a crystal, many find it helpful to hold one, or to hold one in each hand. If you are learning to channel, crystals can help you feel secure about connecting with an energy that seems to be outside yourself. They can't make any connections for you but they can show you how they connect with the creative flow of consciousness that is always available everywhere. Imagine the light from a divine source flowing into your crystal, lighting it up and making it radiant. Then imagine your whole self responding to that flow in the same way. You can also set the crystal in front of you with a light behind or under it to make the image more real, if you like. If you practice meditation with your crystal regularly, I guarantee you something positive will happen. It won't be the same for everyone and it might not be clearly definable.

Any time you ask for light it will be there. Again, don't expect any particular set of events beyond your defined purpose or you might set up limits to what you can achieve. Often the light you invoke feels wonderful for a time, and then, as you use more of it, it begins to light up new areas of self that might have been hidden and now need work. This is a very positive process, although it might be uncomfortable. You need to be able to use all those dark, hidden areas of self in order to have access to your full power.

Crystals, at their conscious level, are very attuned to the vibrations of the Divine Plan. They have a clear awareness of the Creator's plans and hopes for Earth. They work best when you are also striving to be a creative part of that Divine Plan. As they flow with the Creator's love, they will draw you into that flow magnetically. They are quite willing to serve as a focus of love which can guide you as you explore your creative abilities and shape your life and thus your world.

Crystals for Healing

We have already mentioned that self-healed crystals are good for healing. Madagascar Quartz also works very well. Boji Stones are very good at taking away pain and balancing energies. They don't need to be charged, just let them know what you want by placing them over the area that needs to be healed. A small crystal can be charged for healing. Hold it in your dominant hand and imagine love and healing light flowing from the universe through your heart and into the crystal. When you feel that you are finished place the crystal wherever healing is needed on yourself or another.

You don't have to be in contact with another to heal him or her. You will need some sort of request or agreement or the person will not be open to receiving the healing. When you are ready, simply charge the crystal with healing light as before and imagine placing the crystal wherever it is needed. You can also imagine the person standing in front of you and send the light through the crystal to him or her. If you don't have permission, send the energy to the person's soul and ask it to use the energy in an appropriate way. Never use a crystal to try to force on someone else something she or he does not want. If what you want is not part of that person's consciousness or will, it will not work and the person's energy structure will not accept it. Crystals focus energy very specifically and will intensify any negative repercussions back to you.

However, if your intentions are loving you will not have to worry about harming anyone. You do have to allow others to use the energy you send in whatever ways they find best, even if that is not what you desired. As you practice with crystals, the gifts of knowing and seeing how they work will come.

When using crystals for others, be sensitive to their feelings. Crystals have been used as weapons in the past, and if someone who has been injured by one believes you are harming him or her, it is possible that you will. You need to be clear in your motives also. Many of us have subconscious problems that can influence our better, clearer intentions. If something should go wrong, look very carefully inside yourself to see where the problem might be. As you bring more light into yourself by working with crystals, problems will come up that you must accept and, eventually, release. This is good and a benefit of working with crystal energy, but might not always be comfortable. Let the crystals help you clear confusion and negativity out of your light field.

Crystal Elixirs

Elixirs are water that has been charged with the energy of specific crystals. Water is almost magical in its ability to accept and hold various energies and transfer them wherever needed. The simplest way to make an elixir is to set a glass of water in the sun with the crystal in it for a few hours. Two hours is usually enough, but you can go up to twenty-four hours to incorporate the balanced energy of a full cycle. More is not necessarily better here. If you want to store the elixir for a time, make it with at least 50% brandy. Otherwise use distilled water. When you are ready to use it, you need just a few drops in a glass of water.

Minerals or other contaminants might alter the properties of the elixir. Distilled water is best. Use stones that are natural, not stabilized or dyed. Those might be fine or even better for other uses, but not here. For consistent results, the stone should be as pure as possible. Aqua Aura and Rainbow Quartz are exceptions to this rule. The silver or gold that is added is an activator and these stones make excellent elixirs for transformation, healing, and spiritual connections.

All elixirs used to energize and most of those used for healing are best prepared in the Sun. Sunlight is the bringer of life and the primary carrier for divine nurturing and healing. Sunlight emphasizes yang energy, moonlight, yin. If you are treating a fever or wish to emphasize receptivity, use moonlight. This applies also to those used for some specifically female problems. Elixirs prepared in moonlight will be best for conditions where there is too much energy. But, look at this carefully. If the energy excess is caused by blockage, you might need Sun energy to open it and relieve the pressure. Elixirs made by moonlight take longer, one to three nights. Keep them in the dark during the day.

You might want to boil the water and the containers before you use them. This is not always necessary, but everything should be clean and free of any contaminants. Glass bowls are best. Crystal (*not* manmade lead crystal) is excellent if you can afford it but not necessary. Any design on the bowl can influence the energy going into the elixir. Designs or insignia on the bowl have the potential for research. An Om symbol, for instance, might add energy for meditation elixirs or even for healing. We suggest working without them until you are familar with how the elixirs work and feel. In Atlantis bottles or bowls were often carved out of various kinds of crystal for the purpose of making elixirs. Amethyst and Jade were used the most often, Amethyst for spiritual attunement and Jade for healing. But you don't really need anything that elaborate.

A quiet, clear area is best for making elixirs. If there is a great deal of confusion in the area or if you are experiencing negative emotional states, those will be instilled into your elixirs. You can protect your elixirs during their preparation by putting them under a pyramid or a pyramid shape. This can bring in a stronger potential for physical effectiveness. We suggest experimenting with other things. Four Quartz points placed around them will provide protection. You might add Magnetite, Hematite, Obsidian, or Black Tourmaline for grounding and protection. If you are making the elixir for a specific person, placing a crystal nearby that belongs to that person, one that is used a great deal and is attuned to his or her specific energies, will make it more useful. A Ruby or Sapphire will always be useful for developing the maximum potential for your elixir and aligning it with the Creator's Will.

Use your own creativity and intuition always. Remember, working with crystals is helping you expand your CoCreative abilities. Let the crystals and their angels communicate with you and teach you their secrets. You won't learn their secrets by reading books. The most useful secrets come through your heart as you experience working with crystals.

To use your elixirs, put 5-10 drops in a glass of distilled water and drink it, rub it or spray it over an area that is to be treated. If you make your own lotions, shampoos, and so on, you can use your elixirs in them. You can also use them in cooking. After six weeks to eight weeks, your subconscious will adapt to the influence of the crystal energy and they will begin to lose their effectiveness. Rotate a series of crystals that have similar effects, repeating them again in four to six months. Ruby and Peridot are notable exceptions to this and their benefits continue to grow for years.

Amethyst is still an excellent elixir to use generally. Its elixir will help cleanse your cells of impurities and release negativity while bringing in new, higher energy. Peridot elixir is also very good for healing and energizing your cells and balancing their energy flow. It helps the DNA align with the ideal in light and release imperfect patterns of using light. Moonstone makes an elixir that is especially good for calming emotions and bringing in a more balanced perspective. Clear Quartz will help clear and balance your drinking water in general. It is a good idea to keep a Quartz crystal in your water jug all the time, if you use one.

You will never create imbalance or harm anyone with your elixirs if your intentions are to help. If you are completely wrong in your selections, the worst that will happen is nothing, because you will just not be in alignment with the problem and so will be unable to effect a change in it. At best, the effects will be subtle but powerful. You can effect a shift of the body's energy patterns closer to the ideal. The ancient people used many stones by powdering them and taking them internally. With the increased energy levels being assimilated in light, you are able to use stones as elixirs instead. Destroying the stone is not necessary.

Elixirs alone will not change or heal anyone. Chronic disease, or any imbalance, is caused by misperceptions about oneself at the subconscious level. You heal yourself by removing these errors in your body's program and replacing them with unconditional love, joy, trust, peace, and forgiving. Elixirs help you to locate and heal these areas of self that cannot accept these pure qualities of love. They help you hold the ideal pattern in your body, but you must invoke it and do everything you can to make a place for it, accept it as part of yourself and keep it. If you refuse to look at yourself or feel that change is impossible, they cannot help you.

If you are ready to accept that you have the potential to be perfectly healthy and able to use your full creative power, if you are diligent in working with whatever life brings you without letting it get you down or control you, if you sincerely try to cultivate love, joy, trust, peace, and forgiveness in your life, crystals will be invaluable in helping you. They will carry the perfection you seek into your cells so that your physical body becomes, truly, the temple of your soul. Then your soul can really be a part of your life.

Crystal Grids

Quartz is usually the foundation of any crystal grid pattern. Its hexagonal shape mirrors the basic shape of the Divine Plan which flows as light, so three-, six-, and twelve-sided grids are the easiest to work with. Three crystals set equidistant from each other will help you manifest a particular purpose or thing. Three is a number of multiplication and communication. Six is the symbol of balance, so a grid of six crystals is good for healing the mind and calming emotions.

If you are doing healing body work, place six crystals around you and your patient. You will be creating a space that will support balance and harmony. It will enhance receptivity to healing energy and help the body to hold on to the ideal. At least three of the crystals should probably be Quartz. You could make the other three Calcite to make a better electrical connection to the divine flow. Much healing now goes into the mind and etheric brain and Calcite is especially helpful for that. You can add other stones without disturbing the energy framework of the Quartz grid if you add another pattern within the first. Moldavite would bring in an interdimensional approach and awareness of help from beings beyond our dimension. Rhodonite or Rhodochrosite would help heal the heart and open it.

Twelve crystals make a more powerful grid that connects into the divine archetypes at a higher, more comprehensive level. Twelve is totality and completion in a cosmic sense. It might bring more of your divine potential into your life than you are ready for, so work with the simpler patterns first. A circle of twelve is excellent for groups though, because there are more people to handle the expanded potential. Each person's weak areas are supported by the strengths of the others in the group.

Four Quartz crystals make a square configuration that fits into the flow of the plan at the physical level. It brings out your power as a part of the Earth. It interacts at a physical level but is difficult to combine with spiritual purpose. You need an interdimensional approach to do that; thus the pyramid, a square base with triangles on all sides. If you suspend a crystal over the center of your square crystal grid you can bring a more illuminated viewpoint to your work at the physical level.

The pyramid is the first step from a physical perspective to a truly interdimensional awareness; thus the current fascination with them among spiritual seekers. As humanity seeks to expand its awareness and knowledge into new dimensions, the pyramid is the key. If your crystal pyramid grid is large enough, it is good to meditate in it. Quartz carved into pryamid shapes or crystals that form pyramids naturally, such as Fluorite or Apophyllite can be worn. They create a multidimensional energy field that helps you work at levels of expanded consciousness.

If you are a beginner, choose crystals that are similar in size and shape. Use doubly terminated ones for healing grids or generators (crystals that stand upright and whose faces come to a point) for a pyramid base. As you learn to be sensitive to the specific energy of each crystal and how they are interacting, you can be more creative with your grids. You might also discover that some very small crystals are just as powerful as larger ones and can balance their energy quite effectively. Sometimes two crystals of the same or different types placed together form one new energy which may be appropriate in your grid pattern.

You can introduce minerals other than Quartz into your grids to add to their healing, balancing, or inspirational qualities. You can increase the number of Quartz crystals, if you don't change the basic geometric shape, without changing the basic quality of the grid energy.

Crystals like to work together. They know that the more perspectives of understanding you can incorporate into your work, the more creative and effective you become. If you have trouble being part of a group, and many do, crystals can show your subconscious how to link up with and share energy with something outside yourself. They can also help you learn to integrate group energies into a flow that works for you. Working with others magnifies the energy potential exponentially and crystals want to be part of that group.

Crystal Systems

The universe is very structured and orderly at the most spiritual levels. Its structure is a reflection of the perfect knowledge of Source, the Creator. To those of you who are accustomed to thinking in a three-dimensional format, it is difficult to imagine four, five, or more dimensions. You might have an idea that the fourth dimension involves time and a sort of compression of the linear nature of your stream of experiencing into timelessness, where all events occur simultaneously. One event at the third-dimensional level is a reflection of an eternally occurring event that involves all levels. Similarly, at the fifth-dimensional level, all thoughts are one thought. One thought affects all other thoughts. One new thought transforms all other thoughts by its existence.

At the sixth-dimensional level all ideals are part of one universal ideal which generates the thoughts of the fifth. One individual concept about how this ideal works is part of the understanding of the whole about its projection into creation. There is not really any such thing as an individual concept of the ideal, only one expanding ideal.

At the seventh-dimensional level there is a building or bridging that takes the energy, always the basic love of the Creator, from higher dimensions yet and transforms or separates it into specific ideas which are used to form the individual shape and quality of each creative experience. This is a sort of transition point where physical existence really begins to take shape out of the no-thing that is everything. This is also the point where physicality really seems to dissolve for those who are able to experience this level consciously.

This seventh-dimensional level is where the innate knowledge of the Crystal Kingdom originates. Crystals are taking the nonspecific wisdom of what we see as "God" and transforming it into order and beauty. The Crystal and Mineral Kingdoms have not experienced physical existence in the same way humanity has. Humans have free will and make individual choices about how they will use their physical-plane experiences to learn about themselves. This involves personal thought and emotional processes. This process of choosing allows a great diversity in exploring emotions and ideas and a great expansion in the consciousness needed to make choices. It has allowed the consciousness of humanity to evolve through individual effort and growth.

This process of making choices has taken the consciousness of humanity into increasingly specific and isolated experiences, to the point where loneliness and separation are the rule rather than the exception. It is ironic that, in a world which can immediately provide whatever an individual needs and wants, it is often so difficult to recognize that that abundant flow is there for you. The problem is that you haven't discovered what you really need and want, so much of the abundance is spent on trying out lots of things that don't really work or turn out as expected. Well, physical existence is an opportunity to learn by trial and error, so you learn a lot, even though you feel separated from your real providers.

The only choice the Mineral Kingdom made was to become physical. It chose to demonstrate the symmetry and shape of the ideal flow as it comes through the seventh dimension. There is no reshaping of those forms through individual interpretation. The form is as the Creator sees it. This does not allow the evolution in consciousness that is possible for humanity, but it allows the crystals to maintain perfect understanding and awareness of the Creator's original thought or intention. Their physical bodies are direct reflections of perfect thought and transmit Divine Will with little distortion. What imperfections do exist in them are the result of the confusion of thoughts from separated humanity impinging on the creative flow of the Divine Plan. They are innocent and blameless of any distortion of the Divine Plan. They maintain a connection with the flow that is pure and true.

So crystals become the perfect counterbalance for a humanity somewhat lost in their trials and tribulations. They put everything back into a perspective of the absolute truth that applies to this physical world. They become an anchor within the flow of the Divine Plan that can always be depended upon to lead you to its perfection. In that way they can serve as guides or light within the apparent darkness of physical existence. They have never lost the way. They mirror the way. They demonstrate and prove it in their physical form. Humanity does the exploring and expanding in physical bodies, while crystals maintain the connection with the meaning of life. The first seven dimensions are all one dimension for them. There is no separation of the divine ideal into individual interpretations. The connection into the Source is the ideal, is the thought, is the feeling, is the form. All thoughts, feelings, forms are the ideal.

There is some diversity in the form because, at the physical level, it is not possible to do or be everything at once. Physical existence requires separation of the flow into individual atoms which each represent a specific ability of the flow to support physical existence. The Divine Plan is the mechanism that organizes these aspects of divine love back into wholeness through evolution. Crystals don't choose which aspect they will provide. They don't say, "I tried being an atom of iron in hemoglobin for awhile. Now I would like to be manganese and become part of plant chlorophyll for awhile. Or should I try being an oxygen atom? I could move around a lot that way." They just allow the flow to place their consciousness where it is needed and allow their form to develop as the Plan flows through their consciousness. This provides the stability within physical existence which supports the more diverse experiences of the other kingdoms, the plants and animals. The rocks and minerals change, but do so very slowly, allowing the Earth to evolve in cycles which take eons, whereas humanity evolves in cycles of lifetimes.

The Mineral Kingdom as a whole maintains a clear connection for physical Earth to dimensions beyond the seventh. Specific aspects of it serve as "steps" within this flow which make the process of manifesting the physical level more understandable. They maintain a sort of point of awareness at the fourth, fifth or sixth levels which breaks the process of creating down into smaller bits of information. These aspects of the Mineral Kingdom can be generally identified by crystal structure.

The seven crystal systems are defined by the angular relation of the faces of each crystal and their axes. An axis joins the center of a pair of opposing faces. All axes meet in the center of the crystal. The faces and axes are determined by the way the atoms within the crystal are aligned with each other by chemical or molecular bonds. The outer shape (tetrahedral, dodecahedral, rhombohedral, and so forth) depends on environmental factors like temperature, rate of cooling, pressure, chemical environment or presence of other crystals. Many of the shapes are complicated combinations of basic geometric shapes.

The *cubic* system has three axes, all equal, which form ninety degree, or square, angles to each other. Diamond, Spinel, Garnet and Pyrite are examples of minerals that crystallize in the cubic system. This system brings together the third and ninth dimensions. The Divine Flow as it comes through these crystals is bringing the highest perspective of interpretation of the Cosmic Plan and Will. You could call the eighth dimension the one where the Master Plan exists as ultimate truth for Earth. Beyond that lies the Divine Will for which the Plan is created. These crystals bring that ultimate purpose directly into physical manifestation without further interpretation or division. Their method of making this Will clear depends also on the elements of which they are composed, but their action is direct and focused. They are the basic anchors for the Divine Will which motivates the Plan on Earth.

The *tetragonal* system has three axes; two are equal and one is longer. All form ninety degree angles to one another. Zircon and Rutile crystallize in this system as do many minerals that are mined as metal ores, notably Chalcopyrite, the usual source of Copper. These crystals bring together the third and fourth dimensions. When humans began to use metals, the first movement into the fourth dimension began, very slowly at first. With the discovery, creation, and use of radioactive elements, you have recently been blasting holes in the barriers between the third and fourth as well as other dimensions.

Crystals of the tetragonal system make the Plan flow more smoothly at the physical level. They help you understand how to apply the Plan at practical levels. Your consciousness grows gradually by trying out new ideas at the physical level. These crystals help stretch your understanding into new concepts which are the next step in the evolution of your consciousness.

The *orthorhombic* system has three axes, all of different lengths and all forming square angles with each other. Topaz, Peridot, Iolite and Danburite are examples of this system which bring together the third and sixth dimensions. The ideal is clearly understood and manifested through them. They are an aspect of the part of the Divine Flow that makes it possible to bring the ideal into reality. They are a measuring tool against which anything might be compared to the ideal. They also show you what must be changed to transform anything into the ideal.

The *monoclinic* system has three unequal axes; two form square angles, one does not. Kunzite, Azurite, Malachite and Orthoclase are from this system. They unite the upper levels of the third dimension, the fourth and the sixth. Again, they are an aspect of the flow that brings in the ideal, not quite as specifically, but with an enhancement of its movement into your etheric body. It transforms the ideal blueprint into your etheric energy flow so your cells have clearer access to it. Crystals of this system also facilitate creative use of the fourth dimension. They are important in transforming the raw power of the Earth into energy which manifests your personal will and purpose.

The *triclinic* system has three unequal axes and no symmetrical angles between the planes of the faces. Some crystals of this system are Rhononite, Spectrolite, Turquoise, and Albite Moonstone. They are manifesting the part of the flow that blends the fourth and seventh dimensions. They are especially useful for creating openings in consciousness that go beyond what can be seen and proven at the physical level. They are taking humanity beyond the limits of their present entrapment in their physical bodies. They use the heart and emotions to carry you out of yourself and your personal concerns into interpersonal and even cosmic perspectives. They help you understand the parts of yourself that are not physical and that seem to have no practical value. They can make you more comfortable with the unknown as they bring in the absolute truth and love that forms the foundations upon which physical existence was formed.

The *hexagonal* system has four axes, three equal and forming sixty degree (trine) angles with each other, and one unequal axis that forms a ninety degree angle with the others. Emerald (Beryl) and Apatite are of this system. It blends the third, fourth, and fifth dimensions. The number four, of the four axes, is a key to the meaning of this system. Four is connected esoterically with being physical or manifesting at the physical level. It is connected with a deep penetration of divine energy into physical existence. Crystals of this system are part of the flow that brings the order and concept of spiritual intent, the feeling and imagination of the creators into the raw material of the physical plane. They bring the stability and ease of the triangle into the hard but unstable structure of physical reality. There is not one Creator involved here, but one Creator acting as many creators, each with an individual, unique viewpoint. The crystals of this system shape your reality according to divine intent as interpreted by the creators involved. They also blend the feelings and understandings of those creators into a workable whole.

The crystals of the last system, the *trigonal,* are often included in the hexagonal system. There are again three axes forming sixty degree angles and one a ninety degree angle. These crystals, instead of having seven different planes of symmetry within them and seven axes of symmetry, have three and four, respectively.

The perfection and building qualities of the number seven are compressed into the physical power and potential of four and the ease and stability of three, those being the ultimate numbers for creating a reality. This digression on numbers is very abstract, but the universe is built on a system whose meaning is demonstrated most purely by numbers and the Mineral Kingdom is a direct manifestation of them.

This system is simpler in its possiblities than the hexagonal, but more direct in the application of divine intent. It blends the third, fifth, and seventh dimensions. There is not the possibility for emotional interpretation here but the inspiration comes from the movement which changes divine intent into the ideal blueprint. The quality of the inspiration of the Plan is directed into the ideal structure and then into physical manifestation. The movement is translated into perfect form. Understanding is implicit in the shape of the structure. The mind of each individual creator can depend on the shape to fit where it is appropriate because the One Creator intends it to do so. These crystals are the ultimate tools for creating according to the Divine Plan. They bring a message that is direct and aligned with the flow of that Plan. It requires no modification, only the will to use it.

Some of the crystals in this system are Ruby and Sapphire (Corundum), Tourmaline, Dioptase, Phenacite and, most important of all, Quartz. These are the crystals that show you how to organize your potential most effectively to fulfill your divine purpose. They show you how to make the most out of physical existence. You cannot do this without the support of crystals from the other systems. They give you the ability to understand and interpret the flow of the Plan, but these are the elements of active CoCreatorship. These are the crystals that finally make you what you are in a physical sense. They shape your body and the way it responds to the light of the Divine Plan. They are your teachers as you learn to create your reality according to your purpose and will. They teach you to manifest Divine Purpose and Will by exploring your own purpose and will. They show you how to organize all aspects of yourself so that you finally become complete.

Color and Hardness of Crystals

COLOR

Color is a very important indicator of a crystal's qualities. It overlays the properties conferred by their structure and composition. Crystals respond to color and communicate through their own color. You could say that color is the communicative link that allows you to feel what a crystal has to offer and to communicate your purpose to it. Color defines the quality of the communication. A rich deep color often implies greater power or energy, while an ethereal iridescence seems purer and more elevated. Your body responds to the color of the crystal the same way it responds to light. The color of an individual crystal or mineral specimen helps define what it is in an inner sense.

When a crystal is artificially dyed it is not necessarily harmed, although its new color is not a true reflection of the crystal's essence. Some coloring processes, like the Aqua Aura processing, add a new dimension to the crystal's usefulness, partly because of the intensity of the process itself. Treating a stone with a less permanent dye, one which might even rub off as you wear it, often has little effect on the stone itself and more effect on your perception of it. Although dyeing occasionally will block or distort the stone's energy somewhat, if you like the effect and find it useful, the crystal will be good for you to use. If you don't like it, your conscious or subconscious perceptions of its value will limit its usefulness for you.

Color is more a fourth-dimensional quality than one of the third, and it evokes an emotional response from its users. Color goes to the area of emotional blockage or intensity involved with it and the crystal energy can then create movement there. In Atlantis, colored crystals from Earth and from extraterrestrial sources were used to color light and alter or intensify its qualities. Today, that knowledge is being used in a very limited way in color therapy, but as the consciousness of humanity moves back into greater harmony with the fourth-dimensional flow, the use of crystals will be "discovered" again for healing. Lasers are being used by surgeons, yes, but that process is still more destructive than creative. Light and water are the two mediums for transferring the healing and restructuring capabilities of crystals into the human body.

There are many books available about color therapy. The work on the rays by Alice Bailey, for instance, has only begun to be understood and applied. We will give you some general indicators here of the meaning of colors and allow you to expand on them as you wish.

Red

Red is the color of blood and heat. Ruby red is the color of the heart center where the divine spark of your Godhood resides. It is your connection to Source. It carries the greatest life force in the physical sense. Red supports the blood by adding energy to the body. It implies, sometimes, raw, untamed power. It is too much for some individuals to use in great quantities, yet one could live on red energy alone if one were willing to limit himself or herself to basic physical functions. Red gives the power to move out and up but does not in itself help you understand how, why, or where the movement is made. Red is also the color signifying Divine Will and the Creator's purpose.

Red crystals support the blood and its formation. They are also healing to bodily organs which have the greatest blood supply, like the heart and liver, as long as they are not traumatized and losing blood. Many crystals have more of a dark red-brown color. The brown adds energy from Earth to the divine energy source in red and makes the crystal more useful at the physical level. The brown steps the energy of the red down so the body can use it without being overwhelmed. Ruby is an example of the intense pure red that brings in the Divine Will very powerfully, even though it is expressed as unconditional love. The brownish-red of some types of Garnet is a color that is more grounded and empowering for the physical body, although some fine crystals of some varieties might be quite a clear, beautiful red. Pink is quite different from red and is discussed under its own heading.

Red is the energy that promotes the ideal flow of life-giving energy through the base chakra. It is the color of raw creative power as it comes from Earth or Sun. It is the basic will to live and be in physical existence. It will help you release blocks in the base chakra and support it in supplying energy to your body. It is the basic energy for everything from procreation to ascension and it comes to you from Earth through your physical body.

Orange

Orange is a color of the mind and brings it clarity. It helps to shape the dymanic flow of red, being closely related to it in the spectrum. It takes the raw power and begins to confer meaning and control on it. It makes it possible to use power for specific purposes. Orange works at a higher energy level than red but is less intense. It is still difficult for some to use but might feel more like warm sunshine and joyful exuberance. It takes poisons out of the body and supports the immune system. It makes the brain and muscles work more efficiently. It is energizing to the cells without there being as much danger of overheating as with red. Bright orange is about as difficult to find in crystals as clear red. Orange Calcite might be the one most available. Amber is a brownish orange and mirrors creative potential to the body's cells, teaching them to be flexible in the evolutionary process. The brown, again, brings the energy into a form more usable at the physical level.

Orange is the color of the sex chakra, the second one, also called the sacral chakra. It energizes its creative potential, coordinating it with the structural ideal from the universal mind in sexual reproduction and from your mind when you choose to use this energy to create or recreate your life. The expanding creative potential of the new, higher energies is causing increasing stimulation of this chakra in many who are connecting with them consciously or unconsciously. Orange crystals will help you direct that energy into your divine purposes. They also help you to accept your sexuality and to see how to channel its creative potential into many levels.

Yellow

Yellow brings lightness and joy. It elevates the spirits and energizes the mind and body. It can bring your soul's energy into the physical level. It can increase pain if there is a great deal of stuckness and negativity. Grounding stones will help you use its energy. Orange or brown ones help direct it. Yellow is a color of spirit and light made physical. It balances physicality and spirituality. It is creativity expanding throughout physical existence. It encourages multiplication. It stimulates expression of ideas and their creative application. It has potential for structure without imposing rigidity. It flows well and encourages communication within self or with others. It is necessary for growth and thus is the color of sunlight.

Yellow is the essence of vitality which the solar plexus chakra needs to function well. It brings the will to live and supports it in energizing and coordinating all bodily functions at the physical level. By lifting depression it allows the vital energy to flow freely throughout your body. It promotes communication with all parts and levels of self. Clear Yellow Calcite is one example; it brings healing through allowing joy. Yellow Apatite is another that supports the mind in its understanding while encouraging open-mindedness through freer flow.

Green

Green is the color of healing. It sooths the emotions and allows energy to flow easily in the physical body. It balances the bodily functions and the cellular activity, creating a clearer interface with the ideal blueprint as it comes through the subtle, etheric levels of the body's guidance and coordinating system. Green is the flowering of creativity in practical reality. It is the fertility of Earth itself and your connection into Earth's support system for all life. It is the energy that fuels your creative endeavors, supplying you with everything you can use. It helps you feel comfortable in your physical body and with being physical. It is the ultimate healing color for those who are new to physical bodies or who need to come more fully into them. It helps you to physically adapt to new environments. It is the Creator's Love made physical. It demonstrates the potential for creative growth available through physical existence.

Green is the color most useful to the heart chakra at the physical level. It helps you heal any difficulties in using love that have resulted from ages of learning to use physical existence and function as a creative being here. It helps you extend your power into physical existence with love and under the direction of your heart. It will show you how to use your power and creativity for your own highest purposes and how best to cooperate with and assist the evolution of the whole Earth.

Green is not hard to find in the Mineral Kingdom. Emerald is perhaps the ultimate expression of green, but the large number of crystals in many beautiful shades of green demonstrates the abundance of creative opportunities here for growth and evolution, as well as healing. Use green stones to heal the fracturing of your creativity and to resolve difficult experiences. Use it to bring peace and completion into your Earth experience.

Blue

Blue is the color of peace and calm. It is restful and somewhat elevating. It can be the color of sky or ocean, midnight or electricity. There are more possibilities in blue than in any other color. Its tints and tones are beautiful and flowing and diverse. As it shades into violet and becomes indigo, it becomes another of the seven major rays. The variations of aqua, blue and indigo are evolving and multiplying as Earth integrates more of the higher dimensions. Blue takes you out of yourself while bringing you into a state of peace with yourself. It is the color of spiritual love for this planet of love (potentially). The blue ray is the one of the Christ, love, and wisdom. It is also the color of the Earth Mother, Mother Mary and Archangel Michael.

Blue heals, balances, and energizes the throat, or will chakra. It helps open the spiritual vision and intuition through the brow chakra. It is electrical, especially when it is tinged with green to become the color of Blue Topaz or Aqua Aura. It aligns the personal will with Divine Will when it is the color of Azurite or Lapis Lazuli, creating a clear path for spiritual guidance and understanding. It calms and raises the emotions when it is Blue Lace Agate or Angelite. It moves the electrical flow of the ideal deeply into the cells as Dumortierite or Shattuckite. It connects your love into the Earth as Sodalite. The indigo light of Iolite or Tanzanite calms the mind and opens the third eye.

Violet

Violet is the color of spirituality and the New Age. It is the purifying ray that sweeps away everything that is outmoded and no longer useful. It is cool and warming at the same time. It is the most useful color for clearing away negativity and blocks within self. The violet ray is the one bringing in the new higher energies, the new dimensional interfaces and the new form of the divine ideal. It can take you out of yourself if you are not grounded. If you are, it will help you stretch into your potential for creating forward movement here on Earth.

Violet is healing for all chakras, but especially so for the crown chakra. It opens and aligns your spiritual channel, creating the connection you need to align with your soul and all higher aspects of yourself. Then it helps you integrate them at the physical level.

The violet of Sugilite takes you into the next level of understanding your creative potential. As Amethyst, violet is cleansing and uplifting. As Purple Flourite, it carries that cleansing and releasing deep into your cells. As Almandine Garnet, it clears the blood and grounds the electrical potential of the violet ray. As Alexandrite it shows you what the New Age really is.

Pink

As we ascend the vibrational scale of colors, pink is next. It is the color of love at nonphysical levels. It is unconditional love. It is the desire to be in harmony with everything in the universe. It dissolves negativity and creates balanced movement. It encourages your use of your higher chakras through using and expanding your heart. It takes you out of yourself into global or unversal participation. It's a color of fun, even excitement, that puts things into perspective and doesn't let you take yourself too seriously. As the color rose, it symbolizes the deepest opening of your heart and the expansion of your creativity. It heals any part of the body that is lacking in love. Use a great deal of it on yourself if you are lacking in self-love and self-esteem. Pink can mean insincerity and lack of depth in love, but this pink is lacking in life and energy. It feels different to those who are trying to understand love in a more cosmic sense.

As Rubellite, it heals your receptive nature and encourages you to allow love and the bounty of the Creator's love into your life. As Rhodonite, it helps you find ways to express your love. As Rose Quartz, it heals your heart and helps you flow love more clearly and easily. As Spinel, it helps you accept your creative abilities as your contribution to Earth's growth. As Pink Zircon, it makes the love, structured as the creative ideal, easier to use and understand. In some minerals, like Rhodochrosite and Coral, pink is tinged with orange to become coral and encourage the expansion of your heart and your use of love in creative application of your special abilities on Earth. Pink helps you use your eighth and twelfth chakras.

Aqua

Aqua has a particular relationship to electricity and the next level of the energy within light which you and Earth are now learning to use. With light pink, iridescent pearl, silver and gold, it symbolizes the rays and chakras beyond the traditional seven that we already know, particularly the ninth. As Aqua Aura Quartz this ray stimulates your body, emphasizing the new energies and making it aware of them. As blue-green Amazonite, it opens the cells to using more of them. As Larimar, it helps the body accept them and calms any irritation. As Indicolite, it shows your subconscious how to use the new energies in balance with what you already know. As Blue Fluorite, those energies become part of the cellular support system.

White

White can be all colors or no colors. Prismatic White Quartz, for instance, is clear Quartz with more water in the crystal lattice. These crystals, like water, will hold energy until it is needed or release it very slowly. They can be charged for a specific purpose. When you choose to release the energy you might direct it where you choose, according to the abilities of the crystal. Other minerals that form amorphous masses of tiny crystals simply reflect light in all directions. They will also hold a charge but the energy will not be as powerfully focused or directed. They can reflect every part of yourself to you. They can also bring energy from many sources at once. They are useful for expanding your awareness rather than stretching or focusing it specifically. This applies to most opaque crystals of any color.

Iridescent White

This is the light that contains all colors. They shimmer and spiral through the pure energy of this highest of vibrations that can be visualized at the physical level. All colors are blended into one clear flow. This is the color of perfect balance, the colors of your soul's lightbody. Your soul is an aspect of your highest consciousness which has clothed itself with pure angelic energy in order to function as your connection into wholeness. This is the color of the tenth ray, the tenth chakra, and of ascension. When you have learned to use all colors, energies, and aspects of yourself in perfect balance and harmony, you are ready to take up the responsibility of bringing the higher consciousness of your soul into Earth and using it here.

The iridescent light carries the divine ideal and heals the whole body. It brings soul energy into all chakras and into your cells. It is transforming and uplifting. Opal, Pearl, and Rainbow Quartz are examples of crystals that can help you visualize and understand your spiritual light. The rainbows formed from fractures in crystals like Clear Quartz and Clear Calcite make the balance and perfection of the Divine Blueprint more available to your body and its cells.

Clear (Colorless)

Clear crystals, without iridescence, are also balanced light. They are capable of transporting the full spectrum of colors to you. They focus the energy of all rays more precisely and intensely. They are more direct in their action. They also require you to be more conscious of how you are using them, because they will align themselves to your will more closely. Clear Quartz is the ultimate tool for directing the ideal blueprint into your body. Clear Calcite is the best for making the electrical connections you need to use that blueprint. Clear Apophyllite or Danburite, both very sparkling and bright, connect you into all your potentials as beings of light.

Black

Black is the absence of color. Black stones hold all colors and reflect none. Since light is flow, it will not be hindered by black stones if it is pure. They will absorb everything that is not light, everything that is impure or negative. The energy they take in is later released as heat, electrical energy, creative power, or unspecific flow that might be used in any way you wish. Black Tourmaline, for instance, absorbs negativity or pain and transforms it into electrical flow of a high-vibrational order that boosts the power of whatever light is available nearby. Black Quartz that has been irradiated does the same, but natural Black Quartz transforms the negativity into creative power that blends with native Earth energy. They can be enormous reservoirs of power if you choose to channel it into your purposes. If not, it returns the energy to Earth to recharge and rejuvenate her.

Black Diamond absorbs negativity and transforms it into life force that is powerful but nonspecific. It goes in many directions and into many dimensions. It is like playing with fire. You must know exactly what you are doing at every moment you are working with it. Jet is interesting in that when you have worked with it for a time it becomes very personally protective for you specifically. It is good for those who have many conscious and subconscious fears, because it helps in dealing with them. Hematite and Magnetite are black stones that are very grounding. As they release their absorbed energy into the Earth they create a flow that allows you to make a more secure connection with it.

HARDNESS

Color shows the mode of a crystal's energy interaction with your energy structure. It is the crystal's emotional or love expression, how it demonstrates the Creator's love. The crystal's structure shows how it interacts in a conceptual way, how it fits into the Divine Plan and supports it. It is its interpretation of the Creator's original intent, just as you are striving to express your idea of what creation means. It shows its way of responding to and working in physical existence. The final definitive quality is hardness. This is the intensity of the crystal's use of will. It shows how it aligns with the Creator's will.

The hardest mineral, with a hardness of ten, is Diamond and its will is almost absolute. It interprets the Divine Will for physical existence without any allowance for individual variation. That Will is the perfect expression of universal, unlimited love. Anything else will not align with its purpose. You must strive for whatever you know to be the highest and clearest expression of your creativity if you want to use the gifts of Diamond.

Ruby and Sapphire are the second hardest minerals, nine on the scale. Here the absolute truth of the One is tempered by divine and perfect love that is always forgiving and allowing of error. The wisdom and beauty of the love which comes through them absorbs everything into the unlimited love of the One Creator. Ruby teaches you to find perfect love in all creation and Sapphire teaches the perfect expression of love in the knowledge of it.

Topaz and Spinel are next, hardness eight, and they embody the vibration of perfect structure, the perfection of form which demonstrates the Creator's Plan for expressing love. They embody the ideal that is to be used to interact with physical existence from the Source level. They are a sort of lens that focuses love for our physicality. They represent the goal before all evolving consciousness, marking the end of the path that leads back to perfect reunion with Creative Source. They and others of similar hardness help maintain the connection to your divine purpose and your divine potential.

Next down the scale we have Quartz, along with Danburite, Spodumene, Zircon, and others of a hardness of seven. They carry the pattern for actually transforming Divine Love into physical expression. They are the model for building the forms that can eventually learn to use pure light and love to create and express their interpretation of Divine Purpose. There are many more minerals of this hardness because they allow more variation in personal expression. They support the diversity of expanding and evolving creativity. They also hold the light patterns in place so those at the physical level can use them more easily. They serve as the reservoir of knowledge on which is based the creative decisions that have been made at higher levels of consciousness. They are the actual template for physical forms that support and serve conscious expression.

Pyrite, Peridot, Rhodonite, Zoisite and the Feldspars, to name a few minerals with a hardness of 6, aid in adapting the Divine Plan to individual purpose. They are much more tolerant of individual error than the hardest minerals and serve as guide to evolving individual interpretation of divine ideals. They help your cells adapt to your level of understanding and they help you evolve your use of light in your cells to each new level. Without these loving helpers, you would not find opportunities to try out new ideas and go through the process of perfecting them so that they finally express your original intention.

Apatite and the group of minerals with a hardness of 5 carry the creative expression of light through physical bodies into even more personal interpretations. Many of these crystals bring special help from the angelic kingdom. They represent the very personal attention to each individual which the Creator provides and the personal love He or She has for every unit of consciousness. They are personal intercessors into the unlimited love and support of the Divine Plan. There are no depths to which they cannot reach in bringing the special help you need in connecting to your divine potential and releasing blocks to it.

Fluorite, Malachite and Rhodochrosite are a few of the minerals with a hardness of 4. They can work very directly with the cellular emotional levels to connect the perfection of the divine ideal into your body. They give you the biological basis for utilizing light and evolving through love. They allow you to interact more easily with the angels who guide and assist you in evolving your creativity at the physical level. They "mop up" all your mistakes and make that energy available for you as light. They are ever forgiving of mistakes and help you forgive yourself and start over. They remind you constantly that, although you are not yet perfect in your expression at the physical level, you have the potential to be so as part of your creativity.

The minerals of lesser hardness ease the flow of light, soften the expectations of perfection seen in divine ideals, and help you adapt to whatever problems you experience in using the creative resources of physical existence. They won't show you the final glorious fulfillment of your purpose, but they provide the lubrication of the "wheels" that carry you toward it. They won't define the ideal but they will help you adapt to it and use it to create your own interpretation of perfection. They provide a soft pillow to cushion the bumps along your sometimes very hard and bumpy path.

Scale of Hardness

Hardness is defined by Mohs Scale. Specific minerals define levels of hardness, starting with the softest as 1 and going up to the hardest at 10. A crystal of the next higher hardness will scratch the ones below it; that is, everything scratches Talc, nothing scratches Diamond. Some common articles are used as estimates. A finger nail is about 2.5 in hardness and will scratch Gypsum. A Copper coin is about 3 and would be scratched by Fluorite. Window glass is about 5.5, a knife blade is 6 and steel is 6.5.

1	Talc	6	Orthoclase Feldspar
2	Gypsum	7	Quartz
3	Calcite	8	Topaz
4	Fluorite	9	Corundum
5	Apatite	10	Diamond

Metaphysical Properties of Crystals

ACTINOLITE: Integrating the Physical

Hydrous Calcium Magnesium Iron Silicate. Long, light to dark green prismatic crystals or felty aggregates. Translucent with vitreous luster. Monoclinic system. Hardness is 5 to 6.

Actinolite helps the physical body balance the level at which it is working. This is necessary before the body can accept the dynamic new energies of the higher vibrations. It stabilizes the crystallization of your present level. Crystallization is a problem if it involves negative patterns, but it is necessary to provide the structure of your body at the physical level. Actinolite helps to make new patterns available to your cells by integrating them into their working structure. It produces stability in bodily function.

Actinolite helps the emotional body accept the needs of the physical and strengthens the connection between them in a positive way. It can also help the physical body provide a secure support base for the emotional body. It allows each to cooperate with the needs and functions of the other. It also can be very stabilizing for the mind and emotions. It enhances practicality and responsibility.

As an elixir, Actinolite enhances the effects of other crystals at the physical level. It works particularly well with high-energy stones like Diamond and Aqua Aura or with refined energies like Apophyllite and Opal.

ADULARIA (Moonstone)

See Orthoclase. Almost transparent ground, colorless, pale gray to yellowish, with a white to silvery or blue shimmer.

In addition to the qualities given for Orthoclase, Adularia is helpful for bringing clearer connections to the angelic kingdom. Most of you have spent at least some time on other vibrational planes working with or as angels. Since angels do not think or work exactly like those from the CoCreator level, not having "chosen" free will, certain misperceptions might be present in your subconscious about your ability to work with them. Moonstone will help you see them as parts of yourself that are perfectly aligned with Source Will and able to carry out your part in the Divine Plan perfectly. It will help resolve the resistance some parts of yourself might have to allowing them to work with you, serve you, and be part of your energy flow.

Angels are your connectors to the divine flow, and you must be able to allow their energy to flow through you if you are to be part of that flow. Adularia Moonstone can help you make that connection more clearly in the levels of your physical and emotional bodies. It will help clear blocks or resistance to the flow. It will help you accept the energy of your soul's lightbody, as that is angelic substance also. It helps level out the start-stop or up-down swings as you learn to interact with your soul. For most of you, there are varying degrees of fear about allowing soul energy into your physical body, yet that is part of your purpose now on Earth. Adularia elixir dissolves those fears and allows more light into your cells.

Adularia Moonstone brings peace, contentment, upliftment and openness to new thought patterns. It helps the mind integrate new information. It supports and heals the kidneys and lungs.

Traditional and other sources: Brings peace and harmony, sensitivity; enhances clairvoyance and leads one to spiritual concerns. Increases access to subconscious. Calms overreaction to emotional situations, promotes harmony in marriage, relieves frustration. Brings fame and long life. Makes the wearer invisible. If lovers place Moonstones in their mouths when the moon is full, they can foresee their future. Pope Leo X was supposed to have had a Moonstone that grew brighter or dimmer with the waxing or waning of the moon. It benefits agriculture.

Opens flow of feminine energy and aids birth process; aids all female problems. Heals chronic ulcers and burns. Aids abdomen, spleen, pancreas, pituitary gland, and intestines. Weakens ulcers and improves digestion. Use for any disease that causes ulcers. Aligns vertebrae.

The elixir eases anxiety and stress connected with the mother. Opens solar plexus chakra and releases abdominal tension. Integrates emotions and increases sensitivity and ability to listen. Teaches psychokinesis and clairvoyance. See also Moonstone.

AGATE: **Calming and Balancing**

Silicon Dioxide, variety of Chalcedony. Microcrystalline. Translucent to semiopaque. Many colors and patterns. Hardness is 6.5.

In general, Agate supports the emotional and physical bodies. It helps them balance and recognize their strengths so they can integrate the new energies in the way that is appropriate for them. Its energy is very easy for the emotional body to accept and use. It increases the flow of energy between the bodies and helps them communicate with each other. It is particularly supportive of the adrenals and the pancreas, as these glands are involved in converting the light that comes to us as life force (prana) from the Sun into energy that our bodies can use at the physical level. As an elixir it helps transfer the ideal from the light particles into the cells and connect it to the DNA.

Blue Lace Agate, a pale blue layered with gray or white, radiates a peace and calm that can settle an agitated mind and comfort an upset emotional body. It is helpful during the clearing process or in a crisis to smooth the flow of energy and keep it from getting stuck in difficult areas. It makes difficult problems look less difficult. It helps all parts of self feel worthy of accepting soul's energy and capable of using it well. It brings in a great deal of angelic energy that helps make the connections within yourself that you need in order to make realizations and to integrate. Use it during meditation to help create new openings into your unlimitedness that feel supportive and natural. Its elixir is calming and penetrates into crystallized areas within the energy field that create pain and imbalance at the physical level.

Botswana Agate, bands of white and grays, is a very gentle energy that helps body and emotions adapt to change and adjust to new ideas and the energy generated by them. It gives the emotions a way of integrating with the mind and its somewhat different way of using energy. It is useful when worn on your ankle to help you communicate more easily at the emotional level with Earth and to accept its support and nurturing.

It and other banded agates especially help you use the fourth-dimensional flow of Earth's energy by connecting you with those parts of Earth that are using it well, such as the plant kingdom, particularly the trees. It also helps you integrate the strengths of the Mineral Kingdom and basic Earth substances to strengthen your own physical structure. It is not grounding in a heavy or slow way, but it helps the physical level to be accepted as a part of the flow that encompasses all levels. It is especially useful for those who are trying to help their emotional body accept physicality and the great potential in it. Its elixir balances the energy flow of the physical level with the higher energies, producing harmony between them. It helps make the higher energies of transformational stones acessible to the physical level.

Lavender Agate is a gentle transforming energy especially useful at all levels of self during clearing. Since the new, higher energies are stimulating an almost constant state of accelerated clearing, this can be used frequently and in large amounts. It softens the effect of new energy frequencies blazing their own new paths within the etheric and physical brain. It can provide a calming effect which allows the brain to gradually shift into higher activity without the pressure or burning which sometimes occurs during the stretching process generated by your spiritual helpers. It is soothing to the emotions during upset or clearing while encouraging rather than damping the changes going on. It helps the emotional and mental bodies accept change. It is excellent as an elixir to stimulate awareness of which areas of self to work on next to free more of your potential creative flow and alignment with the ideal. As an elixir, all the qualities of Lavender Agate are enhanced for the physical body. It helps heal headaches and tumors, especially those of the brain. It assists the kidneys, liver, skin, and lungs in removing toxicity. It increases personal radiance and joy and enhances positive effects of communication.

Moss Agate, white with tracings of dark green, is one of the stones that has been specially selected to be energized by the angelic kingdom to help humanity recognize its spiritual potential. The angels have placed in it the knowledge of how to connect your consciousness into the highest aspects of self. It activates an awareness of your higher chakras as the bridge to knowledge of all that you are. If you use it over your heart, the angels can help you make actual energy connections to your greater potential. Using it on your base chakra helps you accept physical existence as light. It helps you allow your cells to use the higher energies. Using it as an elixir brings the light of your highest self into your physical body. It helps flow your lightbody into your physical cells if you are willing to continually work on clearing a place for it.

As you work with Moss Agate, visualize the angels who are committed to activating it for you. See them pouring their love through it to you as light which fills your whole being. Allow them to flow with your light to make the connections you need to use it in your cells and on Earth for your divine purposes. Use their love to create joy in your life. You will understand your purpose when the light can flow without any blocks through your whole being. Moss Agate will help you feel joyful and connected to the angels. You will radiate self-confidence and feel peaceful with yourself.

When Agate is carved into a specific shape it gains the individuality it lacked in its natural amorphous state. It is easily imprinted with your specific purpose for it. After you use it for a while, it vibrates to your energies and can be used to help you sort out what you can use now and what needs to be released to move to the next level of use of light. Each variety works in its own special way.

Traditional and other sources: Dependable workhorse of the Mineral Kingdom that brings strength, support and security, whatever your needs. Helps banish fears and brings courage. When powdered, mixed with water, drunk or sprinkled on the wound, it counteracts venomous snake bites; also those of spiders and scorpions. Prevents storms. Quenches thirst and cures fevers and inflammatory diseases. Relieves headaches and eye inflammation, checks menstruation, prevents edema.

If worn when plowing, Tree Agate, or Moss Agate, insures good crops. Also, increases longevity, prevents anger, bitterness, and general bad feelings. Especially strengthening in time of stress. Releases fears, especially about health. Helps you achieve your goals.

Moss Agate elixir improves circulation and enhances cellular absorption of nutrients. Balances body fluids and blood sugar. Eases anorexia nervosa, lymphoma, Hodgkin's disease, allergies, kidney and liver problems, and pulmonary edema. Lifts depression, connects mind and emotions. Aids self-confidence.

Blue Lace Agate is especially peaceful and relaxing. Soothes emotions, softens pain. Good for throat. Makes one more sensitive and aware. Offers encouragement and support.

Botswana Agate enhances physical sexual energy. Gives protection in crowds. Aids self-esteem and ability to handle loss. The elixir enhances and increases body's use of oxygen. Eases depression and lethargy, brings joy. Aligns throat chakra.

Fire Agate grounds, balances, and teaches harmony. Use elixir to expand understanding and learn practicality and discrimination. Connects sex and heart chakras, balancing sexual concerns. (Also see Chalcedony.)

AJOITE: Stimulating, Aids Flow

Hydrated Potassium Copper Aluminum Silicate. Usually found as masses; small, flat crystals are rare. Blue-green. Triclinic system. Found in Quartz where it is most useful, sometimes as phantoms.

Ajoite helps the cells to make the electrical connections that allow a smoother flow of energy and increase your light potential. It is excellent when used with Boji Stones, because they help ground and balance the increased energy flow. When Ajoite occurs in Quartz, it is excellent for enhancing the connections into the ideal flow and the use of its new patterns. It speeds up the healing and restructuring capabilities of all stones. It is one of a spectrum of Copper containing minerals that form a whole system for realigning Earth's energies. As you use it, you connect with the Earth's transformation process. Then, as you work on yourself, your learning and progress flow into the Earth to help it, with no extra effort on your part.

As an elixir, Ajoite in Quartz energizes and vitalizes your whole body. It heals and realigns weak areas and helps them balance with the rest of the body. Water allows the energy to go where it is needed most. It works best with other crystal energies that direct and shape the transformation process as it is mainly energizing.

Ajoite brings hope and belief in your own potential. It creates electrical connections in the brain that activate and optimize your creativity by healing and building the connections you need into the flow that nurtures that creativity. It facilitates the actual accomplishment of your dreams.

ALABASTER
White Gypsum. See Selenite.

ALBITE
See Moonstone.

ALEXANDRITE: Transformational

Beryllium Aluminum Oxide. The green form of Chrysoberyl which truns red under candlelight or tungsten light. Double refractive, orthorhombic system, hardness is 8.5.

Alexandrite was first discovered in the Ural Mountains of the Soviet Union on the day Russia's Prince Alexander came of age. This is symbolic of Earth's coming of age as a member of the Galactic Federation. The stone is quite rare, as is evidence of Earth's (this includes humanity's) maturity. Earth is just now beginning to reach the point of spiritual balance necessary to interact with the rest of the galactic sector so that it can function as a participating member. Alexandrite's properties symbolize Earth's present challenge. The higher energies that are now surrounding Earth are the new light which is stimulating her developing potentials.

Responsibility is the key word here. Humanity must learn that it is responsible for its thoughts as well as its actions. Every thought, conscious or subconscious, affects everything else. Not one goes unnoticed or is unproductive. At this new level of understanding, thought is action and can create good or evil just as surely as selfish action. Fortunately, there are now more individuals focusing on cooperative goals. The group focus greatly outweighs individual ones. Humanity must learn to be balanced in its spiritual awareness and emotional maturity so it can serve as the key to moving Earth to this new level of responsible creativity. The light focused by its combined will and intentions will create the changes desired, in alignment with the Plan.

Those who wear this stone will find they are helped to understand the changes going on and will be helping to bring them in. So, in order to be comfortable with this rare gem, you must be comfortable with change and willing to create it. The angelic consciousness embodied in Alexandrite is itself undergoing a transformation of its will which will lead Earth to the new level. Since angels never resist the flow of Source Will, they make admirable role models for flowing with change.

If you can't afford to own one, just holding or looking at one for a while will help. As you do so ask the Alexandrite angel to be part of your light and consciousness. When you meditate, imagine yourself surrounded by Earth's green, nurturing love. Then imagine this green turning a fiery red which centers itself in your heart as you move into alignment with Source Will, the Divine Plan.

As an elixir, Alexandrite will help create whatever changes are appropriate for you now. You must then be willing to accept them and release the old patterns. The stone is useful at the throat for creating alignment with soul's purpose. Again you must be willing to accept change. It makes you feel confident that you can handle anything. It also increases your ability to feel love for others and for Earth.

Other sources: By day, brings happiness, joy, and success; at night, increases feelings of love and sensuality. The elixir increases self-esteem and the ability to experience joy and appreciation. Opens the spleen chakra, aids leukemia, swollen lymph nodes, and spleen. Aids assimilation of proteins. Eases diseases of the central nervous system and aids regeneration of nerves. Aligns the four bodies and balances emotions.

AMAZONITE: Transformational

Potassium Aluminum Silicate. Variety of Microcline (which see). Medium shades of green to blue. Semiopaque. Hardness is 6.

Amazonite calms the emotions and energizes them at the same time. It opens the emotional body to new vibrational levels and shows it how to flow them. It might stretch you almost to a point of being over-whelmed but then will stop and help you integrate the new level. If you are not ready for that, it will help you deal with what you have at the moment. The color varies from light green to blue-green, deeper ones usually being more intense in their effect, although they might be more subtle.

The blue-green Amazonite can feel very electrical and you might find it necessary to use it sparingly at first. This won't mean you are backward, necessarily, just that at that particular time in your evolution you are particularly aware of energy shifts involved in moving forward at the physical level and must allow yourself to adapt at critical points. All of your bodies do not usually move at the same rate and this stone will help your physical body catch up with the others. The green Amazonite is more healing and integrative. If you have trouble using crystals because of difficult past-life experiences, Amazonite will help heal those broken connections to the Mineral Kingdom. It has been used since ancient times in carvings and for worship and can help you get in touch with past-life experiences and heal them.

As an elixir it can stimulate past-life recall, especially through dreams. It brings you whatever you need to heal your present life. It helps balance the endocrine system and heals the adrenals of exhaustion and other effects of stress. It can also make your sense of touch more sensitive for healing. An elixir of blue-green Amazonite helps bridge the gap between the pineal and pituitary glands which being physical seems to impose. In this way it helps open the crown chakra and brings more soul energy into your body.

Traditional and other sources: Stone of hope. Soothes the nerves. Aids personal expression and creativity. Increases discernment. Helps difficult births. The elixir aligns heart and solar plexus chakras, mind and etheric body. Amplifies thoughts. Increases flow of life force into cells. Enhances other elixirs. Supports male energies, strengthens etheric body.

AMBER: **Calming and Integrative**

Fossil resin of varying organic composition. Usually orange to dark brown. Transparent, often containing bodies or pieces of insects. Hardness is 2.5

Amber is a connector between humanity and the plant and animal kingdoms in physical existence. It removes confusion and imbalance among the bodies. It helps the emotional body accept its place in physical existence and functions as a connector within the four-body system. It can be very useful in helping you to feel more secure as a part of physical existence.

As an elixir it creates flexibility in movement, psychic and physical. It helps to move energy more freely throughout the body. It is healing to joints and ligaments. It can also dissolve anxiety about dealing with daily problems.

Traditional and other sources: Brings warmth of the Sun. Very magnetic. Always feels warm. Eases stress, balances emotions, clears mind. Balances opposites. A connector. Attracts electrically. In dreams, represents electromagnetism and etheric power or quality of energy in etheric body.

Neutralizes negativity. Protects against evil and witchcraft. Makes one invulnerable. An amber cup was supposed to reveal the presence of poisons. Wearing an Amber necklace protects health generally, prevents sore throat (especially tonsilitis) and even goiter, erysipelas (a contagious skin rash), brings longevity, cures fevers. Drives away snakes.

Purifies blood and the aura. Energizes the endocrine system, stabilizes the spleen, heart, and base chakras. Cures coughs, asthma, edema, toothache. Oil of Amber was given for "hysterical affections," rubbed on skin for warmth in whooping cough and to relieve bronchitis or rheumatism. An antispasmodic, it cures whooping cough, hysteria, and infantile convulsions. With honey and rose oil, cures deafness, with honey clears sight. Powdered Amber was taken for stomach diseases, applied to wounds to stop bleeding. Draws out infection or disease. Eases headaches, toothaches, and respiratory problems.

The elixir strengthens the thyroid, inner ear, nerve tissue, stimulates DNA replication, aids in brain and nervous system diseases and viral inflammations. Increases spiritual awareness. Opens the brow and solar plexus chakras. Aids memory, decision-making, relieves anxiety. Stimulates creative action.

AMETHYST: Cleansing and Transformational

Silicon Oxide. Crystalline Quartz colored by traces of iron. Pale violet to deep purple, fades in sun or when heated. Usually forms adjacent masses of hexagonal crystals with pyramid-shaped points. Transparent, lustrous. Hardness is 7.

Amethyst focuses the violet ray and all of the higher rays very specifically, shaping them so the physical body can accept them. The violet ray is the one that is preparing the way for the transformational changes occurring on Earth. Before the new Earth can come in the remains of the old one must be cleared away. Amethyst helps clear out blocks to the new, higher energies so the higher rays can be used at the cellular level. It can be used on blocked areas of the body and on the whole aura to clear resistances or static energies.

Amethyst has its own group of angels that work through it to bring the seventh ray, along with the higher rays, to Earth. The angels are actively working to clear out negative thought forms and to release what is not harmonious with the new energies. They will show you what you specifically need to clear out.

Hold the crystal in your left hand while meditating and mentally direct the flow of light into the area that needs to be cleared. To direct energy to another person or to the Earth, hold it in the right hand or focus light into it mentally. Imagine the violet light flowing from it to Earth or to an image of the person rather than to the person directly. Amethyst generators will help clear the negative vibrations within a whole room and help move the energy there to a higher vibrational level. Amethyst's major characteristic is anticipation. Use it positively to envision positive, forward-moving changes for Earth. Wearing violet can benefit everyone. The crystal intensifies the effects of the violet ray and makes it more personal and easy to understand as transformation goes forward.

Amethyst is an aid to meditation. It will open and clear your channel and help you make the connections within yourself that will open you to more of your spiritual self. Amethyst has been programmed and is being used by the Hierarchy and the Space Command to assist the clearing and transforming that must occur for Earth to be healed and cleansed. These teachers have much knowledge to offer about transformation. You might find that they want to become close friends and have definite ideas about how you can work with them.

When Amethyst is shaped into spheres, wands, and so forth, it becomes more open to your particular needs. Its energy is less focused until you program it to your purposes. Then it can be just as powerful as a natural crystal. Spheres help to fill the aura with the violet ray and prepare it to receive the deep penetration and direct cleansing of other crystals. They will help to release areas of resistance to the new electrical particles in the higher rays and help to open the cellular level to the white light.

The large geodes can be extremely powerful cleansers and their energy will be used more and more for healing Earth. They are particularly useful for transmitting healing energies from groups. They also raise the vibrational level around them and create a spiritual atmosphere. Purple has often been the color of royalty and of spirituality. Amethyst helps you connect with the finest aspects of yourself.

As an elixir Amethyst helps remove toxins from the body. It takes you beyond your perception of what you are now into what you can be. When its vision becomes yours, you can begin to create more ways to use your creativity and to grow. The elixir takes that vision into your cells and precipitates the regeneration of your DNA into the ideal. It works very well with other healing crystals.

Amethyst works especially well with Aqua Aura. The latter is very activating and opens the body to the clearing action of Amethyst.

Traditional and other sources: Enhances meditations, spiritual connections, and feelings of love. Expands psychic vision, brings insight. Helps contact with inner self. Brings mental peace and quiet, chastity, understanding, represses evil thoughts. Stops false visions. Improves memory. Eases fears and guilt. Aids release of karma. Induces sleep. Enhances mental clarity, strengthens will power, aids control of passions and breaking bad habits. Stimulates greater love. If worn by a man, attracts the love of a noble woman. Seen in dreams, symbolizes sacrifice, overcoming karma or healing impossible situations.

Generally keeps negativity away. Protects soldiers and travelers. Prevents drunkenness. Quiets passion. Signifies courage, justice, moderation, self-discipline, balanced judgment, vigilance, and expertise. Brings victory. Makes a man shrewd in business.

Balances four-body system. Aids self-healing. Amplifies all healing energies. Relieves sinus congestion. Expels poison. Relieves headaches, spasms. Aids assimilation of nutrition. Improves vitality and strengthens the immune system. Stimulates endocrine system. Coordinates brain with nervous system. Cures infertility.

The elixir centers, reduces hyperactivity, increases self-esteem. Helps integration with society. Enhances meditation and spiritual awareness. Increases intuition and balances four bodies. Activates brow and heart chakras. Enhances function of pancreas and pituitary, thymus, and thyroid glands. Balances metabolism. Stimulates midbrain and right-brain activity. Balances left-right brain coordination, easing autism, dyslexia, epilepsy, abnormal neurological discharge, and problems with vision or coordination. Use for diseases of pituitary, immune system collapse, diabetes, and hypoglycemia. Dissolves fatty tissue and activated chelation. Protects against radiation.

ANACLIME: Softens, Stabilizes

*Hydrated Sodium Aluminum Silicate. Crystals have a modified cubic shape.
Also occurs as earthy or granular masses. Colorless, white, pink or yellow,
transparent to translucent with vitreous luster. Cubic system, hardness is 5
to 5.5. When rubbed or heated it becomes electrically charged.*

Anaclime is often found with Copper deposits because it works with
Copper to bind the electrical forces of light into the flow of Earth's
energy. It smooths out any misalignments in the merging of the
energies and stabilizes the newly formed composite flow. It will do the
same for you as you integrate higher energies into your body. Its special
process is especially helpful in healing tissue damaged by insufficient
blood supply. It also balances the emotions of confusion, shock, and
separation.

It is excellent in assisting the conscious channeling of spiritual
energies into the physical body. Place three or four Anaclime crystals
around the recipient or group with any other crystals being used and let
them provide a stable environment for realigning the energies of all into
a more ideal configuration. Spray the elixir around the room to remove
discordant energy and provide a quiet, restful atmosphere.

Anaclime works well with all Copper compounds. It makes Azurite
more effective in raising the vibrational level of your intuition and
enhancing it. It makes Turquoise more effective as a protector and
calmer. It elevates Cuprite's vibrations and helps it bring soul's lightbody in. It magnifies the elevating energy of Chrysocolla enormously.
It also makes many very powerful stones such as Ruby, Emerald or
Diamond easier to work with and easier to understand. It will make
you feel grounded, at ease, and increase your awareness of what is going
on around you.

ANDALUSITE: Balancing

*Aluminum Silicate. Trimorphic with Kyanite and Sillimanite. Short,
prismatic crystals, sometimes in rodlike aggregates. Translucent to opaque,
reddish shades, brown, or dark olive green. Might show pink-green pleochro-
ism. Orthorhombic, hardness is 7.5. A variety called Chiastolite contains
crystals in cruciform configuration.*

Andalusite is useful for balancing the four bodies. It shows you
how to accept and use the special qualities of each appropriately. When
worn over the heart, it helps achieve this through the guidance of your
heart. It also balances energy in your body at the etheric level so that
every part is more able to accept the ideal flow.

Chiastolite has the additional qualities of opening the heart chakra to the Earth. It is balancing for all chakras, but especially for the lower ones, helping them integrate with the heart. It encourages love for Earth, nature, and humanity. It helps you see ways to develop a clearer relationship with Earth as part of your creative structure. It grounds your creativity so that you can use it in practical accomplishments. It is especially helpful if you are very mental and tend to talk or think about doing things rather than actually doing them. It helps you carry things to appropriate conclusion.

Chiastolite is very helpful in the ascension process. Because it helps you maintain a heart-centered Earth connection, you gain the physical-level support you need to transform the energy of your life flow into spiritual energy and connect your soul into every aspect of your life. It helps you see the spiritual value and potential in whatever you do.

As an elixir, it increases flow of energy and water through the kidneys. It strengthens the colon and low back muscles. It also encourages a connection of the lower chakras with the head chakras so that pressure headaches are relieved.

ANGELITE: Calming, Elevating

Blue Anhydrite. See Anhydrite.

This is a very spiritual energy. It brings out the harmonics of the physical levels of energy that can provide a "stairway of light" from dense physical to spiritual awareness, with a connecting point on each step to guide you and lead you forward. This is especially helpful for the emotional body as it is shown by Angelite how to connect the physical and spiritual levels. It draws out tension and stress and stimulates the joyous connection to the universal flow as it is seen by the angels. It helps create an opening that allows you to feel the protection and upliftment they provide.

Angels are a mirror of perfect alignment into the ideal. That is the only way they ever work and their goal is to provide such a connection for all of creation into their vision of perfect love. They are always available as a source of guidance for perfect balance and awareness of your divinity. Humanity hasn't always had a perfect relationship with the angels because its desire to experience all the facets of individual will and alignment have often seemed to conflict with their absolute connection into the Will of the Creator. However, one task of all angels is to support the development of CoCreators and care for their needs and wants. If you choose to explore alignment by choosing all the misalignment you can find, they will help you and still be there to help you connect into the ideal when you are ready, because that is the Will of the ultimate Creator.

Angelite helps you see things from the perspective of the angels and will help you find your path into perfect alignment with your own ideal. It helps relieve the guilt of making mistakes and the frustration of not being able to manifest your ideal as you see it. As you explore ways to make your talents work, Angelite will help you understand the help available from the angels.

It is useful for any chakra, especially the third eye and crown chakras, helping them to open to spiritual energies. It is also useful on the sex (second) chakra as it helps to balance your dynamic and receptive energies emotionally and spiritually. It soothes and balances the intensity of the dynamic energy as it seeks to express itself within the creative flow of your being, while giving your receptive side confidence in its strengths.

As an elixir, it opens you to new connections and facilitates the flow between the physical and etheric levels. It can stabilize an erratic nervous system and calm the mind. It creates an easier flow of information through the brain and helps open up new pathways within it, especially those to the higher mind.

Traditional and other sources: Protects from negativity. Healing, restores strength.

ANGLESITE: Balancing

Lead Sulfate. Prismatic crystals or granular aggregates, colorless, white, gray, green, purple (rare), brown, or black (with Galena). Translucent to transparent with greasy luster. Orthorhombic structure. Hardness is 2.75 to 3.

Anglesite is grounding and balances the body's energy with the physical level. It is excellent for those who are in the process of aligning with the physical level. Many of you who feel that you are not part of Earth and belong somewhere else are beginning to realize that you must come to terms with the fact that you are here and must join the rest of Earth. Anglesite will help you blend your consciousness into the energies of Earth. It gives you a grounded foundation for joining the group. It shows your higher energy levels how to harmonize their vibrations with physicality in such a way that they do not lose their identity. No level is eliminated or altered. All become one within you as you learn to recognize and use more and more levels of self, including the physical, as light.

Blue Anglesite can heal your spiritual vision so that you can use it at the spiritual level. It dispells the misperception that your sight is bad and can thus strengthen your eyes. It releases the confusion that new energies can cause, stabilizing your etheric flow. It provides a stable foundation for transforming and regenerating the cells. It can open areas of congested energy, like a headache, by opening the flow into the rest of the body and connecting them with Earth's flow. Anglesite energy moves around your stuck areas and shows you how to release them if that is your desire. By grounding stuck energy and releasing the flow to the Earth, it opens the chakras.

As an elixir, Anglesite opens the physical level to new energy and allows the cells to adapt to it without a shocked or defensive response. It protects the immune system and reduces stress by allowing the body to see new energy as potentially helpful and assimilable.

ANHYDRITE: Balancing, Creates Openings

Calcium Sulfate. (Same chemical composition as Selenite but with no water in the crystalline structure.) Usually forms fibrous masses that break into small cubes. Prismatic crystals are rare. White, blue, gray or reddish. Translucent or transparent with vitreous to pearly luster. Orthorhombic system, hardness is 3 to 3.5.

This material is used to make sulphuric acid. Anhydrite is not corrosive or destructive, but it does dissolve negative or stuck energies as an acid would by gently moving into it and breaking it down. If you desire transformation it will help break down resistance to the ideal and its new energies, creating the openings you need to make it part of your energy structure. It can be a fairly powerful transformer of the physical level if used with other penetrating energies, but does not feel over-whelming or threatening. It will help you accept change.

As an elixir (a weak or new solution is best), it assists the kidneys and lymph systems in removing impurities and helps reduce edema in the tissues. The elixir helps bring many energies into the body so be clear in your intentions when using it and it will be very useful.

Other sources: Strengthens kidneys and ovaries, releases heavy-metal toxicity. Enhances, balances, and clarifies female qualities.

APATITE: Energizing, Balancing

A group of Phosphates, Arsenates, and Vanadates. Crystals colored blue, green, yellow, violet, clear, or white. Hardness is 3.5 to 4. Hexagonal system. Transparent to opaque with vitreous luster.

Apatite strengthens the physical body and enhances muscular coordination. It also helps organize thinking processes by coordinating the physical, etheric, and molecular brain. By molecular, we mean that the separate components of the neurons work together more effectively. The enhanced neurons can better use the guidance of the etheric structure to support the rest of the body. The process is similar for other parts of the body. When each element in a structure can relate well with all the others, it is then ready to move outside itself and expand into greater usefulness within the whole. Sometimes misperceptions in the subconscious do not allow the support from etheric and higher levels of consciousness to reach the physical level. Apatite is one crystal that is very good at helping you reconnect to the ideal so all levels of self work together smoothly.

Apatite also brings intuition or higher knowledge and awareness into practical use at the third- and fourth-dimensional levels. It can help coordinate the channeling process so that the message comes through more clearly. During or after any clearing, physical or emotional, it helps coordinate the new structure with the new flow of light in your body. It is not especially grounding, but it will help you flow with your Earth connection by helping you feel more coordinated and balanced within it. It will help you use Earth's power as your creativity grows and evolves.

An elixir of Apatite is often useful to loosen heavy metal deposits in the tissues so they can be eliminated. It should be used with something like Fluorite to complete the cleansing, as it is better for loosening than for complete releasing. A few grains of salt added to the elixir would also be helpful for cleansing. It assists coordination as an elixir or by being carried on your body. Placing Apatite crystals on your wrists, ankles, and base of the neck will assist other crystals used for healing and will help you coordinate your whole body with the ideal. It also gives self-confidence and trust in self's abilities.

Traditional and other sources: Strengthens muscles and improves coordination. Eases hypertension. Clears thought. Increases personal power. Aids in the healing of muscle and bone degeneration due to radiation exposure. Opens throat chakra and stimulates expression and reduces stuttering.

APHRODITE STONE.
See Cobalto-Calcite.

APOPHYLLITE: **Uplifting, Angelic Connection**

Hydrated Potassium Calcium Silicate. Pyramid-shaped, cubic or octahedral crystals. Clear, white, pink, green, or yellow. Translucent or transparent with pearly luster. Tetragonal system. Hardness is 4.5 to 5. Perfect basal cleavage.

Apophyllite has a beautiful, spiritually uplifting energy that assists in bringing in the soul's radiance, your light-body. It makes the flow of that light through your body feel more real at the physically conscious level. It will lift your spirits if you feel "down" and help restore hope. If you wear it or carry it frequently it will help release negativity by helping you flow and use more light. It will put problems or negative traits in their proper perspective so you can release them more easily. There is simply no room for negativity or darkness in the radiance of angelic light it brings to you.

As an elixir it can help relieve symptoms of asthma or emphysema. It is healing for the lungs. It raises the energy of your colon and bladder, which are not often regarded as spiritual parts of yourself, and helps release beliefs about heaviness or lack of spirituality in being physical. It shows your subconscious the rightness of everything that happens and helps you use every experience for your upliftment and evolvement. It is highly recommended for helping you realize that you already know how to use all the new energy levels and your spiritual potential for the uplifting of all of Earth. It shows you how to be aware of your divine qualities while remaining centered in where you are at any moment. That is the job of its angelic flow, to help you connect to your divine light.

APPLE CALCITE: Grounds Electrical Flow

Especially helpful to the emotional body in making you more comfortable with the transformational flow. See Calcite.

AQUA AURA: Energizing, Stimulating

Clear Quartz, Silicon Dioxide, treated with Gold. Physical properties the same as Quartz, but it is more fragile (brittle).

Clear Quartz has been processed under heat and pressure with Gold vapor so that the Gold becomes part of the crystalline structure of the Quartz, filling in the spaces in its crystal lattice, incidentally giving it more sparkle. Often, crystals that have been artificially altered or treated are of less value metaphysically. However, this process produces a stone that does not replace natural Quartz for healing and transformation, but gives it a whole new ability to facilitate the process. It focuses more of the higher rays, particularly the ninth and tenth. It helps you connect with your eighth chakra. It can energize you out of your personal perspective. Hold it in your left hand to stimulate greater receptivity or in your right for a greater dynamic flow. Its powerful charge will go deeply into the cells to wake up those that have stuck energy. It will shatter patterns that do not accept its flow. It is at least ten times more powerful than it was before the Gold bonding so use it carefully until you become familiar with it and what it does for you.

You might be able to use it for only a few minutes on your chakras, particularly if you have many deep and sensitive areas associated with any of them. Learn how much stimulation is good for you and allow your nervous system to rest when necessary. Amethyst works particularly well with Aqua Aura to clear out the "debris" it stirs up. It also helps make the higher energies easier to handle. Hematite or Jasper would be useful also to keep the energy grounded if you get too energized by it.

Aqua Aura spheres gather light into themselves and multiply it until it reaches a dimensional level where it can escape the bounds of the Gold coating and radiate the higher rays into your whole aura. They fill it with the higher-vibrational energy and help the four-body system accept the gentle stimulation. These are gentler in their action than the points and can usually be used for a longer time. Basically, they filter out the lower rays and let only the higher rays interact with your own vibrational level, therefore aiding in raising it.

Quartz has been treated similarly with Silver. See Rainbow Quartz.

AQUAMARINE: Calming, Elevates Emotions

Variety of Beryl, Silicate of Beryllium and Aluminum. Pale blue, blue-green, or green hexagonal crystals, pleochroic, transparent, with vitreous luster. Hexagonal system, hardness is 7.5 to 8.

Aquamarine helps release negativity, pain, anger, and depression, replacing them with beauty, peace, love, even joy. It especially helps you activate the beauty of your heart energy. Use it on your solar plexus chakra to calm or balance, on your heart to strengthen your awareness of its beauty, on your root chakra to help accept the beauty of Earth as part of the Divine Plan which you helped create. It helps your polarities work together in harmony. It brings mental peace and clarity through opening your brow chakra. Use it on your throat to help flow the potential of your creative power in a beautiful, harmonious way. It helps the emotional body blend its energies with the soul's and soothes the heart and the emotional body. It keeps the emotional body balanced with the mental body. It helps the emotional, "child" self grow up, open to more light, and see itself as a divine being, responsible and able to handle power.

The angelic essence of Aquamarine is one of beauty and peace. When you wear it, visualize these qualities flowing from every cell and from your heart. With practice and the help of Aquamarine, these qualities will soon be a part of what you are.

As an elixir it dispels negativity and helps release dependence on drugs or other habit-forming substances. It brings your higher emotions into your cells as connectors with the ideal. As you use the finest aspects of yourself you learn to recognize and cooperate with them rather than with the more negative ones. Aquamarine helps heal the effects of degenerative disease and assists in the transmutation of your DNA into the ideal. It can be sprayed on your skin for tissue rejuvenation or into a room to create an atmosphere of peace and alignment.

Traditional and other sources: A sacred stone. Symbol of happiness and eternal youth. Also moderation and self-control. Makes sailors fearless and safe at sea, protects everyone on water. Insures a good catch. Eases fear, confusion. Opens spleen and throat chakras. Aids self-expression. Gives inspiration and desire to explore and integrate self. Preserves health and function of upper body parts, especially jaw, teeth, throat, and neck. Aids digestion and reduces fluid retention in body. Cools, calms, relaxes, clears emotions. Aids meditation. Smooths the flow of life. Strengthens liver, spleen, thyroid, and kidneys. Stimulates white blood cells.

ARAGONITE: Grounding

Calcium Carbonate. Elongated, prismatic crystals, colorless, white, yellow, red-brown, and other colors. Often found in hot spring deposits or fossilized skeletons of marine animals. Hardness is 3.5 to 4, orthorhombic system.

Aragonite helps your physical energy to flow more smoothly and is healing for the base chakra. It will help calm and direct erratic dynamic physical energy, as in hyperactive children or prematurely aroused kundalini energy. This is one of only a few stones that are also quite useful if ingested in concentrations greater than those you find in an elixir. Try letting a piece soak in a glass of water with one teaspoon of vinegar for about twenty-four hours. Drink about one ounce every four hours. It will help you feel more integrated into the flow of practical life at the physical level. As a regular elixir, it helps restore the ability of the base chakra to make secure connections into the flow of Earth's creative energy so you are more effective in being a part of it. It will help you use your heart at the physical level, because your heart needs to be able to flow its energy through the base chakra in order to be wholly effective at the physical level. It is part of the ideal structure that needs to be incorporated into it in a balanced way.

Aragonite has the same electrical properties as Calcite, but it can sometimes reach deeper into the vibrational levels of physicality. It also helps nourish the adrenal and pituitary glands with the electrical flow they need for ideal balance and function.

AVENTURINE: Healing

Microcrystalline variety of quartz. Green, pinkish-brown or grayish-white with sparkles of mica. Translucent.

Aventurine is a very valuable healing tool right now. It magnifies the Divine Blueprint so the cells can align with the electrical flow of the new energies as well as with the parts of the old ones that are still needed and are still part of that evolving Divine Blueprint. It provides a soft, easy connection with them. Its specific, soothing energy absorbs negative patterns that are not part of the blueprint. Each time you hold it, it focuses on deeper and deeper levels until the blueprint is clear and better understood.

It is willing to work with you if you wish to focus healing into specific areas of your body or aura. Place it over the area that requires healing. Placing it on your shoulders, hips, and ankles helps to magnify your ability to align with your light potential. Sleeping with it every night helps the bodies release old blocks and heal resistant areas. It is a gentle energy and you probably can't overdose on it.

Aventurine is capable of channeling very specific and complicated energy sequences that help the body connect into the many levels of dimensional experiencing that are available within physical existence now. It is very excited to be working with humanity at this beginning of the New Age.

As an elixir, it heals and supports all bodily functions. It helps you use the dynamic, creative aspects of Earth power known as kundalini energy. It balances and stabilizes your use of your base chakra.

Traditional and other sources: Symbol of visionary power. Gives an Earth-centered comfort and support. Stabilizes and calms emotions. Relieves buried fears, anxiety, and psychosomatic illness. Aids development of emotional tranquility and positive attitude toward life. Promotes general well-being and brings opportunity. Brings good luck in gambling. Opens heart and throat chakras. The elixir is cleansing. Stimulates nerve and muscular tissues. Very helpful in psychotherapy.

AZEZTULITE: Grounding, Opening of Higher Chakras

A form of Quartz, which see. Found as small, clear, flattened, irregularly shaped crystals, not usually more than one inch long.

Probably contains trace minerals that have not been identified at this time.

Azeztulite opens a clear flow of all your energies into the Earth. It invokes an increasing flow of higher energies throughout your whole body. It will stretch your willingness and ability to use more light, but it will never overwhelm you or produce a shutdown of your subconscious control over the flow. It opens the higher chakras, especially the crown chakra, allowing the guidance of your soul in regulating, directing, and using the energy it brings in. It expands your whole aura and helps you release energy blocks by bringing energy through them as if they did not exist. It trains your subconscious to use light in the ideal way, with no limits placed on your ability to be light.

Azeztulite's effects are powerful, but repeated use of a particular stone will allow it to work with you more personally on specific areas. It helps you choose the next appropriate areas within yourself to clear and brings in whatever light you need to take the next step. It creates a very real connection into your energy structure, so if others use it, it might bring their problems to you. This could be helpful or not; you can decide. You can wear it all the time as a necklace, once you become accustomed to its energies, or you can place it on whatever part of your body seems to be especially stuck.

As an elixir, it opens your cells to using more light and expands their ability to connect electrically into the universal flow. It also helps you develop conscious awareness and control of your spiritual power to create your dreams and ideals at the physical level.

It accelerates the ascension process, but be careful here. What you don't understand about yourself can create confusion and doubts about your abilities or clarity. You must be patient with the process of exploring and learning to use your full potential as a CoCreator. The most important thing Azeztulite teaches you is how to work with your soul as a partner at the physical level. Then it helps you learn to work together, integrating your soul's spiritual wisdom with your knowledge of physical existence.

AZURITE: Balancing, Understanding Light

Hydrous Copper Carbonate. Forms bright blue, prismatic crystals or earthy, granular or concretionary masses. Transparent to translucent with vitreous luster. Monoclinic system, hardness is 3.5 to 4. Used to be crushed to make pigments. Often found with Malachite or Chrysocolla.

Azurite in the earthy or granular forms is gentle and soothing. The crystalline forms are more energizing and create movement that leads to balance if you are ready for it. It helps to blend the flow between the heart and third eye. It makes them more receptive to higher energies of the soul by helping the system understand how those flow patterns can be used at the physical level. It helps open the heart to the higher rays and stabilize it within this increasing electrical flow. It is healing to the endocrine glands, especially the pituitary and thyroid, and balancing for the whole electrochemical system of the body.

Azurite clears the mind, making it easier to coordinate your intuition into your conscious thought. It will also make dreams more lucid and help you remember them. It helps you to allow the third eye to open. It enhances meditation by helping you understand the qualities of divine light so you can use them through your heart, consciously. It is bringing through a quality of light, much needed by Earth right now, which helps you see how much light is a part of physicality. You might notice when you wear Azurite you feel more connected with Earth through love.

It will help you develop your own individuality as a creative consciousness within the focus of Earth and physical existence. It is one of many crystals that can help you recognize your own unique creative qualities as you look for places to use them within your Earth experience. You will be able to open to the creative ideals and the creative potential that is available to you as you interact with light at the more subtle levels of vibration.

Azurite can be powerful in its own right, and when it is used with more powerful stones like Aqua Aura, Herkimer Diamonds, Moldavite or the precious gems, it helps to anchor their light into the physical, cellular level.

As an elixir, Azurite aids the assimilation and use of trace elements necessary for healthy metabolism. It is sometimes useful in hypothyroidism. In the bath, it stimulates an awareness of where to direct energy in your body for healing and helps the body use the light you direct to it in the appropriate way.

Traditional and other sources: Enhances and improves spiritual and psychic awareness, raises consciousness, clears and stimulates mind, brings insight, visionary power, and pure thought. Improves mental control and aids decision-making. Enhances and clarifies dreams, healing, and meditation. Aids hypnosis. Gives courage. Intensifies energy flow of nervous system but acts in a calm, soothing way to reduce stress and confusion. Rub it to lift spirits.

The elixir stimulates and helps with problems of the skin, bones, thyroid (hypothyroidism), and spleen. Eases joint problems and arthritis. Stimulates calcium absorption. Strengthens the etheric body, stimulates the mental body, opens the spleen and solar plexus chakras to bring in more life force flow.

AZURITE/MALACHITE/CHRYSOCOLLA: Balancing, Integrative

Azurite is often found blended with these and other Copper-bearing minerals. The combination helps balance and smooth the interaction of the mind and emotions. It shows the mental body the beauty of the emotional flow and how to work with it. As the bodies learn to work together, they begin to allow the spiritual body into the flow and to share the creative process with the physical. Then you have what you need to create what you want here in your physical reality. If you are actively involved with working on clearing your subconscious of unproductive patterns of behavior and thought, this stone will help you integrate each learning experience, balance the use of it between the bodies and anchor more light into the physical body. It helps you feel more comfortable with all aspects of yourself.

As an elixir, this stone is transformational and regenerative. It brings knowledge and awareness of the divine ideal and makes them available at the cellular level. It can be used for balancing emotions and for clearer dreams. When you carry or wear this stone, it makes your light connections more stable and consistent with whatever you are doing. It aids communication and helps release negative programming about being with or working with groups.

Other sources: Helps control abnormal cell growth and malignancies. Cleanses negative thought forms. The elixir enhances the dream state and astral projection. Gives much patience and discipline. Increases clairvoyance. Eases anxiety. Benefits the skin, liver, thymus, muscles. Alleviates anorexia nervosa and compulsive eating, hyperactivity, muscular dystrophy, cirrhosis of liver. Facilitates bile action and increases absorption of copper, zinc and vitamins A and E.

BARITE: Softening

Barium Sulfate. Found as tabular crystals, granular or earthy masses or as rosettes. Colorless, yellow, red, green, black. Crystals are transparent or translucent with vitreous luster. Orthorhombic system. Hardness is 2.5 to 3.5.

Barite is grounding but is unique for its ability to soften the effects of high-vibrational or intense energies. It doesn't mute their effects, just makes them easier to handle. As an elixir it aids elimination and aids digestion. It also enhances other elixirs that are used for detoxification.

BENITOITE: Integration, Completion

Barium Titanium Silicate. Forms stubby, prismatic, dipyramidal crystals of various shades of blue. Translucent to transparent with vitreous luster. Pleochroic, blue to colorless. Very fluorescent in ultraviolet light. Hexagonal system, hardness is 6.5.

Benitoite is wonderful for helping you reach a completion or integrated point in your understanding. More importantly, it helps you realize when you have reached that point of completion so that you have full use of the knowledge gained. It also helps resolve emotional problems so that you can apply the newly transformed energy into positive use. It helps you direct the energy toward your goal. It then helps you carry the transformation into the physical body and assists in the restructuring process. It works very well with other stones: Kyanite to integrate a heart-centered perspective, Ruby to integrate your special gifts into your understanding of how to achieve your purposes, Aventurine to heal the physical body and increase its light potential, Topaz or Shattuckite to restructure the DNA.

When you wear Benitoite you will feel energized but calm and clearly aware of everything around you. You will find it easier to connect into whatever you need. You will also find that it is easier to apply love to any situation. As an elixir, Benitoite reduces fevers and inflammation. It enhances the electrical conductivity of the nerves without overstimulation and it clears your mind. It can also help blend the energies of a group or between partners.

Other Sources: Stimulates pituitary gland and aids connection with higher self. Increases spiritual awareness and knowledge of self. Enhances clairvoyance.

BERYL: Strengthening

Beryllium Aluminum Silicate. Forms hexagonal prisms, is transparent, has a vitreous luster. Often opaque, milky white, or pale yellow, pale green, or pale gray. Some crystals are over three feet in length. The bright, transparent colors are the precious gems, Emerald, Aquamarine, and Morganite. There are also bright yellow (Golden Beryl), yellow-green (Heliodor) and, rarely, red (Bixbite) or colorless gems. Hardness is 7.5 to 8. Hexagonal system.

Beryl strengthens the etheric structure of the body and aids its alignment with light. It strengthens the endocrine system, especially the pineal and pituitary glands. It aids all assimilative functions. It helps the small intestine assimilate nutrition, it helps the lungs absorb oxygen, it helps the brain assimilate new information, and the mind and emotions to accept new perspectives.

Beryl processes the information about the ideal conveyed to the cells by light. It is one of the keys that unlocks the new information focused by Quartz and grounded by the heavy metals and other slower vibrations. There are enormous, transparent crystals of Beryl of blue, green, yellow, and red buried deep in Earth. They serve to anchor and make available the power of the seven rays which are continually maintaining (or recreating) Earth's existence. They are somewhat etheric now, but as Earth evolves to a clearer use of the higher vibrational levels they will be more real to you. They will be discovered and become somewhat accessible, although they will remain where they are. It is helpful to visualize them as the sides of a pyramid with a brown and gold base that radiates energy for Earth's physical and spiritual support. Imagine yourself at the center of this pyramid, balanced within the universal flow of love as focused by the spiritual teachers who help you flow with that love. You can travel into this pyramid now in your spiritual or higher astral body. One day, many will be able to take their physical bodies there.

Golden Beryl supports the heart and the solar plexus. It heals and strengthens the solar plexus and the organs associated with it, especially the liver, stomach, and small intestines. Its elixir is healing, strengthening, and stabilizing for them. It is very useful in clearing and cleansing as it helps to bring in the ideal that immediately replaces what has been released with the new patterns, locking them into the restructured flow.

Heliodor heals the heart, helps it to accept the new energies and assists it in coordinating their use throughout the whole body. It helps bring the soul's healing into your body and your life. Its elixir strengthens and stabilizes the heartbeat. It also assists the coordination of heart and mind. It heals your feet and your Earth connection by helping you accept the creative flow of love from Earth that nurtures your life.

Red Beryl can be used to activate the kundalini energy and direct it into your conscious purpose. It strongly focuses your spiritual purpose for you. If you are working toward a more perfect alignment with the ideal, it will automatically bring up the creative resources you have available through your heart and your experiences. It would be best worn just above the heart to assist you in your alignment with your soul. Its elixir is healing for the heart and releases the physical effects of depression and grief.

Large, clouded or opaque Beryl crystals can serve as aids to meditation for you or a group by helping to create a stronger spiritual connection (your spiritual channel) and a clearer alignment into the wisdom or message encoded into the light that you allow through it. They powerfully ground the light and hold it in focus for you. If you or a group works with them long enough they grow clearer as your channel becomes stronger and clearer. They help to integrate the energies and purpose of the group, and they help to manifest the group purpose.

See also Aquamarine, Emerald, and Morganite.

Traditional and other sources: Symbolizes eternal youthfulness, good luck, and cooperation. A favorite oracle stone. Stimulates mind and intellect. Brings marital harmony. Cure for idleness and stupidity, especially Heliodor. Strengthens the will. Gives protection and increases receptivity. Aids problems with jaw and throat. Cures tonsillitis and swollen glands of neck when it is rubbed on them. Heals diseases and injuries of eyes (with powdered stone). Eases tonsillitis, bowel cancer, and swollen glands. Keeps liver healthy.

The elixir aids cardiovascular system problems and restores elasticity of its cells. Cleanses intestinal tract and eases its overstimulation during flu or diarrhea. Strengthens the pituitary gland. Relieves anxiety and overstimulation of mind. Eases tension in physical body. Supports receptive energy during activation of dynamic. Stops hiccups.

BLOODSTONE (HELIOTROPE):   Cleansing

Variety of Jasper (see Quartz). Deep green with spots of bright red.

Bloodstone is grounding and protective like other Jaspers but with a significant addition. It is good for cleansing the liver and blood and balancing the elements in the blood. When used with Aqua Aura it can help the red blood cells carry more oxygen to the tissues for their regeneration and transformation. So, while it it not a particularly high-energy stone, it holds the light at the physical level while the other stones bring in the ideal for reshaping and re-energizing the DNA. Its elixir is specific for energizing the availability of oxygen at the physical, cellular level. When used with "heart stones" like Rose Quartz, Rhodochrosite, Rhodonite, or Kunzite, Bloodstone is healing to the heart and emotions.

Traditional and other sources: Brings out inner Christ Light. Symbolizes the Passion and Sacrifice of Jesus Christ. Pliny is said to have used a mirror made of Bloodstone to view eclipses, thus the name Heliotrope. Also it was thought it changed the Sun's image to red when immersed in water.

Gives courage and mental balance. Helps expression of feelings and heals anger. Powerful mover of blocks within self. Aids self-confidence. Adds harmony to aura. Brings riches and fortune. Encourages caution. Protects from deception.

Stops bleeding and heals wounds. Prevents injury and disease. Aids diagnosis of disease. Reduces tumors and hemorrhoids. Purifies blood, detoxifies kidneys, liver, and spleen. Relieves blood disorders, leukemia, acute stomach and bowel pain. Clears bloodshot eyes, relieves sunstroke and headaches. Promotes healthy bone marrow, spleen, and heart. Supports good circulation and boosts physical and mental energy. Balances predominant male or female energies, aiding testicles or ovaries, cervix and uterus.

The elixir connects mind and circulatory system, allowing one to increase blood flow to specific parts of body. Opens and aligns heart and base chakras. Brings in spiritual aspects of life force flow if one wishes to use them. Is balancing and healing for bone marrow and blood cells, spleen, heart and capillaries, testes, ovaries, cervix, and uterus. Enhances cell replication and blood supply to endocrine glands.

BOJI STONES: Balancing, Calming, Energizing, Integrating

Sedimentary in origin, with bits of fossil and metallic compounds, usually Iron Sulfides. Colors are black to brown, often with gold or blue iridescence. Varieties of these are found in many places, but the name Boji is copyrighted and applies to ones found in Arkansas at the base of a natural Earth pyramid. They are gathered by their "mother" who specially prepares them for our use, making them superior tools to work with.

These fascinating stones have been brought from the womb of the Earth by angelic beings who offer them as a gift to those who love the Earth and have served her for so long. They will help you accept being a part of Earth and her love. They can help you blend into the flow of Earth's new energies with the support of all her divine resources.

They are essentially balanced, but they like to work in pairs or even groups. The smooth ones are considered to be female and the ones with pointed projections male. One "male" can make the energy of a group of "females" more penetrating. Any of them can help you balance your male with your female polarities and your physical body with your spirit. They also help balance your mind and emotions as well as your head and heart. If there could be one stone that does everything, this one comes close to accomplishing that. It helps integrate the new, higher energies but is very grounding. It keeps you "down to Earth," connected to your purpose on Earth.

A Boji is like a newborn baby. It is unlimited potential, yet it needs the nurturing of your willingness to serve as a part of the Divine Plan for Earth. It needs your friendship and companionship to accomplish its part in this Plan. It works through your love. In return it will help you evolve the highest expression of your love, and help you connect into whatever you need to accomplish your purpose on Earth. At the same time, its wisdom contains the profound accumulation of eons of Earth existence. Bojis have gathered it from many sources within Earth and integrated it into a system of using light that is very appropriate now, in this time of transcendence.

You can use Bojis by holding them, preferably one in each hand, or by placing them on your chakras for balancing and calming. They calm an overactive chakra by channeling its energy to the others and balancing the flow with the whole system. You can also put them on or under your pillow for protection and divine guidance while you sleep. They will help you remember your dreams. Place them under or on your feet while you meditate to make a good connection to the Earth and to balance your channel.

Herkimer Diamonds work very well with Bojis. They emphasize the higher energy potential that is inherent in the Boji but not always easily available. Boji Stones plus Herkimers provide a full spectrum of light connections which activate the flow in a very balanced way through all twelve of the chakras in use on Earth now.

Bojis make the ideal pet. The more you use them and love them the more they will be able to love and serve you. They should not be stored in contact with each other as this causes them to crumble. Contact with other stones is not harmful; they like that.

Traditional and other sources: Were used in Lemuria to build new plant forms. Attune you to nature. Healing and balancing. Raise spirits, bring joy. Grounding. Protective. Heal holes in aura. Increase vitality. Regenerate tissues. Align four bodies. Open spiritual channel, access to subconscious mind and communication with physical body. Aid understanding of needs and diseases of plants and animals.

BUSTAMITE: Power Enhancing

Calcium Manganese Silicate. Forms masses, sometimes fibrous. Pale flesh-pink to red-brown. Transparent to translucent, vitreous luster. Triclinic system. Hardness is 5.5 to 6.5.

Bustamite pulls the vital flow of Earth's energy into your body, particularly the lower chakras. It helps you make a more secure connection with Earth and with your power. It grounds sexual energy, directing it into whatever purpose you desire. It encourages a connective flow among your three lower chakras and provides a basis of power that you can consciously use creatively. It allows a clearer support of your spiritual purposes by your personal power structure. At the same time, it helps you direct your desires into alignment with the ideal, if you will allow that.

Bustamite helps you feel more comfortable with using your dynamic power, your yang energy. It stimulates it and helps you channel it into your purposes and control it. It is grounding, without damping the energy flow. It amplifies the power of all other stones, especially violet or yellow ones. Its purpose is to help you become part of Earth's spiritual group purpose. It helps women feel comfortable with being dynamic and assertive and more able to handle responsibility for their own lives. It helps men channel their power with conscious awareness of their spiritual obligations.

CALCITE: Electrically Connective

Calcium Carbonate. Hardness is 3. Many colors, including crystal clear, yellow, rust-red, blue, green, orange, and brown. Trigonal system, appears in masses (microcrystalline), or in rhombohedral, scalenohedral or prismatic crystals. Transparent to opaque with vitreous luster. Splits easily along cleavage planes to form perfect rhombohedrons. Very birefringent, sometimes fluorescent.

One of the most valuable of all the stones. It helps align and connect the electrical energy of the soul into the physical body, aligning into the Divine Blueprint at all levels. A dynamic flow of energy is invoked through holding Clear Calcite and the connection into the cells is facilitated so they can learn how to use it. It also helps to integrate the energy flow in the cells, releasing old flow patterns or illusions in the flow of your creativity. Each time Calcite is held, it thrusts the cell into contact with a more dynamic, creative level. This is helpful to the ascension process as you proceed, step-by-step, through the integration of each aspect of yourself that your soul requires to function effectively at the physical level.

Calcite helps open up new energy pathways within the brain and heart chakras which aid in the integration of the whole system. If used near the throat, it can help integrate the heart and head by directing more light through this upper triangle and into the whole system. In other words, it is grounding, in that it connects the higher chakras with the rest of the system so they can realize their purpose of aiding the flow of light into the physical level.

Calcite is often helpful in creating more movement in stuck areas. This will show you what is buried so that other stones that are more helpful for removing negativity can help release it. It helps sort out the various levels of energy so your subconscious can see how to use them appropriately. It can show you the vibrational level of specific things you find in yourself so you can decide how or whether to use them.

Calcite will help you feel light, joyous, and at peace with self, others and Earth. It enhances the flow to others physically, especially in loving and healing situations. It heightens group energies, making more of individual energy available to the group purpose. It helps you find more positive things or energies around you to connect with.

Clear Calcites are more intense and electrical in their effect. They often have many "rainbows" which show you clearly the nature of your soul's energy, your lightbody, and help you accept it and use it at the physical level. Most important, it can help you release feelings of unworthiness about being acceptable to your soul and using its light. As you look at its rainbows, imagine yourself filled with them and surrounded by them.

Yellow Calcite helps establish connections between the mind and emotions, energizing the mind and clearing or healing the emotions through the ideal blueprint.

Pink Calcite is especially good for making new connections into your heart and assisting the expanding flow between the solar plexus and heart so necessary for ascension. It facilitates emotional clarity.

Mangano Calcite is translucent to opaque, showing bands of soft pink and white. It is very soothing to the emotions and calming to the whole body, especially during an emotional crisis.

Blue Calcite is similar and calming to mind and emotions, bringing in easy levels of the electrical, higher energies that can be integrated as you are able to handle them. It can help heal the effects of intense clearing or emotional crises. It helps re-energize the cells with the ideal after releasing the old patterns.

Green Calcite is the most healing of all. The electrical energy it invokes is accepted well at the physical level. It facilitates a balancing of the life force flowing to the etheric-physical body through the spleen chakra. It is used most readily by healthy cells, strengthening them if they need to compete with some imbalance of energy in the body. All varieties of Calcite are useful as elixirs, but green is especially so. All of its healing properties are enhanced and made more available by water.

Brown Calcites, including the redder tones, are grounding. They stimulate the electrical flow in the base chakra, stepping it down to levels that are useful to the physical body and physical Earth. They help you feel more comfortable with bringing the electrical flow of the higher energies into physical existence as you align the new sequencing of time and space that they are bringing. They help focus the fourth-dimensional viewpoint into the third-dimensional framework, so you can integrate the two. They help you realize your creativity at the physical level by allowing the electrical flow of the creative energy to be shaped by your intention and to connect in at all levels so that it reaches the physical as a complete and well-integrated format, capable of being effective within physical existence.

Gray Calcite has a soft energy that nevertheless can bring in much of the electrical flow of soul and help you connect with your light-body at the physical level. Just having it in the same room helps you flow with the love that is available on Earth now. This helps you connect with the rest of the CoCreative system on Earth so you can find your place in it and be supported and challenged by it at the same time. It helps the physical-etheric structure to adjust its electrical flow to a higher level of energy. It helps stuck areas connect with other areas that are using the flow well. It gains a broader perspective when used with other types of Calcite and in return blends the electrical flow of each.

Orange Calcite aids in integrating your four bodies by helping the mental body to understand how they fit together. It facilitates a good communicative flow among them and creates a receptive openness in them that creates an understanding of all the viewpoints of your various parts of self. This moves you toward your goal of integrating all these parts into one. It moves stuck energies in the brain and brow chakra, facilitating clearing there. If there are blockages in the throat or lower chakras, you might find brown Calcite used with Hematite or some other grounding crystal helpful for releasing any pressure buildup.

Honey Calcite looks just that, a light honey color. It energizes the dynamic, electrical flow but is healing and calming at the same time. It creates a balanced but clear and alive feeling. It would be useful with many stones to expand their effect and create a wider viewpoint of any problem or potential. It works by opening your aura outward electrically, expanding it while you see how to blend it in with the rest of Earth's energy flow.

All the above Calcite qualities are enhanced as elixirs. In addition, they strengthen and "electrify" the skeletal structure so that it holds more light. They can also help heal weak or decayed teeth and might even be able to regenerate damaged root and gum tissues, if you are willing to learn also to accept life as an opportunity for assimilating light into your total being.

The spiritual teacher, Vywamus, recommends all types of Calcite, especially the clear ones, as the "most useful stone right now."

Traditional and other sources: Amplifies thoughts. Calms mind and increases intuition. Relieves frustrations and fear. Increases mental abilities, improves memory, aids astral projection. Balances yin and yang energies. Aids kidney function and their elimination of toxins, also spleen and pancreas. Alleviates syphilis.

CARNELIAN: Strengthening, Grounding

A variety of Chalcedony, colored rusty red by bits of iron dispersed among the tiny grains of Quartz. Properties similar to Quartz.

Carnelian has been popular since ancient times since it holds a polish very well. Its function now is to help guide humanity into the flow of the fourth dimension by strengthening the body, through the blood, to sustain a more energetic flow of life force. It strengthens the liver and pancreas and is healing to these organs, expecially when combined with green varieties of Aventurine or Calcite. It works by making the cells more open to the multidimensional qualities of the nutrient supply received in the blood.

When it is placed on outer parts of the body, it draws energy into the heart where it is then available to the rest of the physical structure. As the physical body, with the help of Carnelian, begins to cope more effectively with the changing energy levels, you will feel more optimistic about being here and being effective as light.

As an elixir Carnelian's healing qualities become more available to the cells' level and makes them more ready to receive the nurturing elements of light. It grounds the transformational energies and helps the cells assimilate them.

Traditional and other sources: Symbol of joy and peace, dignity and power. Promotes courage, releases sorrow and fear. Gives ambition, motivation, and direction. Improves memory. Stimulates curiosity. Grounds and focuses thoughts. Strengthens voice and confidence in speaking. Balances emotions. Generally grounding. Brings prosperity. Balances male-female energies.

Protects against illness and poisoning. Stops bleeding. Aids birth process. Aids infertility and impotence, cleanses reproductive organs. Strengthens respiratory system. Promotes healthy intake and assimilation of food. Aids stomach problems. Purifies blood and liver. Used to activate energy of other stones.

The elixir increases oxygen in the body, strengthens respiration and circulation, promotes tissue regeneration, takes out excess radiation, aids assimilation of nutrition. Opens heart chakra and strengthens etheric body.

CASSITERITE: Balancing

Tin Oxide. Found as opaque, black or translucent red-brown crystals, square with pyramidal tops or as granular masses with wood-like bands. Tetragonal system. Hardness is 6 to 7. An ore of tin.

Like other metal ores, Cassiterite can feel very energizing, but its final effect is balance. It energizes the energy flow through or around blocked areas and diverts energy from areas that are overstimulated. It reads the ideal at the astral level and directs energy according to it, bringing in the intensity necessary for ideal functioning of your energy system. It works very close to the physical level, not bringing in information from particularly high levels, but translating what is directly appropriate or needed for ideal functioning at the physical level.

You will feel it differently, according to your needs. Sometimes it might be very grounding, as it helps you create a better connection at the base chakra level of energy. Other times it will feel energizing, as it helps you use the energy patterns of the solar plexus that supply your body with vital energy. It can even feel calming if you are generally overstimulated, as it disconnects you from the stress or imbalance that is affecting you.

Cassiterite allows the soul to communicate with the physical body to tell it what it needs to do to allow a clearer connection with the light-body, while it does not actually create the connection. It is most useful in transformation for assisting the step-by-step process of integrating higher energies that occurs as you work on clearing yourself and under-standing your own energy structure and how it works.

As an elixir, Cassiterite helps balance the endocrine glands, especially the adrenals and thyroid. It can be useful in cancer and autoimmune diseases for its ability to direct energy away from areas or patterns which do not support healthy bodily function. It is useful with regenerative elixirs for its ability to show the cells how to use the ideal patterns in the most effective ways. It usually needs the additional information on interpretation of the ideal from other stones, but it can be very important in using that information.

Worn or carried on the person, Cassiterite brings a balanced, practical perspective that is open to outside knowledge and guidance.

It can help connect you to answers to practical or communicative problems, if you are actively looking for them.

CAT'S-EYE or CYMOPHANE: Understanding

A form of Chrysoberyl (which see), that is chatoyant, hence its name. Has inclusions of fine, parallel, crystal needles. Yellow, yellow-green, gray-green, or honey-colored.

Also called "Noble Cat's-Eye," it will help you see your strengths and give you confidence in their value. Cymophane aids understanding, not just at the mental level, but at the emotional and physical as well. It creates an interface between different levels of self or of understanding that allows you to know something in a very integrated way that involves many levels of self other than the mind. In this way, it allows understanding to involve your whole self, carrying it into your cells and integrating it into soul's perspective as well.

Placed on your forehead, it will help balance your mind and emotions and release the limitations of your physical consciousness. It then opens your consciousness, not only to your higher mind, but also to the true value and meaning of your physical self. Wearing it makes you feel comfortable with yourself and with others. It helps you accept others as they are. It bring stability to relationships. Use it in your bath to release self-doubt and lack of confidence. Use it as an elixir to promote transformation and regeneration of cells through balanced integration of light.

Traditional and other sources: Protects wearer from evil spirits, protects health and guards against poverty. If pressed against the forehead between the eyes, gives foresight.

CAVANSITE: Grounding

Calcium Vanadium Silicate. Forms small, bright blue-green to sky blue prismatic crystals, or rosettes. Transparent, vitreous luster. Orthorhombic system. Hardness is 3 to 4.

Cavansite encourages the electrical flow through your energy system by strengthening the connections with Earth and eliminating, at least temporarily, any blocks that would create the pain and heat which cause the subconscious to stop the flow. It shows the subconscious that the resistance is not necessary and that you can handle whatever energy is available and necessary for your soul's purposes. It helps you find practical ways of achieving your purposes within a physical-plane perspective. It brings practicality, discretion, and acceptance of being physical. It shows you that being physical is a spiritual state of being and helps you live your life as a spiritual activity.

Cavansite encourages communication and improves relations. It not only helps you accept others for who they are, but it helps you accept yourself and any inconsistencies within yourself. You must recognize and accept whatever is there before you can resolve any problems.

Cavansite elixir is best used by spraying it lightly on your body. It balances your energies and grounds any excesses, stabilizing all systems and processes.

CELESTITE: Calming, Elevates Thoughts

Strontium Sulfate. Prismatic crystals, orthorhombic system. Colorless, milky white or pale blue, transparent to translucent, vitreous or pearly luster. Also occurs as massive aggregates. Hardness is 3 to 3.5. It is used as a source of strontium which adds red to fireworks displays.

Celestite is very much a New Age stone. The angels have endowed it with special properties to help raise the consciousness of humanity. It can help you rise above the fear and negativity of the mass consciousness. Earth cannot be transformed unless there are enough people who can maintain a level of consciousness that is not immersed in old fear programs.

Celestite helps the physical and emotional structures work together to use the higher energies and increasing activity of the cellular level. It facilitates cooperation and understanding among the four bodies so they don't work against each other. It is soothing to the emotional body and helps you relax into a clearer spiritual connection to the Earth and to the light coming in from many directions. Having it near you will give you confidence in your ability to adjust to changes.

It supports the lungs and breathing, helping you bring more life force into your physical cells from the energy in the air you breath. It can bring peace if you are stressed and will calm and balance your mind. It also helps open your mind to new ideas and higher levels of consciousness. It produces calm and protection during sleep and brings pleasant dreams. It aids transformation and regeneration by making your cells more open to healing available from the angels and the many spiritual beings who work with them. Carrying or wearing it makes you feel vitalized and sure of spiritual help and guidance.

It is so integrated with the fourth- and fifth-dimensional energies of the angels that it does not need water to release its most healing qualities for your body's cells. It is best used by having it near you when you meditate. If you reach a state of being open to cosmic energies, your body will take in enough of what it needs from Celestite to last for a time, which varies with different people. It is, however, good in your bath for bringing angelic energy into your cells for healing.

Traditional and other sources: Eases breathing and helps adjust body at high altitudes. Reduces fevers.

CHALCEDONY: Expressing Love

Name given to the microcrystalline varieties of Quartz that form concretionary deposits. Fibrous crystals of Quartz are cemented together with Opal (Hydrated Silica). All colors. The clear yellowish and brownish-red varieties are called Sard. Hardness, like Quartz, is 7.

See Agate, Jasper, Onyx, Carnelian, Chrysoprase, Bloodstone, Gem Silica.

Chalcedony often forms "roses," rounded, flat nodules, usually shades of gray or white, which are used in their natural state. They are an expression of Nature's love and creativity. They will help you find ways to express love creatively. They help you connect with your own heart more completely. They help you bond creatively with Earth and to recognize her beauty and potential as well as your own. They are nice companions and will help release loneliness and hopelessness. They disconnect you from negativity and gently raise your spirits if you are tired or depressed. They work well with all other stones to bring love into your life. Used in an elixir, they give patience and feelings of joy.

Other sources: Opens heart chakra and inspires spiritual and artistic creativity. Links mind and emotions. Aid to dealing with traumatic memories. Clears mind and increases objectivity. Clears anxiety and sadness. Gives optimism. Promotes maternal feelings and increases lactation.

The elixir stimulates bone marrow, spleen, red blood cells, and heart. Aids assimilation of iron, silicon and vitamin K. Strengthens the etheric flow.

CHALCOPYRITE: Grounding, Balancing

Copper Iron Sulfide. Usually forms microcrystalline masses. Dark or brassy yellow and opaque with metallic luster, might have an iridescent film. Tetragonal structure, hardness is 3.5 to 4.

Chalcopyrite is grounding but in a way that is energizing and even electrical. It brings Earth's energy into the cells like other metals, but it particularly balances the Earth energy with incoming energy from extraterrestrial sources. It stabilizes the cells as they integrate higher energies. It can be quite calming and uplifting as your body realizes that it can use these seemingly destructive energies creatively. It balances by interacting with the cells through the body's whole etheric flow, where other minerals work through the etheric level of each cell. It is the Copper in it that gives it the whole-body approach. The Iron in Chalcopyrite then takes the energy into the cells. The Sulphur blends the elements and strengthens the flow.

As an elixir, Chalcopyrite brings into physical reality the electrical network that allows you to function effectively as part of Earth and gives you access to its creative power. We can't stress enough that since you have made Earth part of your evolutionary growth as a CoCreator, you must become part of Earth and learn to use its power as your own before you can complete this level of experiencing and pass on to the next. You can do it without Copper, Iron or Chalcopyrite stones, but they will help because they have already done it. They show you how to connect with the physical meaning of your vast experience and integrate it into your whole consciousness. Chalcopyrite heals by increasing the potential flow of healing energy through the physical level as well as all higher vibrational levels. It helps connect them all into the physical level. It is a valuable grounder with all transformational stones.

Chalcopyrite makes you feel strong and in control. It lets you know you have the power to do whatever you want. It brings perseverance and makes you sure of your purpose. It also makes you feel able to interact with others in whatever way is necessary.

CHAROITE: Strengthens Spiritual Flow

Calcium Potassium Silicate with Hydroxyl and Fluorine. Bright violet, mottled with white and sometimes black. Discovered in the 1970s. Opaque, amorphous.

Charoite is one of the best stones for balancing the energies of your crown chakra, helping it to open and helping you become acquainted with and use the energies of your eighth and ninth chakras. It also helps you flow the perspective of oneness and wholeness from your twelfth chakra. It clears and releases stuckness or negativity in using the energy vibrations of all the higher chakras and then brings their energy into your cells. It helps anchor light into these newly opened areas as they become available to become part of your light potential. It prevents some of the rebound that often brings you down after a peak experience. It tends to level out the ups and downs of the transformation process.

Like other violet stones, it focuses the violet transforming ray very effectively, allowing it to bring in the new levels of the ideal that Earth is learning to use now. Charoite can be breathtakingly beautiful in the finest stones, just as your light can be stupendous when it begins to shine as the ideal. It is channeling energy from Sirius and the spiritual center in Orion where the Divine Plan is coordinated for this part of the Galaxy. It is excellent when used with Quartz as it clarifies even more the ideal for human DNA and helps the cells use it in rebuilding your bodily structure during transformation. This ideal is being focused on Earth by the Galactic Center.

Charoite heals the pineal gland and assists in integrating this physical aspect of your seventh chakra into a perfect crystalline structure that allows you a clear connection with your soul and brings its full participation into your life. This is the purpose of Christ Consciousness: to allow you to function at the physical level with the same perfect alignment into light that you use in the higher dimensions.

Charoite can energize stuck areas in the body and promote healing. As an elixir, it helps the cells accept the ideal and release negativity and resistance to new levels of light. It makes the higher vibrations easier to assimilate. It aids digestion and is healing for the whole alimentary tract and the kidneys. It stabilizes the action of the spleen and strengthens the pranic flow to the heart. An elixir of Quartz and Charoite will help bones heal and help prevent osteoporosis by emphasizing the structure of the ideal as it manifests at the physical level. It also softens the effects of light throughout the body, making the more intense energies less damaging if your incomplete understanding and use of light are damaging your immune system or your DNA.

Charoite has its own special angelic consciousness which has been activated to help Earth make the transformation leap which is occurring now. It is a special gift to Earth, a new energy for Earth's growing creativity and expanding awareness of its place in the spiritual universe. It will make you feel free and open to accepting new ideas.

CHABAZITE: Elevates Physical Energy

Hydrated Calcium Aluminum Silicate. Forms rhombohedral crystals, often as interpenetrating twins. Colorless, white, greenish or reddish gray. Transparent to translucent with vitreous luster. Hexagonal system, hardness is 4 to 5.

Chabazite opens mental communication with the physical level. It can help you understand your body and it will help you listen to it. It will help you see the light potential that is there for you. Being physical is an immense source of spiritual strength if you accept your physical body absolutely as a part of your divine self. Chabazite will help you see through your misperceptions and misunderstandings about physicality and life on Earth so you can recognize the love and light that are its final essence.

Chabazite creates a supportive energy for the physical part of yourself that allows it to climb up the vibrational ladder of light, stabilizing each new level and opening your understanding of the next. It might give you a feeling of being powerfully grounded because it focuses higher energies into the physical level. If you stretch your awareness beyond that feeling you will understand how those energies have become more available to you at the physical level.

As an elixir, Chabazite makes healing energy more available to areas that are out of balance or lacking enervation. It supports breathing and enhances oxygen intake.

CHIASTOLITE.
See Andalusite.

CHRISTOBALITE: Balancing

Silicon Oxide.   Octahedral crystals are rare.   Usually forms masses of microcrystals.   Colorless, white or gray, translucent to opaque.   Tetragonal system alters to cubic above 1470 degrees Centigrade.   Hardness is 7.

Christobalite is stabilizing and balancing. It helps maintain a focus and concentrates thought. It prevents the fluctuations in your use of new energies, as you adapt them to your use, by damping the effects of uncertainty and fear about whether or not your body can tolerate them. As an elixir, it will help reduce mood swings and stablize your blood chemistry.

Carrying or wearing it will help focus your energy on whatever you are doing. It will help you see more efficient ways of doing things. It will help you feel capable of achieving the task. It helps you put everything into proper perspective, understanding the spiritual impor- tance of small tasks.

CHRYSOBERYL: Reduces Stress

Beryllium Aluminum Oxide. Usually appears as twinned crystals, cloudy or transparent and lustrous, various shades of yellow to greenish or brownish. Orthorhombic system, hardness is 8.5.

Its outstanding quality is its luster. See also Alexandrite and Cat's-Eye (Cymophane).

Chrysoberyl can help you relax and move more easily with the variations in the flow of the ideal as you and Earth seek alignment with it. It takes away stress by helping you see that you are already part of everything that is, and all you need to do is accept that you have what you need within yourself. In that sense, it will help you feel more at ease with yourself. It will boost your self-confidence in situations where you might tend to doubt your ablilty to cope. It activates the flow through the solar plexus and connects it into the rest of the chakras in a balanced way. In this sense, it balances the emotions but does not restrain them.

Chrysoberyl is an energy support for the nervous system, helping it to work more smoothly. It is valuable in the transformation process for helping you use new etheric, electrical connections in the brain and other cells. For this, wear it on hands, wrists, ankles, or toes. It supports the heart by facilitating the flow of energy from the physical body to it, allowing you to support yourself more effectively. It then facilitates the flow from the heart so it doesn't have to work so hard and so you support yourself with confidence. For this, wear it over your heart or neck.

As an elixir, it works differently, bringing the light connections through the cellular membranes and flowing them around the DNA strands very closely, in the ideal way to help you align with the ever-evolving ideal. It is useful for healing every deviation from the ideal and creating perfect health. It is also rejuvenating when used as an elixir to drink, on skin, or to breathe in with air.

CHRYSOCOLLA: Healing, Expanding

Hydrated Copper and Aluminum Silicate. Microcrystalline masses, monoclinic structure. Bright green to bluish. Translucent with vitreous luster. Hardness is 2.5.

Chrysocolla helps heal the emotions through the ideal perspective as seen by the heart. It helps integrate the ideal of the heart into the emotional flow so you can flow as perfect love. It helps resolve the negative emotions so you can transform their energy into positive ones that can flow in balance with the ideal. This helps heal the split between your physical, conscious self and your ideal self that doesn't allow you to see all parts of yourself as divine and as part of the Plan.

Chrysocolla assists other crystals in interacting with all your bodies.

This is a universal energy that is healing at all levels, but with a third-dimensional focus. It can make physical existence seem transcendental as it elevates your understanding of it. This can expand tremendously your perceptions of the cosmic, spiritual potentials within physicality. It has been programmed to bring through a particular aspect of the Divine Plan for the New Age which is designed to expand Earth's great potential to share love. It helps you connect into that love within the Plan and Earth. Its energy is Earth-centered but also very connected to Galactic Center.

Chrysocolla can be healing and relaxing to the heart and other vital organs in a crisis. It is useful as an elixir, but will be most effective if the crystal is placed in water for just a few minutes. Visualize the water being activated by it and then remove it. The energy that is being transferred is so high that too great a concentration of it makes it less active, "weighs it down," in a sense.

Wearing Chrysocolla gives a feeling that everything is as it should be. It helps you share that feeling with others so that they begin to accept themselves more easily. It is especially helpful for people who work with others who need a great deal of emotional or psychic support. Your energy will flow to them as needed, without depleting you, and it will be under the direction of your heart. You can't do anything for them, but you can reflect the ideal connection and flow to them so they can learn to support themselves eventually.

Traditional and other sources: Supports music and musicians. Aids prosperity, luck and shrewdness in business. Calms emotions and stimulates mind. Increases intuitive and analytical ability. Expands mind, relieves confusion. Aids practical application of creativity. Brings peace and harmony. Aids flow of emotions. Eases stress and hypertension. Releases fear and guilt.

Stimulates lungs. Clears liver, relieves digestive upsets, ulcers, and arthritis. Aids digestive organs, lungs, coccyx, medulla oblongata. Stimulates hemoglobin formation.

The elixir strengthens the lungs, thyroid, coccyx, and medulla oblongata and stimulates hemoglobin. Cleanses subconscious blocks.

CHRYSOLITE.
See Peridot.

CHRYSOPRASE: Elevating, Having an Angelic Connection

A form of Chalcedony Quartz, colored by Nickel. Apple green to yellow green.

Chrysoprase has a specific mission. It is ready to prepare your physical-emotional-mental vehicle to integrate your lightbody, which is the ultimate expression of the divine ideal Quartz is bringing to Earth. It brings a sense of peace within the confusion of change. It gives you a feeling of upliftment that is grounded in the awareness of what must be done at the physical level. Its angelic spirit is dedicated to helping you transform your body into the ideal expression of light and your full potential.

Chrysoprase brings an aura of acceptance of healing and transformational energy into the cells. It can be used to create a healing space where other, more specific or direct crystal energies will be used. It works best with clear Quartz, preparing the cells to receive the ideal blueprint. Wearing it will help you accept the vibrational variations that you encounter in your daily activities and that come from your subconscious as well as from without. You are creating these distortions in the ideal flow and Chrysoprase will help you transform them through understanding and by dealing with them at the emotional and physical levels. When you can be totally accepting of everything around you, you are able to make it part of a learning process that is transformational. Everything becomes power that you can use for your creative purposes. Chrysoprase makes this understood at the physical level.

As an elixir, it lifts the spirits and removes the negative feelings aroused by difficult relations with others. It helps create connective "spaces" for clearer relationships. Use with heart stones like Rose Quartz or Rhodonite to create receptivity to heart-centered connections in your aura. The elixir assists other crystal elixirs that remove toxicity from the body. It also is healing to your emotional body and your emotional relationship to Earth. It locks into negative emotional patterns and lifts them to heart level, transforming them into positive energy.

Traditional and other sources: "Manifests the supreme heavenly love of truth" (Swedenborg). Stimulates creativity, wit, and imagination. Reveals hidden talents. Brings mental peace, enhances intuition, and gives insight into personal problems. Gives prudence, adaptability, and versatility. Lessens greed, selfishness, and carelessness. Eases hysteria. Increases fertility. Enhances healing by strengthening etheric body.

Strengthens eyesight and eases eye problems. Relieves pain and gout. The elixir supports the prostate, testes, fallopian tubes, and ovaries. It increases fertility and alleviates associated diseases. Eases venereal diseases. Opens the second chakra and strengthens the etheric body. Lifts depression.

CINNABAR: Strengthens Self-Awareness

Mercury Sulfide. Opaque, dull, scarlet, microcrystalline or earthy masses. Hexagonal system. Hardness is 2 to 2.5.

Cinnabar works from the mental level of vibrational frequencies to strengthen your connection to the ideal. It can help you understand the flow as it comes to you and you interact with it. It stresses your essential needs and identity within the cosmic flow. It shows you how to blend with others creatively, retaining awareness of your own gifts and giving appreciation of others' gifts.

Cinnabar should probably not be used as an elixir; however, it will radiate its special gifts more strongly when placed in a pyramid, even a small one. It might give a feeling of heaviness until you are ready to share your creativity with others and with the Plan. It will help you do that. For others, it will immediately open the aura so that you receive communications from many levels. It enhances all communication by creating a flow system at the cellular level that supports your awareness of all messages.

CITRINE: Supports Mental Activity

Quartz with microscopic inclusions of iron hydrates that color it yellow with varying degrees of brown. Clear and lustrous, its properties and form are those of Quartz. Natural Citrine is not so common. Much of what you will see is Amethyst that has been heated. But color is important and this material is still very useful.

Citrine is specific for aiding the mind. It helps it expand and open to new ideas, including those of soul. It helps the mind expand so it can encompass the ideal your soul is seeking to bring into physical existence. It helps the mind put it into a conceptual framework that has meaning at the physical level of consciousness. It helps ease the flow of energy through the mind, aiding in the removal of mental blocks. It has been programmed by the spiritual teachers for the purpose of connecting into the spiritual ideal and awakening the mind to it. It helps bring the energy of your creative flow through the mind into the other bodies, facilitating communication with them.

Citrine clears the mind, delineating the concepts that are being formulated. It helps you feel confident in recognizing the ideal and using it. It also energizes these concepts so they find their place within the creative flow on Earth. It literally strengthens the electrical flow in the brain itself, helping it form new connections and new patterns of thought and extending those lines of thought into all dimensions. It is helpful for exploring your creative potential.

Citrine helps the emotional body understand how the mental body works and shows it how it can energize the mind's creations, making you more productive. This is particularly true if the Citrine is used with green or orange Calcite, as they help the emotions form the electrical connections with mental energy.

The elixir stimulates cellular activity, promoting regeneration and healing. It supports the kidneys and muscles and aids assimilation of nutrients from digestion. It also stimulates the brain cells, making you more alert. It removes toxic substances that result from poisoning or infection. It also helps dispel the negative thoughts that predispose you to such problems. It is a gentle energy that can be used liberally and which combines well with other elixirs or stones. It can also be used to heal other crystals that have been damaged by mishandling. Place the one to be healed in the elixir or spray it with it.

Traditional and other sources: Stimulates mental abilities, aids focus, clears mind, aids mental discipline and emotional control. Enhances intuition and wisdom. Aids communication and voice projection. Enhances creativity and abundance. Relieves emotional distress and suicidal tendencies. Improves will and channels creativity. Stimulates healing. Aids heart, kidneys, liver, and muscles. Removes toxins from body. Light colors of Citrine affect physical body, darker ones affect spiritual self.

The elixir alleviates self-destructive and suicidal tendencies. With meditation, rejuvenates the physical and eliminates toxic thought forms. Increases connection to higher self, giving true self-confidence. Aligns four bodies, stimulates the etheric system. Stimulates the base, heart, and throat chakras.

Elixir also stimulates physical healing and eases karmic cellular disease patterns. Relieves effects of radiation. Aids absorption of antioxidants. Supports heart, kidneys, liver, and muscles. Stimulates regeneration especially of red and white blood cells; also lymph system and brain tissues, somewhat. Removes toxicity from infection such as in appendicitis, gangrene or autotoxemia.

COBALTO-CALCITE (Aphrodite Stone):   Balancing

Cobalt Calcium Oxide. Forms spherical masses or crystalline or radiating crusts. Bright rose-red to gray, brown or black. Transparent to translucent with vitreous luster. Trigonal system. Hardness is 3 to 4. Aphrodite Stone is the name for the bright, rose-red variety.

This variety of Calcite creates an awareness of flow beyond the physical-etheric levels. It opens the next level of vibrations which is that of emotions and subconscious communications. It expands your awareness of the potential of balanced emotions to create a larger sphere of influence energetically. It helps you build a foundation of higher-energy pathways that open your ability to extend your power and influence beyond your presently perceived limits. It finds and stabilizes whatever energies you need to expand your creative influence. It also serves as a connecting point for energies from many levels and coordinates their use at the emotional level. It does not stir up negative emotions. It sees flow as love and expands your ability to use the higher emotions and your heart.

Cobalto-Calcite especially opens the flow between the solar plexus and the heart and creates a more secure connection between them. It can then bring an enormous amount of energy from your upper chakras into your lower chakras, energy that might not have been available before. This expands your power base by integrating spiritual energy with Earth power. It will help resolve lower emotions or emotional imbalance into higher emotions. It stimulates the flow of love between individuals and creates bonds of love. It makes communication a positive experience for everyone involved. If you or someone around you is in the habit of subconsciously using the flow between you in inappropriate ways, it will protect you from psychic draining, manipulation, or attack. It also helps you release blocks of fear, mistrust, or unworthiness which make clear communication difficult at all levels. It will open you to using your heart in all relations with others and balancing the use of mental and spiritual levels with emotions for a more complete communicative flow within yourself.

The ablity to use emotions at the ideal level of unconditional love and selflessness is a major key to attaining spiritual control of your life at the physical level. It puts you completely within the flow of the Divine Plan that is already set up to allow you to use your full potential as a creator. It allows you to consciously ulitize and direct the flow of the ideal into your purposes without any limitations. This stone brings the connections with the universal flow to perfection within you. As you work to clear and balance your energies it will help you come closer and closer to perfect alignment with the ideal flow.

These crystals are ideal for cleansing the aura for yourself or in healing sessions with others. Use it in sweeping movements from top to bottom, or in circular movements around trouble spots. If you finish off your treatment with it, you will leave your subject feeling lighter but more connected.

COPPER: Electrical, Grounding

Usually forms large masses or dendritic or filiform masses. Crystals are rare.
Coppery-red, black or green on exposed surfaces, opaque with metallic luster.
Cubic system. Hardness is 2.5 to 3.

Copper's most outstanding property is its ability to conduct electricity. It conducts all energies well. In its natural form it provides a good electrical connection with Earth in both directions, to and from you. It removes discordant vibrations in your light flow and realigns it with the ideal. It is healing because it mirrors to your subconscious how to flow energy freely. It helps break up areas of negativity in the body by bringing light into them. Quartz and Copper are an excellent combination for flowing light into the body. Copper helps carry into the cells the ideal blueprint that Quartz brings, grounding it there. Copper can activate a good connection with any crystal, making it more effective. Energies flowing through Copper retain their specific properties while being adjusted to blend with those at the physical level.

As an elixir, Copper increases the body's ability to transfer energy from one part to another. For instance, it aids the transfer of energy from oxygen into the hemoglobin and then into the cells. It assists the cells in using the etheric energy in the oxygen you take from the air. It is energizing in general. It helps the body use the new, higher energies rather than rejecting them, thus helping the restructuring of the immune system into one that works well with them. By using Copper, you provide a more effective connection with your friends and helpers in the Space Command as they help you heal and transform your body.

Traditional and other sources: Increases self-acceptance and balances the emotions, aligning spiritual and mental bodies. Makes you less restless, excitable, apathetic, neurotic, hysterical, and eases early stages of psychosis. Eases fear of death, poor memory, and improves mental focus. Balances and harmonizes the astral and physical bodies.

Strengthens and balances reproductive organs in men and women. Helps heal cholera, edema, eczema, flu, gallbladder disorders, hernia, jaundice, neuralgia, sciatica, scarlet fever, schizophrenia, chilliness, dizziness, nausea, night fever, pneumonia and pulmonary imbalances, heart palpitations, and low heart rate. Improves function of endocrine glands and promotes red blood cell formation and capillary action. Alleviates throat problems, coughing, hoarseness, laryngitis, difficulty in swallowing. An overnight infusion of Copper plate and lime water clears eyes. Cleanses wounds. Dissolved in vinegar and mixed with lard it heals ulcers and fungus infections. Eases cramps, convulsions, nervous disorders, and mental or physical exhaustion resulting from overactive mind or lack of sleep. Eases arthritis and rheumatism. Aids assimilation of Copper. Alleviates intestinal disorders and stimulates metabolism.

The elixir is helpful in all inflammations, including those of the cerebral cortex and inner ear. Aids breathing by strengthening diaphragm. Increases flexibility in bones, ligaments, tendons, sinuses. Balances right and left brain, easing autism, dyslexia, epilepsy, coordination, and visual problems. Balances all levels of self, especially the lower five chakras, and opens the heart. Facilitates all electrical functions in the physical body as well as in the etheric and higher. Eases effects of cosmic radiation. Amplifies thought.

CORAL: Supports Life

Calcium Carbonate with protein binding agents. Skeletons of marine organisms. Red, pink, white, coral, black, brown or blue, mostly opaque. Trigonal system, hardness is 2.5 to 4.

Coral helps the physical body use the nourishment provided at the physical and etheric levels. It particularly aids the flow of the basic etheric energy (prana) which supports life. It enhances the flow between the physical and emotional levels of the body, facilitating release of old energy and the intake of new. It can be soothing for the emotional body and support its needs to communicate and flow. It can loosen any tendency to withdraw from contact with others at the emotional level.

As an elixir, it strengthens bones, teeth, and skeletal alignment. Pink and Pink-Orange Coral especially promote healing by helping the body assimilate nutrition, particularly sugars. It helps balance the pancreas and the liver functions having to do with glycogen formation and distribution. Black Coral helps the colon heal and function well. Brown coral removes toxic materials from muscles. White and Blue Coral are healing for nerve and brain tissues. Red Coral makes muscles stronger. All Coral is useful in the bath for removing toxicity, which is especially helpful for relieving arthritis pain.

Traditional and other sources: Relaxes mind and emotions. Raises vibrations and brings attunement to nature and creative forces. Stabilizes personality. Promotes a good disposition. Prevents nightmares and madness. Releases melancholy and worry. Orange Coral helps release pent-up energy, boosts self-esteem.

Protects travelers. Protects against witchcraft, the evil eye, and depression. Protects anyone from thieves and storms, all accidents of fire and water and disease. If it breaks while you are wearing it, it has given its life energy in protecting you. Protects dogs from rabies. Powdered and mixed with seeds, protects crops from thunderstorms, disease, caterpillars, and locusts. Protects children from danger and epilepsy if given before anything else at time of birth.

Deepens in color if worn by a man, lightens if worn by a woman. Also pales if worn by an ill person, darkens when health is restored. Balances body. Releases tension, boosts energy, relieves vocal strain. Red Coral protects against sterility, strengthens and supports growth of children.

Cures almost everything, external or internal. Dries, cools, binds. Used for fevers, leukemia, diseased gums, spleen imbalances, ulcers, asthma, constipation, coughs, emaciation, eye problems, indigestion, jaundice, lack of appetite, obestity, and rickets. Stimulates fertility. Aids childbirth. Stops hemorrhages, menorrhagia, and any abnormal discharges. Stops watery eyes and clears sight. Strengthens the heart primarily, also the stomach and liver. Acts on mucous membrane secretions and bile secretions. Worn as a cure for indigestion. Stops convulsions. Reduces scarring. Neutralizes poison and bites of scorpions and snakes.

Powdered and mixed with Pearl for children with colic, vomiting; protection from disease. Dissolved in acid, is used to cleanse the blood. Powdered Coral taken in fairly large doses produces violent coughing and cures whooping cough and chronic convulsive coughing in children.

The elixir balances all levels of self and the use of male and female aspects of self from the spiritual level. Strengthens the etheric structure and supports its nurturing of the blood cells; also the heart and circulation, easing anemia, hemorrhage, varicose veins, and contraction of arteries. Increases capillary action. Stimulates reproduction of red and white blood cells. Strengthens the spine, lessening its degeneration and stimulating its regeneration. Lessens senility and increases concentration.

Red Coral activates the thyroid and stimulates the metabolism, thus releasing toxins from muscles and aiding emotional balance. Pink Coral increases sensitivity and aids white blood cells, lymph system, spleen, and thymus, specifically. Gurudas says Coral elixir should always be treated with blue light before using, to make its qualities available.

CORDIERITE
See Iolite.

CORUNDUM: Strengthening

Aluminum Oxide. All colors including black, any shade, opaque to transparent, as masses or tapered, prismatic crystals. Trigonal system. Hardness is 9.

While Ruby and Sapphire are the most popular and well-known forms, all varieties are useful. Corundum gives courage to use your special talents and wisdom to know that you must find your own way. It shows you that success in unfolding your divine purpose will not come by following another but from unfolding your inner self in creative ways only you can discover. Your part in the Plan cannot be carried out to best advantage by anyone but yourself and you must find out how to fit it into the whole. But the Creator has placed part of Himself and Herself in you and will give you unlimited support in discovering yourself fully. Corundum will help you find your special purpose. Your experiences on Earth act as the polishing material that reveal your inner truth and power and Corundum, all varieties, will help you reap the rewards of that process.

Corundum is very useful as an elixir. It provides the strength you need to find solutions to your problems. It also helps free the body of toxic accumulation of heavy metals according to homeopathic principles, replacing them with the materials needed for health.

Rubies and Sapphires sometimes develop six-rayed stars. Some degree of opacity is necessary to see a star, so often these stones are not as valuable as the clearer ones, but they are always wonderful aids to meditation. They help bring a clearer mental and emotional connection with your soul and help you hear its message more clearly. Just gazing at their perfect balance and beauty helps ease the merging of soul's energy structure within that of your body.

See also Ruby and Sapphire.

COVELLITE: Stimulating, Expands Energy

Copper Sulfide. Usually forms masses of little plates. A deep, iridescent, indigo-blue, opaque with metallic luster. Hexagonal system, hardness is 1.5 to 2.

Covellite enhances the electrical flow through your body. It will energize the body part it is near. It assists the transformation process by helping to break down the barriers that limit your ability to use the higher energies. It works exceptionally well with Quartz to facilitate the flow of the ideal into the cells. Covellite enhances the electrical potential in the cells' walls so they attract and receive the new energies more completely. It can also stir up a lot of blocked energy, so be ready to work with what comes up. It is not ordinarily recommended as an elixir.

CROCOITE: Stimulating

Lead Sulfate. Forms striated, translucent, red-orange, prismatic crystals which might be hollow. Hardness is 2.5 to 3. Monoclinic system.

Crocoite is fairly rare, but is a powerful stimulator of the dynamic, creative flow. It can blast holes in your resistance to using your dynamic energy. It can be sexually stimulating and energizing for the whole body. It brings in a great deal of healing power which is helpful in transforming the self-destructive patterns of illness into self-healing. It stimulates self-love and encourages expansion through understanding how to respect your own abilities. It is not recommended as an elixir.

CUPRITE: Grounding

Copper Oxide.   Octahedral, cubic or dodecahedral crystals, dark red, sometimes altered to Malachite on the surface. Translucent, becomes opaque when exposed to air. Also occurs as masses of fine hair-like crystals. Cubic system. Hardness is 4.

Cuprite energizes your electrical connection to Earth and helps your root chakra draw power from it. It energizes and magnifies your dynamic energy. It helps you validate your own power and your right to use it creatively. It gives you courage to act dynamically. It can help energize you if you are tired. It can also help open your spiritual channel by providing the grounding needed to bring its energy into your body and consciousness. Many of you would rather forget how much your physical body is a part of your spiritual wholeness. Earth is part of your consciousness that you must learn to use to be complete. Other crystals will help you see how to do that and Cuprite will then help you connect with and use the new sources of power you discover in your Earth connection.

Used over the second (sex) chakra, Cuprite will help focus your energy into a specific purpose. On the solar plexus, at the navel, it will often bring up issues about power that you need to deal with. It is not ordinarily so useful on the higher chakras. It works on them through being placed on the lower ones. It is valuable in crystal grids for grounding and intensifying the combined energies of the other crystals and helping you to integrate your energies with them.

As an elixir, Cuprite also stimulates the formation of red blood cells and increases their efficiency. It is healing for the adrenals and sex glands. It helps stimulate the efficiency of the blood flow to muscles.

Other Sources: Alleviates overintensification of the etheric energy which often occurs in thyroid excesses. The elixir increases absorption of Copper and Gold, aiding the heart, thymus, bones, and nerves. Used for tachycardia, heavy metal toxicity and female pelvic disease. Stimulates and regenerates muscle tissue. Balances difficulties about masculinity. Opens the heart chakra, especially in men, releasing its higher properties. During therapy, can help bring out problems with parental imaging.

DANBURITE: Integrates, Creates Openings

Calcium Boron Silicate.   Clear prismatic crystals with wedge-shaped terminations, occasionally tinged with pink or yellow.   Transparent with vitreous luster. Orthorhombic system. Hardness is 7.

Danburite is a very important stone for those who are working on clearing and integrating themselves. It helps build bridges into all parts of self, then brings the parts into the whole and helps you integrate them. It will also open areas that you have not been willing or able to look at before. This can be overwhelming if they are large areas.

As you begin to use it or wear it, you might notice that you feel irritable, depressed, or even angry. This indicates that your emotional body is feeling some degree of overwhelm or resistance to what is being revealed in yourself. It might be something "negative" that you need to work with and clear, or it might be part of your potential, a talent that you have never before recognized. Persisting in the judicious use of Danburite will help you look at what is causing those feelings and resolve them. If you feel too overwhelmed, stop using it for a while. Yellow Labradorite can help you rebalance. When you are ready to use Danburite again you will find that the area has been partially desensitized and is easier to work with.

Danburite accentuates the emotional flow and magnifies it, so you can use it to see into each area of self more clearly and understand it. This can be a powerful aid in clearing. It is also a powerful tool to use in integrating your strengths into the use of your whole power structure. It will help you integrate your creative power into the flow of the Divine Plan.

Using Danburite with Quartz helps the flow to stay within a structure that you can understand. Some of the grounding stones would be useful in conjunction with this to help utilize the Earth itself to allow you to use the Earth's energy-integration structure to help you integrate.

Ruby is an especially good partner for this stone as it emphasizes your strengths and your creative power in the integration process. It helps you use your heart. Danburite with Emerald is a potent combination that activates the flow of your dynamic power into whatever you are doing. We recommend that you not use that combination until you have worked with Danburite for a while and have completed clearing whatever it is bringing up. It is best to clear most other issues before you begin with power itself. Rose Quartz would be an especially good energy to help smooth the flow of your work with Danburite at all levels. Any colored stone helps it do its work. Yellow Labradorite or Spectrolite are notable for their ability to help overcome any overwhelm you experience with it and to make the integration process easier.

As you work with Danburite for a while, you might find that it restructures your whole environment, because you will be using more of your potential and integrating more of your potential. Like Calcite, this stone helps the cells integrate the electrical flow and heals breaks in it. It works at a higher vibrational level than Calcite, but it is gentle in integrating the higher frequencies into a flexible framework that is adaptable to the changing flow of the Plan; that is, if you are diligent in watching for what it brings up and cultivate a habit of willingness to work on clearing yourself of anything not pertinent to your ideal and your divine purpose.

As as elixir Danburite penetrates into the deeper energy levels and helps release any subconscious misperceptions that are crystallized there as disease or imperfection. It prepares the cells for transformation according to the ideal. It works at the etheric levels to bypass connections into wrong thinking and create new openings into the pattern for perfect health and balanced living. It can help your body overcome destructive habits and teach it to desire what will allow it to be perfect.

DIAMOND: Crystallizing the Ideal

Carbon. Occurs naturally in octahedral forms. Transparent, very lustrous. Clear, yellow or brown tints are common. Blue, pale green, pink, violet, or even red tones are rare. Cubic system. Hardness is 10.

Diamond is the king of the Mineral Kingdom. Its hardness and brilliance make it traditionally the favorite precious stone, although fine Rubies and Emeralds can be more expensive. Its energy is difficult to use. You must know exactly what you want and be specific in your invocations with it because it is so accurate in creating the structure of your thought. It invokes the potential in your whole being to help bring what you desire into realization. Once a diamond has been programmed, it will hold the structure of that idea until it is specifically asked to change it. If it is programmed with love, you will invoke assistance of the Divine Plan, since that is the ideal pattern for using love.

Diamond stimulates or augments any state of being. Use it or visualize it in or on any area of the body that needs to be restored to full circulation. It personifies the first ray (Divine Will) but combines all the rays within itself, so it might be used with all other stones to augment their qualities.

Diamond symbolizes ideal balance of male and female polarities within the life flow. It wants to eliminate any blocks to achieving that ideal. It enhances partnerships only if you are willing to work on yourself to release barriers to achieving perfect balance between you and your partner. If you cling to selfishness and self-centeredness, your search for the ideal will cause it to dissolve the partnership. To maintain the flow between partners you must be willing to maintain loving communication. This job has traditionally belonged to the woman, so it is she who is given the Diamond. With the growing realization that both partners need to be responsible for the health of marriage, Diamonds might not be used as much any more.

As an elixir it strengthens the whole being at all levels, making it more radiant and clear. It can be ruthless in bringing up anything that is not part of the ideal and forcing you to deal with it. It does not stint in its quest to create that ideal.

Traditional and other sources: Seen in dreams, symbolizes initiation and the higher self. Also symbol of kingship and power, virtue, purity, innocence, and mental clarity. Corresponds to Saturn. Symbolizes constancy and purity and enhances love in marriage, but if its wearer sins or is unfaithful, it loses its power. Brings power, friendship, wealth, everlasting youth, success, good fortune. Activates personal power and will. Enhances power of other stones. Is a pure focus of Source energy if you are not materialistic. Promotes clear thought.

Dark-colored diamonds are supposed to be male, light ones, female. They were said to be able to produce offspring. Has an affinity for Gold and is found with it often; it even attracts Gold. Has an antipathy to Lodestone. It protects from snakes, fire, poison, sickness, thieves, flood, and evil spirits. Confers cleverness, protects from strife, sorrow, witchcraft and attack by animals. A man should carry it on his left side where it protects his limbs and promotes virility.

Works from highest spiritual levels into physical. A master healer.

Removes all diseases, taking their life force. Cooling. Generally absorbs energy. Strengthens all bodily functions. Heals insanity. Powerful remover of blocks and negativity that interfere with other vibrational remedies. Removes poison from drink if dipped in it. Sweats in the presence of poison or venom. Also was once powdered and used as poison. Flawed stones cause lameness, jaundice, pleurisy, or leprosy. Good ones bring strength, courage, and victory in battle.

The elixir balances and heals the brain. Use for brain fever, brain tumors, pituitary and pineal gland problems, hemorrhage, inflammation, and left-right brain disorders including autism, dyslexia, epilepsy, abnormal neurological discharge, lack of physical body or visual coordination. Adjusts the cranial bones. Releases tension in head and shoulders, TMJ, upper cervical spine. Eases syphilis, strengthens the testicles.

Elixir also removes the life force from most diseases. Draws out energy, aids removal of toxicity. Aids other stones and elixirs in recharging their energy. Removes blocks in crown chakra. Stimulates the brow and sex chakras. Strengthens self-esteem security and eases anxiety. Promotes clear thought and aligns one with the higher self. Cleanses the etheric body and aligns it with the physical. Enhances protein absorption.

DIOPSIDE: Healing, Softening

Magnesium Calcium Silicate. Prismatic crystals or aggregates, shades of green, bright to blackish or yellow. Transparent or semi-opaque with chatoyancy or asterism. Birefringent. Monoclinic system. Hardness is 5.5 to 6.

Diopside facilitates flow in an integrative way. It helps bring things together. This can be parts of yourself that you are working with or the energy of substances that you wish to bring into your body. Other stones will facilitate the connections, but Diopside will increase the flow between them so they communicate well. Its green color is the key that tells you that it works from your heart, allowing you to use love more easily to carry out the process. It flows the connections from all parts or elements back through the heart, making it an integral part of the communication process.

Diopside works from a perspective of unconditional love, making it very adaptable to many uses. Its potential is still developing, and the use to which humanity puts it will help it decide its future purpose. It will help you expand your heart and teach you to be flexible and allowing of others. As a connector into the will of Source it provides you with the abundance Its love has for you.

Diopside can help you digest your food and assimilate it more efficiently. It can help you integrate new information by making the mind more receptive. It can help you use the love of your higher self in your life if you choose to focus on learning to do that. Diopside works well with all other crystals, helping you to assimilate their energy and stretch into the ideal more completely. As an elixir, it helps you relax and feel that everything is all right. It will also be the best form to aid digestion. It helps you derive more spiritual support from the planet through your food. It will relax a nervous stomach and help you sleep more peacefully, promoting healing during that time. It also helps your liver and kidneys eliminate negative or inappropriate energies from your body.

DIOPTASE: Relaxes Resistance

Hydrous Copper Silicate. Bright emerald green crystals, transparent to translucent, vitreous luster. Trigonal system, hardness is 5.

Dioptase will increase the energy flow in your body by decreasing resistance to it. It is good at going around stuck areas and helping to dissolve them. It is especially effective at releasing blocks in the lower chakras. It is of fairly high vibrational level, but it harmonizes well with energies concerned with drawing and using energy from Earth. Remember, you are part of Earth, and Dioptase will help you flow as part of it.

It is especially good at helping you accept abundance, because abundance is an important part of the universal flow of Source energy. Your body was meant to be supported by it. You are the ones who chose to limit the ways you can nurture your energy needs. Dioptase will help you rediscover many ways to use light as energy. When combined with Quartz, especially Clear Quartz, it brings this new energy directly to the parts of your cells that need it most and enhances their particular function. It also helps you reach out and connect with whatever you need to accomplish your purposes.

Dioptase will also help you deal with issues about using the dynamic energy (yang) for your own purposes. Many of you have the subconscious misperception that it is safest to allow whatever "gods" you are working with to use it for you. But the gods, if they are evolved ones, are here to help you become one of them, to help you evolve into your infinite potential. To do this you must learn to act as if Divine Will were your own will and take full responsibility for it. You are here to become more creative and to learn to do what the gods have previously done for you. Your dynamic energy, in balance with your receptivity, is the tool you use to grow and learn more about yourself. Dioptase can help you learn to stop allowing or expecting somebody else to create your life for you.

Dioptase is especially strengthing to the heart, immune system, and adrenals. As an elixir, it strengthens the evolving structure of your being as you rebuild it into the ideal. It helps you flow your purpose and learning with the new structure, so it helps the transformation process by making new connections more immediately available. It enhances the healing qualities of other crystals.

DOLOMITE: Calming, Draws Out Confusion

Calcium and magnesium carbonate. Colorless, white, pink or yellowish, rhombohedral crystals or masses. Transparent or translucent with vitreous or pearly luster. Trigonal system. Hardness is 3.5 to 4.

Dolomite is formed from the sea, often from the remains of marine amimals, and so provides a watery, flowing energy field that feels like home to the emotional body. It helps the emotional body achieve balance during change. You can hold it and allow it to remove stress and confusion from your body.

DRAVITE
See Tourmaline, Brown Tourmaline.

DUMORTIERITE: Transforming

Aluminum Borosilicate. Usually occurs as columnar or fibrous masses of blue or violet, sometimes red-brown. Crystals are rare. Orthorhombic system. Hardness is 7.

Dumortierite is useful for restructuring the DNA. It provides a link that holds the ideal in place until the cells figure out how to use it. So it is also useful for healing and regenerating altered or damaged DNA. It stabilizes the chemical processes in the body and emotions. It transforms emotions as well, helping you see the truth of misperceptions so you can release or transform them. It helps you see transformation as a step-by-step process that takes careful attention to each layer of misperception and habitual ways of flowing light that might not be serving you well.

As an elixir, Dumortierite selectively dissolves old structures and the connections to old behavior patterns. It helps release toxins and old energies. It makes it easier for the red blood cells to release their etheric levels of nutrition to the rest of the body. It also strengthens connections between new structure and patterns so they function more effectively as a transition into the use of the ideal by the whole body.

EILAT STONE: Memory and Knowledge

A combination of Chrysocolla with other Copper-bearing minerals, including Turquoise. It came traditionally from Israel, but much of it now is from Peru.

This combination of materials integrates mind and emotions into the fourth-dimensional flow and provides a link to the higher mind. It helps bring the higher perspective into your creative activities at the physical level. It shows mind and emotions how to interact as a practical working unit. When your mind and emotions are balanced and integrated you will have more than knowledge of facts. You will have wisdom which is the understanding resulting from resolution of experience by mind and emotions.

When you misuse your spiritual power, question it, or fail to use it, rejecting your physical potential as light, you lose some of it. This is reflected into the interface among the lower chakras and it affects your adrenals and your protein and sugar metabolism. Eilat Stone heals the interface among the first three chakras, making physical power more effectively available for channeling light into purpose or creativity through directed thought. By bringing you the wisdom to recognize your power and knowledge and use it well, it heals your body.

The elixir dissolves karmic patterns having to to with misuse or denial of power. It helps form a clearer understanding of creative personal and group relations. It also builds self-esteem. It corrects relationship problems at the cellular level, providing balance and communication between aspects of self as well as with others.

See also Azurite/Chrysocolla.

Traditional and other sources: Detoxifies body, aligns subtle energies, balances yin and yang. Integrates thought patterns between two individuals in a relationship.

The elixir aids regeneration, especially in bones. It aligns the body at all levels so other elixirs work better. Aids nutritional assimilation. It brings inspiration of the higher self, eases depression, and helps one accept life's circumstances.

ELBAITE.
Gem Tourmaline. See Tourmaline.

ELLESTIAL QUARTZ (Skeletal Quartz):   Emotional Healing

These crystals are a form of Smoky Quartz that form rapidly in a more watery environment, and have a shape with many overlying faces and multiple terminations.

These crystals can provide a connection to your own angel (or angels). Special healing qualities have been added to the energy of these crystals by the angelic kingdom. They are especially useful for healing emotions and balancing the whole four-body system. They help the subconscious mind flow with and adapt to the transformational process which is occurring now, whether you choose to flow with it or not. Ellestial Quartz helps the subconscious accept and adapt to change. It is an excellent choice during any kind of transformational, healing, or balancing work. It has all the properties of regular Smoky Quartz, and as an elixir is very similar, with the added emphasis on extra help from the angels.

EMERALD: Supporting Dynamic Energy

Beryllium, Aluminum, Chromium Silicate. Transparent to opaque green with vitreous luster. Color might vary to bluish or yellowish. Hexagonal system. Hardness is 7.5 to 8. See also Beryl.

Emerald connects you to the power that supports and nourishes you on all levels. It helps you validate your Source connection and release the blocks and resistances to recognizing yourself as a cosmic being. It gives you confidence in your own creative abilities. It is a powerful aid in bringing the Plan to Earth. The clear stones are more powerful, but all will show the subconscious how to bring the infinitely abundant Source flow through all levels of your being. The darker ones are better at helping to anchor that abundance into Earth and into your life.

Emerald helps you learn to be confident of your potential as a divine being and helps you bypass the blocks and resistances to recognizing that you are a cosmic being with infinite potential and that you are being supported at all times by the abundance of creation. It helps to strengthen your confidence in your own creative flow and to use it as a divine creative being who happens to be a part of physical existence.

Emerald helps all of your cells see the balance and the divine connection in all levels of energy that are coming to Earth now and helps them feel comfortable in using them. It works from the CoCreator level, expecting you to be willing to assume responsibility for your part in the Divine Plan. It helps you keep moving to each new level during the transformation process. It is powerful and you might find your body cannot use it for long periods. You need periods of rest to integrate each new level.

Emerald feeds and provides balance for the chakras and all aspects of self. It helps regulate the energy flow so that each part supports the four-body system wherever its energy is needed. It makes an excellent elixir that can promote confidence in your own abilities. Water softens its energy and makes it easier to use. Emerald elixir builds cell walls that are strong enough to contain and flow with the new energies. It strengthens the alignment of the whole body with light. It transforms negativity, going deeply into stuck and crystallized areas, freeing the energy there to be used positively.

Emerald is a powerful aid in bringing the Divine Plan to Earth so its healing and transformation can proceed. It activates the dynamic creative flow through each person who wishes to contribute to achieving this, activating a clearer understanding and acceptance of his or her purpose.

Emerald is the favorite of the spiritual teacher Djwhal Khul.

Traditional and other sources: Symbol of divine order, universal attainment, psychic power, and immortality; also of love, prosperity, kindness, goodness, hope, faith, incorruptibility, and triumph over sin. In dreams it represents innate healing energy of blood or extension of healing power. Incan stone of royalty. Link to spiritual self. Stimulates sense of movement and motion. Gives tranquility and calms a troubled mind. Promotes love and security in love. Makes its owner eloquent and persuasive. Stimulates love and self-truth from others. Increases prosperity. Brings joy. Encourages chastity. Encourages patience. Increases concentration. Expands consciousness. Brings inspiration. Balances will and wisdom. Brings universal wisdom.

Aids work with high energies. Grounds excess energy, relieving anxiety, hyperactive behavior, sexual frustration, and muscular tension in head, neck, and shoulders. Wear from neck to release useless fears and negativity. Calms worries. Gives knowledge of the future and increases psychic faculties generally. Improves memory, increases intelligence, strengthens insight. Promotes deep sleep.

Changes color or breaks if a lover is unfaithful. In fact, it generally shatters in despair if unable to bring its possessor good or prevent evil. Turns pale or changes color in the presence of deception and treachery. Warns of danger or illness by falling from its mount.

Heals whole body. Balances. Nurtures. Stabilizes. Absorbs negativity. Cleanses aura. Removes energy blocks. Facilitates healing energy of all other stones. Aids function of liver and cures dysentery. Used as laxative. Strengthens and heals heart. Aids circulation and neurological disorders. Also strengthens kidneys and pancreas. Protects eyes. Relieves eye strain. Restores sight; gazing at it improves the eyesight, cures eye diseases generally. Used as antiseptic. Protects children from epileptic convulsions, breaks up if the disease is so violent it cannot be overcome. Antidote for all animal, mineral, and vegetable poisons. Tie to a woman's thigh to hasten birth process.

The elixir balances the heart chakra and aligns the etheric and emotional bodies. Brings better understanding of dreams. Eases mental illnesses. Improves meditation and eases hidden fears. Aids formation of hemoglobin and plasma. Strengthens the heart, kidneys, liver, and pancreas. Supports heart and kidneys during cleansing process. Heals skin. Clears radiation toxicity. Aids resolution of problems with father image and allows growth in this area.

ENSTATITE:　　　　　　　　　　　　　　　　**Balancing**

Magnesium Silicate. Usually occurs as fibrous or platy masses, yellowish, green, olive or grayish. Prismatic crystals are rare. Translucent, luster is vitreous to pearly, might be chatoyant. Orthorhombic system, hardness is 5.5. The more opaque variety contains increasing amounts of Iron, is more brown, and was found in Moon rocks.

Enstatite brings balance to all levels of self. It is usually carved into cabochons and can be worn to provide emotional and mental balance. The elixir helps to balance the body's chemistry. When worn over specific chakras, it helps them to balance with the rest of the system. It is particularly good for bringing an underactive endocrine gland up to normal function, but it is sometimes able also to assist in calming an overactive gland. The chatoyant varieties can help you see into yourself and to open your channel.

Wearing Enstatite will make you feel cheerful and helpful and will assist meaningful communication. It helps you see another's viewpoint without proving yourself wrong. It can help communications with animals and show you what they need for healing. This is because one of the undertones of its vibrations is compatible with those of the animal kingdom, especially of mammals.

As an elixir, it heals emotional splits or shattering, grief and loss of love. It balances heart rhythms, physical or etheric, and opens up breathing, helping to clear lungs or open sinuses.

Other sources: Brings victory in mental competitions. The elixir strengthens the emotional body, gives self-esteem, security, and capacity to love. Stimulates heart, lungs, and kidneys. Alleviates tuberculosis, cardiovascular disease, leukemia, and kidney dysfunction. Lessens rejection of transplanted organs or tissues.

EPIDOTE: Grounding, Strengthening

Hydrous Calcium Aluminum Iron Silicate. Forms prismatic, columnar crystals, green or green with gray or yellow tints. Also found as granular or fibrous radiating masses. Translucent with vitreous luster. Monoclinic system, hardness is 6 is 7.

Epidote brings a solid awareness of your own identity and makes you feel more secure in it. It helps you accept yourself as you are and helps you value yourself and your abilities. It will slow down precipitous actions and help you to evaluate each action fully and clearly. Then it helps you feel the confidence to proceed as you see best. It strengthens the dynamic, yang part of self and supports the receptivity, or yin, with readiness to do whatever is needed at the moment. It also stabilizes emotions and provides help in controlling them or using them constructively.

As an elixir, Epidote supports all glands and bodily processes concerned with action. It strengthens the adrenals and the muscles. It supports the thyroid with the proper energy levels to balance it. It reduces stress on the immune system by making it easier to eliminate negative or discordant energy from your body.

EUCLASE: Focuses Light

Hydrous Beryllium Aluminum Silicate. Forms prismatic crystals, colorless, white, green or blue, transparent to translucent with vitreous luster. Monoclinic system, hardness is 7.5.

Euclase helps you break light down into its component parts and use it more effectively and with greater understanding. In healing work, it helps you understand how to direct the healing flow and the appropriate intensity to use. It allows the healing angels to interact with the body more precisely without subconscious interference. It also helps the person being healed to retain the ideal state by showing the subconscious which patterns must be released or altered to allow permanent healing.

It also helps you focus your higher potential into your life. Euclase is an elevating energy. It raises your perceptions to a point where you see their realationship to your higher aspect. It helps you connect with the energies of your higher chakras (eighth and up) and integrate them into the light you use at the physical level. This can make you feel as if you raised your energy into new levels, but you have really brought the higher energies into a better relationship with your physical reality. So it brings an elevated perspective into physical existence. This is the true essence of ascension in this time of Earth's transcendence.

It is helpful when analyzing or diagnosing a problem. It increases mental clarity and breaks up negative emotional patterns. The green variety is somewhat more effective for physical and emotional healing. The blue expands the mind and increases mental capacity. The colorless one shows you specific aspects of soul perspective that can be applied to a situation. White Euclase helps analysis by providing balance in a multiple focus.

As an elixir, Euclase balances the chakras through the heart energy. It can raise the spirits, dispell negative emotions, and make one feel more open to communicating with others.

FLUORITE: Releases Negativity

Calcium Fluoride. Found as cubes, octahedrons, and dodecahedrons or as undefined masses. Transparent to translucent with vitreous luster. Colorless, yellow, green, blue, purple, pink or black, sometimes in bands. Cubic system. Hardness is 4. Cleaves into perfect octahedrons.

Fluorite moves into the cellular membranes and "loosens" the bonds of its molecules so there is a freer flow of energy into and out of the cells. It especially promotes a clearer flow at the fourth-dimensional level where emotions operate. It draws negativity into itself and releases it as balanced energy. Your desire to be clear and to align with the ideal provides the energy that allows it to do this. It helps you ground yourself with Earth by showing you that you are part of its flow of light, and it helps release misperceptions that you don't belong here or don't fit in.

Holding Fluorite brings blocks and negativity to the surface and then releases them from the body and the aura. It promotes a triggering effect in which, as one cell releases old programming, others find it easier to do the same. Holding or wearing Fluorite helps the cells be more aware of the joys and opportunities in life. Used on the throat it helps release blocks or misperceptions about using your creativity. Used on the sex chakra, it makes more creative energy available to your whole body and channels sexual energy into creative processes other than procreative ones, if you so choose.

Green Fluorite promotes healing. The Purple stones bring in a great deal of the transforming violet ray and are best for general clearing. Yellow Fluorite is the best for emotional releasing. Blue Fluorite takes you to higher levels of awareness of the clearing process and is the easiest to use for all bodies. It can be very calming if you are stressed, confused, or unable to communicate.

The octahedron is one of the basic shapes used in the act of creation. Fluorite's natural cleavage planes allow it to be easily formed into this shape, which enhances its innate ability to help you flow with the natural "shape" of the Plan as it applies to physical existence. It helps you make a connection with the Plan that shows you how it fits into your life on Earth. The undifferentiated spiritual life as it flows through Fluorite is focused into the third- and fourth-dimensional levels of light because that is where Earth needs to integrate the Plan now. So it can help you integrate these levels as light and utilize these levels for transformation. Fluorite doesn't create flow so much as it emphasizes the structure that guides flow so you can move as you desire.

Fluorite elixir is even better at clearing negativity, releasing negative thoughts, and even protecting against them. It strengthens teeth, bones, ligaments, and muscles, especially heart muscle. It makes breathing more efficient. It balances positive ions in the body by helping you understand your body's nutritional needs as part of your whole being. It reduces the effects of toxicity.

Other Sources: Helps shape the human form in childhood. Absorbs negativity. Cleanses aura. Removes energy blocks. Facilitates healing energy of all other stones. Increases concentration. Expands consciousness. Grounds excess energy, relieving anxiety, hyperactive behavior, sexual frustration, muscular tension in head, neck, and shoulders. Aids in working with high energies. Brings universal wisdom. Promotes deep sleep.

The elixir alleviates anxiety, sexual frustration, and hyperactivity. Aids perception of higher realities. Strengthens etheric source of life force in the physical body. Strengthens bones and teeth. Stimulates mucous membranes and lungs. Eases bone and dental disease, pneumonia, viral inflammations, and tuberculosis. Use in bath to ease arthritis.

FOSSILS: Understanding the Past

Fossils are the preserved remains of various animals. Some are the original shell or bone which might have added materials such as Calcium Carbonate. In others, all the original material is replaced, commonly by Pyrite, Hematite, or Silica. In any case, they take on the qualities of the new composition.

Fossils are interesting, but do not have great metaphysical properties beyond that of the material comprising them. They serve as a sort of bridge between the animal and mineral kingdoms, but lack the strengths of either. They can sometimes stimulate past-life memories or take one into the basic flow of life on the planet. There are special cases in which forms of exceptional beauty create an individuality of their own. It is difficult to make generalities about them. If you are fascinated by Fossils, you are close to and appreciative of the possibilities of life in physical existence. You are also close to the development of evolution on Earth.

FUCHSITE: Healing

Hydrous Potassium Aluminum Silicate (variety of Muscovite). Bright green, composed of small, opaque flakes or laminae; Hardness is 2 to 2.5, Monoclinic system.

This stone is very healing to the physical body. It draws out the innate healing abilty from each cell, particularly during cell division, so it balances degeneration or disruption by correcting cell replication and can be a very important part of regeneration and rebuilding. It helps the cells align with the ideal light flow and heals the crystalline alignment of the etheric body. Fuchsite helps smooth the connection of more electrical stones like Rutilated Quartz and grounds the rejuvenating qualities of Aquamarine.

You can place it on any area that needs to be healed for as long as you wish. Keeping it near you while you sleep will help the rebuilding of the cells that goes on then. It also helps balance the emotional and physical bodies, making the emotional body feel more secure in being in physical existence. It helps the cells sort out energies already assimilated or just being received but not needed. It heals and balances the emotional body during stress. It harmonizes discordant cellular vibrations and helps the energy flow more smoothly.

Fuchsite is useful with clear Quartz or Aqua Aura to help cells adapt to the Divine Blueprint. It makes the dynamic energies of some of these crystals more acceptable.

GALENA: Grounding

Lead Sulfide. Lead-gray, cube-shaped crystals in compact masses. Very heavy, opaque with metallic luster which blackens after long exposure to air. Cubic system. Hardness is 2.5 to 2.8. The principal ore is Lead, but it is often found with Silver.

Galena and Lead are the ultimate grounders. They absorb all unrecognized or unused energy and so protect Earth from the effects of over-stimulation or accumulation of energies which it is not ready to use. It absorbs negativity and transforms it into heat, radiating it, into the etheric level more than the physical. It is stabilizing in environments where there is much contention, confusion, or uncontrolled emotion. It can draw out pain. It blends diverse energy patterns by providing a common ground.

Other sources: The elixir strengthens lungs, thyroid, parasympathetic nervous system, and white blood cell reproduction. Alleviates emotional blocks to spiritual progress. Aids regulation of breath in meditation and visualization. Balances male and female aspects of self.

GARNET: Strengthening, Grounding

Silicates of Magnesium, Iron, Aluminum, or Calcium. Pyrope Garnet is bright to dark red or brick red. Rhodolite Garnet is pinkish red. Almandine Garnet is deep red-violet. Spessarine Garnet is orange-pink, red-orange, or yellow-brown. Grossular Garnet is yellow-green, blue-green, or light orange shades. Andradite Garnet is black, honey-yellow, green, brown-black, red, or black. Often found as perfect rhombic or dodecahedron-shaped crystals, transparent to semiopaque, lustrous. Cubic system. Hardness is 6.5 to 7.5.

Garnet is strengthening for the physical and emotional bodies. It helps to ground the light, to balance and use it in the ideal way. The dodecahedron symbolizes the direct manifestation of Nature from the Will of the Creator. It is form, pure and undistorted by misunderstanding or misuse. Garnet, through its direct use of this shape, helps you to connect into the Plan in a way that makes it understandable and workable at the physical level. It helps you understand every level of the ideal with your physical consciousness. It focuses a third-dimensional perspective that is open to all other dimensions and so mirrors to your cellular level a way of allowing the higher dimensions to flow and blend with the physical.

Garnet is especially good at bringing more energy and light into the lower chakras. It can help you make a clearer connection between your heart and the lower part of your body which often is seen as less spiritual and not supportive of spiritual purposes. You must balance light throughout your whole body to transform it and reach the ascension point.

Garnet also helps clear out old energies or toxins that can accumulate when your subconscious hasn't understood how to use the available energies. Garnet strengthens the blood and physical-etheric heart as a support for physical existence. It also strengthens liver, kidneys, muscles, and the flow of life force at the cellular level. It interacts with the whole etheric body, strengthening it and providing energy for it to expand. It strengthens the communication and balance between the chakras and helps the physical structure see itself as a mirror of all that is divine.

This is an important stone for anyone who wants to cooperate in manifesting the Creator's Plan on Earth now. It not only helps you connect the Plan into physical existence, but also helps provide the stability through the changes that are necessary in order to bring about that Plan now. The natural dodecahedron shape of the crystals is symbolic of the presence of the whole within each part of creation. In this way, Garnet supports your growing awareness of yourself as a functioning part of Source within this creative experience, supporting the creative process and your part in it. It is particularly helpful to wear it on your left side, where it can help your inner female bring Earth's resources into use in your creativity.

As an elixir, Green or Yellow Garnet helps clear out infectious processes, especially those due to sexual disease and those resulting from abortion or childbirth. This applies to consequent guilt or other emotional pain also. Brown Garnet strengthens the blood by activating the hemoglobin, increasing the energy transferred by it into the cells. Red-brown Garnet strengthens the muscular system and its nervous connections. The pinkish Almandine is most specific for strengthening the heart. The violet shades promote clearing and acceptance of a clearer perspective of physical existence.

All Garnet is easy to use. Your body integrates its energy easily, and you can probably not overdose on it, unless you have subconscious misperceptions about Garnet itself. For some, its dark red color might stir past-life memories of blood sacrifice. In that case, use it to help yourself see that you now know how to support the Earth through love and no longer have to bleed to death to do it. Garnet would like to help humanity learn this lesson.

Traditional and other sources: Symbol of faith, truth, and fidelity. Enhances and stimulates creative imagination. Brings prosperity. Brings success in business and helps business relations and realization of goals. Attracts profound love. Makes you positive and popular. Very grounding.

Relieves depression, increases self-esteem and will power, and relieves psychosomatic imbalances. Calms anger and discord. Prevents loss of security and fears about it. Brings up deep energies, then soothes and integrates them. Heals emotional problems. Sleep with it to remember dreams. Eases bad dreams. Can become pitted and dull if it absorbs too much of your fear and insecurity. Powerful protector.

Keeps energies moving. Balances energy of body. Strengthens heart, liver, kidneys, and thyroid. Protects heart against poisons and plague. Used for hormonal problems. Balances spinal disorders. Protects from wounds and toxins. Removes toxins from body. Stops bleeding and heals wounds and inflammatory disease. The Hunzas of Asia used Garnets as bullets as they were supposed to be more deadly than lead.

Rhodolite elixir increases blood supply to the lung tissue, intestinal villi and skin, enhancing their functions. It also eases nausea from detoxification. Helps alleviate precancerous conditions. Balanced etheric and emotional bodies.

Spessartine elixir strengthens the heart, liver, kidneys, and thyroid. Increases plasma components, hemoglobin, and white blood cells, alleviating anemia and heart and liver disease. Used for sexual disease or sex-related psychological disorders. Makes one less self-centered and reclusive. Enhances one's own self-awareness while increasing willingness to serve others. Brings out the spiritual qualities of relationships with others. Stimulates the heart, throat, and sex chakras.

GEM SILICA: **Calming and Elevating**

A dense variety of Chalcedony colored by Copper Oxide. Various shades of green.

Gem Silica, like Chrysoprase, is specifically working to bring angelic light into physical existence through humanity, but it is a finer energy. Its perspective is more centered on the spiritual aspects of universal understanding. It wants to lift you out of all worry or limited thinking. It makes the soul perspective more tangible, more a part of you. It will make you feel lighter, less stressed, more accepting of whatever is happening.

Your lightbody is the angelic form your soul, which is pure consciousness, uses to express itself in physical existence. When you have cleared out everything that is not light from your body, you will be ready to allow your soul to bring its light in completely. Of course, it is already willing to use as much of your energy field as is light now. You have only to invite it in. But those parts of yourself that still are using or hiding negative thoughts and emotions are not available to it.

Gem Silica strengthens your light and magnetizes it so it becomes easier to understand yourself as light, and the light can then grow by attracting more light. It makes the light part of yourself more believable and real, so you gradually release everything that is not light.

Gem Silica is excellent worn on wrists or fingers where it helps draw the highest and best aspects of self out into your aura where you can use them creatively. But wear it on any part of the body you feel is appropriate or needs more light. It helps focus angelic healing energy into your cells and your emotional flow. It elevates thought and emotion into clear expression of what it is to be light.

As an elixir, it is rejuvenating and transforming. It carries the ideal blueprint into the cells and connects it in wherever there is clarity, using the special help from its extra angelic connections. Use it with clearing, cleansing stones to transform the area being healed. Other stones might be better at the actual clearing and releasing, but Gem Silica is one of the best for reprogramming into the ideal. It facilitates the healing energies of all other stones, especially Quartzes.

Other Sources: Has great power. Brings peace and compassion of the universal female prototype. Aids menstrual disorders, pregnancy, birth. Helps one get in touch with feelings.

GOLD: Ideal Connector

Usually occurs as small flakes or sheets. Opaque, yellow, with bright metallic sheen. Cubic system. Hardness is 2.5 to 3

Gold is the revealer of essential identity. It brings out the identity or ego awareness of individual consciousness. Those who wear much Gold are often attempting to validate themselves to others. Wearing Gold says, "I am who I think I am, a worthy person." Gold will help you accept yourself. It also brings out the essential qualities of crystals, enhancing their ability to communicate them to you. Gold never gives up its own intrinsic value by enhancing your self-worth. This is its lesson for you. By respecting the worth of others, you validate your own. As you accept your own worth, you will attract the unlimited abundance that is your share of Earth's and the universe's resources.

Gold is an excellent conductor of heat and electricity. It helps release negative energy and increases the flow of positive energy in any system. It is warmer and responds more to personal concerns than Silver. It does not differentiate between "lower" or "higher" energies, accepting and flowing them all equally. It is grounding as well as elevating. It really just helps you flow as exactly who you truly are. It helps you be. It heals by connecting you with all your best aspects of self.

As an elixir, Gold enhances any other elixir and strengthens its effects. It heals any disease that originates with lack of self-esteem. It makes the heart chakra more radiant and helps it balance and integrate with the other chakras. It brings the perfect acceptance and allowingness of the Sun and the Solar Logos, that great being who fills our lives with light so abundantly.

Other sources: Once part of Sun's ether (Steiner). Symbol of the universal spirit in its perfect purity (Heindel). Symbol of our desires. Gold talisman implants have been found in Egyptian, Chinese, Incan, Mayan, and European mummified remains. Gives sense of responsibility and conscience. Resolves ego conflicts, frustration and too much responsibility. Eases self-reproach and thoughts of suicide, mania, megalomania, excitation, and rage. Restores balance, self-confidence and self-esteem. Opens heart and brow chakras and amplifies thoughts.

Purifies the physical body. Rebuilds the nerves and alleviates multiple sclerosis. Improves circulation and breathing. Stimulates brain and digestion. Relieves anemia, eye problems, headaches, paralysis, pneumonia, syphilis, and spinal problems. Used for tuberculosis, heart and cardiovascular disease and sexual dysfunction. Increases warmth. Eases chills, fevers, heat flashes, and night sweating. Use for skin cancer, leprosy and as salve for lupus. Eases overexposure to radiation.

The elixir balances and supports the heart chakra and the thymus. Aids assimilation of all vitamins and minerals. Regenerates physical body.

HALITE: **Protective and Grounding**

Sodium Chloride (Rock Salt). Square crystals, white, clear, yellow, violet, red, brown or black. Transparent to translucent with vitreous luster. Cubic system, hardness is 2.5. Fluoresces under ultraviolet light.

Salt is a traditional substance for protection. It has a distinctive aura, or light structure, which blends into other patterns and facilitates the flow of energy that is aligned with the ideal, and blocks the rest. At the etheric level it selects energy that is of practical value to your intentions and purposes and takes it into your cells. It works powerfully at the physical level. Too much of it confuses the flow and brings integration to a halt because you cannot assimilate any more. Eating too much salt symbolizes an unresponsiveness to your body's needs and a failure to provide everything it needs, such as the cleansing and releasing necessary for growth. Salt tends to hold on to the connections it makes. It requires a good flow of light at the subtle levels and water at the physical level to do its job properly. It is so important to all life that it is found in almost everything you eat.

Carrying Salt or Halite crystals grounds the protective qualities of other crystals. It can be very stabilizing for the lower chakras, particularly the base chakra. Salt in solution tends to absorb all other energies, positive and negative, rather powerfully, so it is somewhat overrated and misused as a cleansing agent for crystals. Cleansing with salt water is only necessary for crystals that have been severely misused; they then require a period of readjustment as they rebuild their energy. One or two grains of sea salt added to your elixir stock bottle is more useful for cleansing the body than larger quantities.

Other sources: Holds the emotional level (astral body) to the etheric body. Relieves sadness, irritability, depression, and hysteria. Also anemia, chilliness, constipation, headache, fistula, or dryness of mucous membranes in the intestinal tract.

The elixir stimulates the soles of the feet, the sacrum, and the whole etheric body energy structure. Lifts depression and clears negativity within the personality.

HEMATITE: Grounding

Iron oxide. Found as stubby, rhombohedral crystals or as earthy masses. Heavy, opaque, metallic black, often with streaks of red. Trigonal system. Hardness is 5.5 to 6.5.

Hematite focuses an earthy perspective which is very grounding. It will help you function more effectively at the physical level because it brings everything down to that physical perspective. It helps you see how everything relates to the physical level of your being and your purpose. It can keep you from getting lost in dreaminess, nonproductive energy use, or vagueness in purpose. It keeps you focused into practicalities.

Hematite helps bring the electrical flow of the lightbody into your physical cells, stabilizing them at the same time and not allowing them to fear or scatter the energy. It is a specific help in overcoming old electrical (kundalini energy) blocks from past lives. It soothes the emotional body as it attempts to align with the soul's desire to move into the physical level. Its strength is its desire to help you flow with your Earth connection.

Hematite is very effective in grounding when worn on your feet or ankles. It is also strengthening and energizing for the whole body when used as an elixir.

Traditional and other sources: An astringent. Aids inflammation or tumors of the eyelids (used in water or in egg white if condition is severe). Heals ulcers and spitting of blood. Specific for gall bladder problems. Aids burns. Heals wounds. Strengthens blood and heals blood disorders. Strengthens kidneys and enhances their blood-cleansing functions. Very grounding, reduces "spaciness." Increases intuition. Calms mind and emotions. Enhances personal magnetism and will. Raises self-esteem. Aids flow of yin and yang energies in nervous system.

The elixir increases self-esteem and ability for astral projection. Stimulates the spleen chakra and strengthens the etheric body. Supports other crystal energies in tissue regeneration. Supports the red blood cells and the kidneys in their blood-cleansing functions. Helps gonorrhea. Increases physical vitality.

HEMIMORPHITE: Cooling, Calming

Hydrated Zinc Silicate. Small, colorless crystals, different at each end, are rare. Transparent to translucent with vitreous luster. Usually forms masses or crusts, blue-green, white, yellow or brown. Orthorhombic system. Hardness is 4.5 to 5.

Hemimorphite brings things into focus at the physical level. It allows you to understand how you can exist within the limits of physical existence and still be unlimited. It calms and cools the frustration of not being able to do everything you want to do or feel you should do. It puts your desires and feelings into proper perspective. It helps you accept that even though you have unlimited potential you must deal with present circumstances or states before you leave your limited perspective. It is valuable in understanding and clearing yourself because it makes you feel less like justifying yourself and your limitations through defensive, egotistic actions.

As you struggle with difficulties in your life, heat sometimes builds up in your emotions, causing frustration or even anger. Hemimorphite can relieve this, allowing you to face your problems from a more constructive point of view. It allows a creative blend of mind and emotion to channel positive energy into them. In this way, it supports your creativity. It can be very helpful in transformation and ascension, as it helps you solve the problem of channeling into your soul's purpose energy that is tied up in experiencing pain and stuckness.

As an elixir, Hemimorphite acts at the higher etheric and emotional levels to help you integrate your use of the ideal DNA codes into your body. As the emotional flow balances through acceptance of the ideal, it connects more directly with the physical level during DNA replication. During this process the cells gradually learn to recognize the ideal rather than any damaged DNA as the template.

HERKIMER DIAMONDS: Activation of Higher Chakras

Silicon Dioxide. Double-terminated quartz crystals that contain microscopic bits of carbon. Clear, very lustrous. Named from the location where they are found, Herkimer, New York.

Herkimer Diamonds are a very special form of Quartz. Eons ago, energies from three galactic and universal centers were focused on Earth by an avatar who brought the gift of clear vision. His birthplace is marked by the presence of these wonderful crystals in the Earth. They still carry the gift of clear vision from the Universal Logos.

Clear vision is not just what we think of as seeing. It involves the highest possible connection into light where there is no distortion from perceptions of limitation. Herkimers help you flow with the energies of your higher chakras to attain the highest possible viewpoint. They can help transform your vision beyond mere physical or astral sight into one of absolute truth and clarity. They will help anchor this clear vision into your understanding of physical existence as light and unlimited potential.

Herkimers are electrical and will activate any chakra. They are especially helpful in opening the brow and crown chakras and can bring an enormous amount of light into the physical. Use them to help open your channel and to bring light into your physical, emotional, mental, and spiritual bodies. Their energies blend with most crystals and enhance their effects. They are not difficult to work with and do not usually create excesses of energy that you cannot handle. They know how much you can use and bring you what you need. Large ones or clusters can help each person in a group find his or her own individual patterns of light that allow that person to express his or her own creative contribution.

Herkimers can be healing at any level in that they encourage the flow of the ideal in you. They are especially powerful in transforming your DNA patterns to correspond to the new levels of energy use on your expanding Earth. You can use them to reprogram any negatively altered DNA molecules in your body. The angelic energy of Herkimers is being emphasized and supported by the Galactic Center now to aid the integration of light into the physical level. Using Herkimers with Moldavite and Rhodochrosite helps achieve this. Moldavite opens the cosmic connections and Rhodochrosite opens the heart as the ideal part of yourself to anchor that connection as your Herkimers channels its light into physical existence.

Each Herkimer Diamond has its own individual focus and, like the Bojis, its own personality. There might be special examples within other types of crystals that achieve individuality through some perfection or focus in themselves, but Bojis and Herkimers are born as individuals. Bojis and Herkimers work well together, forming a nearly perfect balance of energies, the Herkimers bringing the completing spark of the light from the galactic level to the Bojis' very balanced and spiritual focus at the physical level.

Other Sources: Stimulates dreams and visions in meditation. Brings in much light. Broadcasts energy; Diamond strengthens this ability. Clears subtle bodies. Works well with Moldavite. Reduces stress and tension in body, especially muscles. Helps body release toxins. Enhances other crystals in healing and other work. Use as a pendulum to locate and draw out toxicity in body (Gurudas). Protects from radiation.

The elixir draws forth past-life memories. Stimulates clairvoyance, balances the personality and increases healing ability. Releases stress and tension, especially in muscles, by cleansing the subtle bodies and relieving conditions that lead to cancer and malignant tumors.

HIDDENITE: **Opens Creative Flow**

This is the green form of Spodumene. The best pieces are bright emerald green, but it might also be lighter green or slightly yellow. Hardness is 6.5 to 7.

Hiddenite might resemble other green stones at first glance, but its subtle qualities are distinctly its own and it has a special energy. It has its own angelic energy which operates independently from that of Kunzite or Spodumene, as well as from the rest of the Mineral Kingdom. Not that it does not work within the framework of the whole Plan, but it has its own special task that is somewhat independent within the whole. It has the responsibility of bringing the evolving energies of Source's creativity to Earth and directing it to those who are ready to use them.

You do not have to own Hiddenite in order to work with its energies, although it surely helps. One outstanding aspect of the creative flow, as it is developing now through humanity on Earth, is its universal availability through the structure of the Plan itself. If you are striving to work with your divine purpose and the Plan, then its energy is automatically available as part of the Plan's response to your desire to serve. This stone was first discovered about one hundred years ago, symbolizing that the universal sharing of creative effort at this level is new to Earth. When humanity really begins to learn to share its creative resources, more of these stones will be found.

If you possess even a small piece of Hiddenite, it can help you get in touch with your own creative potential. It will also demand that you find ways to share it and use it for the benefit of the whole. In this sense it could be said to bring wealth, but only if you are guided in its use by your heart. While we would not consider its energy as male or yang, it does bring out the dynamic aspects of love required to manifest the creative flow. Its sister stone, Kunzite, would be the ultimate guide and partner in using it well. She would provide the knowledge and wisdom of self needed to find your own creative potential in the way you flow your love. Each stone works best with the other, supporting your ability to adapt and adjust your creatitivy with your growing knowledge about it. Together they manifest the eighth ray and help you connect to the expanding creative potential of your higher self as it seeks to manifest at the physical level. Hiddenite will thus help you find the spiritual potential within physical existence and experience, which is the ultimate source of creativity. See also Spodumene.

HORNBLEND: Stabilizing

A complex Silicate with Calcium, Sodium, Magnesium, Iron and Aluminum. Forms stubby, prismatic crystals or aggregates, dark green or black, translucent with vitreous luster. Monoclinic system, hardness is 5 to 6.

Hornblend brings your four bodies into a unified perspective by minimizing the differences and emphasizing their common purpose. It helps disconnected parts of self find connection with your spiritual center through the physical level. It is grounding, helping you feel centered.

Hornblend can help you channel sexual energy into creative purposes other than procreative ones. It can put the physical and emotional aspects of sexually stimulated activity into a perspective that allows love and the higher mind to participate. It makes the spiritual perspective more meaningful in physical terms. In this way, it generates a constructive love and acceptance of self. Its action is introspective rather than expansive, but it provides a stable basis for stepping out of oneself and one's own concerns.

As an elixir, Hornblend assists other crystal energies by helping your cells to accept and use them. It increases heat in the body.

INDICOLITE

See Tourmaline.

IOLITE (Cordierite):   Clairvoyance, Creates Movement

Silicate of Magnesium and Aluminum with Iron. Short, multifaceted, prismatic crystals, blue-violet to light or grayish blue. Pleochroic, transparent with vitreous luster. Orthorhombic system. Hardness is 7 to 7.5.

Iolite is specifically helpful for the brow chakra, not just to enhance vision, but to expand its perspective of the whole chakra system and its place in it. It can help open a rigid or closed mentality that does not allow cooperation with your own four bodies or with others. It gently creates openings in your seeing and thinking processes which help balance the whole system from a conscious perspective. It helps balance the sixth chakra into the integration process and release pressure buildups and headaches. Its is a sixth-dimensional energy that helps you fit all of the pieces of any puzzle into the ideal. It helps you feel comfortable and secure in being that ideal and using it with trust that the Plan will guide you into doing what is right. It guides you into being in the right place at the right time. It helps you appreciate physical existence as part of the Plan.

All stones have their own angelic energies connected with them. Iolite helps you direct other angelic energies into the flow of the Plan and into your creative ideas. It helps you see the structure of your ideas in relation to the ideal as your soul is focusing it for you. It provides a nice balance between your desire for transformation and your desire for peace and oneness with yourself. Iolite helps you connect with the angels whose job it is to make transformation a part of your life at the physical level. They also show you how to relax into the flow without stress or strain in your body. Iolite can be very uplifting.

It is calming for the brain. It energizes the breath and balances the metabolism. Its elixir decreases swelling or inflammation of the brain. It softens the crystalline structure of the endocrine glands at the higher etheric levels so the individual cells join together as one integrated energy, harmonizing with the will of your soul.

Other sources: Aids dominance and leadership.

IVORY: Strengthening

Calcium Phosphate. The tusks or teeth of the elephant, hippopotamus, walrus, and other mammals. Hardness is about 2.5.

When Ivory comes from animals that have died of natural causes, or from fossil material, it imparts the strength and deep connection to Earth on a spiritual level of these very intelligent and highly evolved animals. You recognize some of the intelligence of elephants, but the others have their own great wisdom which evolved in past ages on Earth. They are just as aware, in their own ways, of their places in the divine whole as you are. When animals are killed for their Ivory, it carries a very strong connection to the karma of not respecting life as a divine gift and the right of each divine being to evolve in its own way to its fullest potential.

If you are completely free of the karma of destroying life in any way, you might be able to use any Ivory to help heal your own and humanity's tendency toward violence against what it does not understand. This work might also require practicing strict vegetarianism and nonviolence. As an elixir, Ivory is excellent for promotion of healthy growth and healing of bones and skin. It also provides the ideal pattern of structure within bone marrow for its function of producing healthy blood cells. It supports the balanced flow of kundalini energy through the whole body for its proper function. It could also be ground up and taken as a calcium supplement, but there are easier, cheaper ways available to accomplish the same thing.

Wearing Ivory brings love of life and respect for the power innate to spiritual use of physicality. It can help you anchor your spiritual ideals and accomplishments in your physical cells. Ancient peoples used it as a source of sexual potency. As evolved, spiritual persons, you can learn to see beyond personal, materialistic desires to awareness of your true purpose of using your physical body as a vehicle for your soul's purposes on Earth. If you can wear Ivory without condoning or supporting the killing of animals for it, it will serve you well. However, there are many other stones that serve similar purposes.

Other sources: Soothing, lifts spirits.

The elixir aids discipline and relieves anger and frustration. Encourages appropriate self-sacrifice. Opens the solar plexus, strengthens the etheric body and aligns the emotional body with it. Amplifies thoughts and encourages emotional expression. Stimulates bone structure and increases its strength, flexibility and resiliency. Releases toxicity and increases general health. Use for leukemia, bone cancer, skin cancer, internal and external ulcers, and heavy-metal poisoning.

JADE, JADEITE: Cleansing

Jadeite Jade (as opposed to Nephrite Jade) is a Silicate of Sodium and Alumi-

num. Granular aggregates of crystals, off-white or grayish brown, yellowish brown, orange-yellow, reddish orange, lilac, blue-gray or gray and green. Monoclinic. Hardness is 6.5 to 7.

Jadeite is an old energy and not of especially high vibration, except when carved by someone who can draw out its full potential for beauty. It is somewhat protective. It is grounding in that it can help you realize the flowing continuity of your Earth experiences and your deep involvement with Earth. It is an energy that helps you distinguish what was useful in the past from what is available for the future. It could be useful for helping young people who want to throw out the whole system to see that some continuity with the past is necessary to provide a foundation for stable transition into the future.

Jadeite Jade was used in Lemuria when humanity was just learning to be conscious of emotions and was learning to use the astral body. It can be helpful in resolving negative programming or fears that are related to those times. It strengthens the solar plexus and helps channel its energy creatively. For those who are overly mental and reject or neglect their emotional selves, it can re-establish the connection there. Since humanity has gone past this, for the most part, and is now perfecting a balance of mind and emotions with the heart, it is not so useful now. It will be re-energized sometime in the future when humanity has begun to integrate the new level it is just now moving into.

It is useful as an elixir for healing and cleansing.

Traditional and other sources: Most revered stones to the Chinese. The essence of Heaven and Earth. Gives long life and peaceful death. Reminder of the integrity of mind and soul. Helps one draw on the strengths and knowledge from past lives, especially Oriental ones. Brings the vision of benevolence, knowledge, righteousness, harmlessness, virtuous action, purity, endurance, honesty, morality, and music. Also clarity, modesty, mercy, courage, justice, and wisdom.

Calms and quickens the mind, aids decisions, brings wisdom. Worn as a pendant, aids difficult birth, protects against snakebite and other diseases. Jade from Iona, Scotland, protects from drowning. Drinking Nephrite Jade throughout life prevents decomposition of body after death. Also brings endurance of heat, cold, hunger, and thirst. Carving into symbolic shapes enhances its qualities. A Jade butterfly strengthens romantic ties. A Jade scarab brings longevity and prosperity. Jade amulets placed in mouth of a corpse protected body from decay and served as heart in the afterlife.

Aids general health. Makes men more fertile. Aids childbirth and female concerns. Healing, especially for eyes. Aids heart, kidneys, larynx, liver, parathyroid, spleen, thymus, thyroid. Cleanses blood. Eases immune system disorders. Strengthens voice, muscles, the whole body; hardens bones. Makes hair shiny. Prevents and relieves kidney pain, aids passage of kidney stones and strengthens kidney functions. Relieves stomach pain, asthma, and thirst. For treatment of fractured skulls, fevers and reviving the dying (powdered and mixed with herbs). The variety with yellow and black spots is good for diseases of spleen or liver. Reddish varieties aid blood disorders and stop bleeding.

The elixir generates unconditional love. Brings out psychic abilities, discrimination and altruism. Aids emotional expression. Aligns emotional and etheric bodies. Aligns biological functioning and consciousness with Earth. Integrates etheric body with physical and emotional bodies. Strengthens the first cervical vertebra. Supports heart, kidneys, larynx, liver, parathyroid, spleen, thymus, thyroid and parasympathetic ganglion. Improves iodine assimilation. Cleanses blood through kidneys. Eases immune system disorders, kidney diseases, and petrochemical toxicity.

JASPER: Grounding

Variety of Chalcedony Quartz, deposited in massive microcrystalline forms from water, might contain organic elements. Reds, browns, greens, yellows, or black. Often has multicolored striations or patterns. Opaque. Hardness is 6.5.

Jasper comes in too many patterns and color combinations to list. Each geographical area yields its own variety. All are grounding. Jasper helps lock energies from all levels into the physical and into Earth. It helps you use the strengths of Earth to see your own strengths as a physical, spiritual being. It can be especially helpful for the emotional body in grounding and focusing into any problem or idea that you need to look at. It will help ground the energies of other more energetic or electrical stones. It is calming, protective, and helpful in drawing out negativity in a gentle way.

Jasper's grounding ability is valuable in helping you to use your knowledge of Earth and your physical connection to it as a foundation for building the light structure which allows you to accomplish your divine purpose here. It helps you find places for your special talents and guides you into the connections within yourself that reveal your potential. The red and brown varieties, particularly, can help you connect with the potential power in physicality. They are excellent to use as grounding stones to tap into the Earth's dynamic power while other stones raise your consciousness to levels where the meaning and purpose of power is understood.

Hold it while you meditate or keep a piece in your pocket to help you ground the spiritual energies into Earth and to prevent getting disconnected from Earth or life. Jasper can help you connect with life in a way that allows you to get the most from it. It helps you appreciate being physical and helps you appreciate the simple things that give meaning and quality to your life. Leopardskin Jasper is especially helpful here. Picturing Jasper helps you appreciate the flow of life and its cycles.

Jasper elixirs help carry old energy and toxins out of the body. They support the kidneys and help connect other healing energy there.

See also Bloodstone.

Traditional and other sources: Symbol of happiness, strength, and stamina. Gives caution and aids control of passion. Reduces insecurity, fear, sorrow, and guilt. Aids development of sensitivity and understanding for others' needs. Makes wearer fiery and ardent. Prevents inappropriate emotional attachments or expression. Makes wearer victorious in battle. Can bring rain. Protects at night.

Stimulates sense of smell. Balances mouth, digestion, and respiration. Strengthens bladder, liver, and gallbladder. Eases constipation, ulcers, and intestinal spasms. Prevents and heals wounds. Stops bleeding (mostly red Jaspers), slows pulse, reduces desire, and calms mind. Red Jasper balances body's metabolism. Brown Jasper brings security and stability. Green Jasper gives feeling of personal security and strengthens the stomach and heals its disorders. Rose Jasper soothes emotions. Best set in Silver.

Green Jasper elixir activates healing and tissue regeneration. Aligns all bodies and increases life force. Balances healer and activates his/her intuition. Yellow Jasper elixir stimulates and regenerates the endocrine glands, particularly the thymus and pancreas. Reduces toxicity.

Brown Jasper elixir alleviates suppressed fears, overactive dream states, and hallucinations. Stimulates throat and brow chakras aiding clearer visualization. Balances emotional and etheric bodies. Strengthens skin, kidneys, thymus, and their nerve supplies. Reactivates immune system and slows premature aging.

JET: Protective

A black fossil wood related to brown coal. It will take a high polish. Hardness is 2.5 but might be as high as 4.

Jet absorbs negativity, as do other black stones. However, it has the capacity to adapt to your energy structure, to get to know you, so to speak, when you have used it or worn it for a time. It knows your personal fears and will protect you specifically from them. It is helpful for those who have a lot of fears, conscious or subconscious. It will help them deal with fears and eventually see how to bypass or release them. It relieves pain that originates from fear. It teaches trust. It protects from nightmares that originate from fear. It can be used to balance and clear Diamonds and to remove the effects of their misuse.

Traditional and other sources: Wear it to connect body with soul. Calms passions, fear, delusions, hysteria, hallucinations, depression, and delirium. Protects your personal space. Protects against negative energies. Wearing it prevents nightmares. Drives away venomous beasts. Brings safe journeys. Should be used by only one person. Burning it drives away the most virulent disease, also hysteria and epileptic tendencies.

Use for female problems, to ease stomach pain, for colds, edema, epilepsy, swollen glands, fevers, and hair loss. Powdered and mixed with wine, it cures toothache. Also, used as dentifrice, makes teeth and gum strong. Mixed with wax or burned, it cures tumors.

The elixir eases anxiety and depression, especially manic-depression. Increases clairvoyance and awareness of higher self. Opens base chakra. Stimulates the coccyx, legs, and pancreas. Aligns lower spine. Increases fertility. Alleviates heavy-metal toxicity.

KUNZITE: **Love Focus, Heart-Centered**

Silicate of Lithium and Aluminum. The violet-pink variety of Spodumene. Pleochroic, transparent, long, flat-sided crystals with uneven terminations. Orthorhombic system. Hardness is 6 to 7.

Kunzite helps the heart to open and reach out to interact with others on the CoCreator level. It helps individuals to understand their place in the group and function in it through their heart. It helps the heart chakra to balance into all levels and serve as a support during the transformation process. Kunzite helps you attune to your higher emotional qualities and to bring them to a more focused use through your heart. It can help stabilize a strained heart or one that beats erratically by showing it how to move into the correct attunement for the new energy levels. It smooths the alignment into those higher energies and makes the process more comfortable for the whole four-body system through the support from the heart. It promotes a more balanced use of your heart energies by all bodies.

Kunzite helps the emotional body to open to a clearer connection with the other bodies through love. It can be calming and soothing to the emotions, helping to transform them into higher, love-centered ones. It heals a "broken heart," elevating the emotions to a higher plane where difficult losses or experiences can be better understood and resolved. It helps the mental body utilize the heart qualities to balance the heart and third eye, thus opening a flow of light between them. Use it on or near the heart for extended periods to help train the four-body system to use the heart more comprehensively. In meditation hold it in the left hand to bring new ways of using the heart qualities.

Hold Kunzite in your right hand to send love to another person or an area of Earth. It invokes the infinite healing capabilities of Divine Love. It helps all chakras connect more clearly with the Soul Star. Carved into a gemstone it is particularly helpful in opening any chakra, especially the heart. The shaping and polishing reveal the full beauty and radiance of its potential, just as life shapes your love, revealing its full creative potential.

As an elixir, Kunzite's healing qualities are enhanced. It also helps you to flow more easily through daily life by enhancing communication through your heart.

Other Sources: Vibrations of very spiritual love. Awakens highest Heart consciousness. Brings compassion, peace, trust, and understanding. Comforts and heals heartache. Steadying, aids discipline. Helps one deal with stress. Soothes anger. Strengthens circulatory system, lungs, aids tissue regeneration. Use for eye, kidney, and lumbar area problems.

The elixir opens the heart chakra and increases spiritual self-esteem. Strengthens the etheric body, increasing the life force flow into the physical body. Balances the whole cardiovascular system and alleviates associated diseases, especially aplastic anemia and other blood disorders. Enhances blood supply to and regenerates tissues.

KYANITE: Gives Understanding

Aluminum Silicate. Long, tabular crystals, light to medium blue but might be gray or green. Transparent, vitreous to pearly luster. Triclinic system. Hardness is 6 to 7 along cleavage planes, less across them.

Kyanite is very healing for emotional and mental relationships. It serves as a connector between differing perspectives. It can help your cells understand the divine blueprint and see their place in the Plan, literally showing them how to use it. It keeps them connected into the ideal, promoting healing in that way. It helps draw out the DNA prototypes from the light, making them available to the cells and clarifying them.

Kyanite helps move energy through the brow chakra and relieves blocks and pressure in the head so that it can interact more easily with the other chakras. Holding it can help awaken or expand your creativity. It allows your soul to reach into your mind, emotions, or cells and draw out their creative potential. Large pieces of Kyanite can fill a whole room with an aura of understanding and promote a balanced mental perspective in a group. It brings an awareness of the ever-present love and support of the Creator and His/Her presence within you always.

Misperceptions and negativity change the energy flow in your body and alter the shape of cells at the etheric level. As an elixir, Kyanite releases those and promotes healing and transformation by reshaping each cell to align perfectly with its ideal. Then the pattern and energy of the ideal is perfectly received and integrated by them.

Other sources: Use for centering. Removes energy blocks in body. Helps clear sinus congestion. Allows access to Akashic Records.

LABRADORITE (Spectrolite, Sunstone):   Relieves Depression & Overwhelm, Uplifting

Sodium Calcium Aluminum Silicate, a Feldspar. Amorphic masses, colorless, yellow, green, pink, red, often very iridescent, especially the dark green, red, and blue variety called Spectrolite. The clear yellow variety often has very thin layers of Hematite in it which produce rainbow iridescence. Triclinic system. Hardness is around 6.

Labradorite is exceptionally useful now in helping you adapt to the new energies and integrate them into your creative structure without impact or overwhelm. If you feel depressed and overwhelmed by new energies, your own emerging potential, or the amount of work remaining to be done, Labradorite will cut through all the negative emotions and leave you feeling positive, ready to move, and in control. It helps put things into their proper perspective, find the cause of problems, and create solutions. It helps you reveal your best side.

The clear yellow variety is especially useful with very powerful, sometimes overwhelming energies like those of Danburite, Moldavite, Aqua Aura, Phenacite, or any crystal you have difficulty working with. It helps you integrate their energies and potential at all levels. It helps you accept the framework of the new structure and relieves you from the anxiety of letting go of the old one. Sleeping with one or more pieces of Labradorite will help you awake feeling rested and eager for each day's adventures. They will have made your dreams more powerful, positive, and aligned with the joy of your higher self.

The darker, iridescent Spectrolite helps to integrate the higher vibrations into the flow of your daily activities. It is more grounding than the clear variety, yet more powerful in creating openings into the higher energies.

Both varieties help open, balance, and stabilize the flow within your spiritual channel. They make channeling or communicating with higher levels seem more natural and comfortable while helping to differentiate between what is coming from your present level of consciousness and what is coming from those you are expanding into. Most of all, Labradorite relieves the emotional and mental bodies of the anxieties that come from letting go of self and letting higher self into your life.

Labradorite brings in the clear understanding of your soul's creative framework and illuminates it at the emotional level so you can flow with it more easily. It lights up that framework so brightly that it seems easy to follow and appropriate to use. Depression and hopelessness vanish and life looks inspiring again.

As an elixir, Labradorite stimulates release of the endorphins that block pain and create feelings of well being. It creates balance in the whole body. It dispels negativity and creates connections for you into positive emotions. It dissolves and disperses patterns that involve you in negativity. It creates harmony at the cellular level as well as at mental and emotional levels. It is a very important tool now for transformation and ascension.

LAPIS LAZULI: Expansive

Silicate of Sodium, Calcium and Aluminum, containing Sulphur and Tin. Made up of Haüynite and Sodalite, which make Lazurite, the blue component, with specks of Pyrite and white streaks of Calcite. Occurs as aggregates of crystals, bright blue, opaque. Cubic system. Hardness is 5 to 5.5.

Lapis is very much an Earth stone, in that it helps you attune to Earth's creative flow and communicate with it as a CoCreator. It is grounding, but it brings light into physical existence with awareness of its full potential. You must learn to work with Earth's light as well as your own if you are to master physical existence enough to totally control your own life. Lapis is eager to help you do that. It has always been valued throughout Earth's history, but was given extra power to aid creativity during Egypt's time of spiritual leadership. At that time it was used very well by certain spiritual leaders to instill greater awareness of the Divine Plan and its potential to guide Earth's evolution. This experience gave the group soul of Lapis great wisdom in channeling the power of physical existence, Earth power, into manifesting spiritual ideals. It was used well by some of the great pharaohs who lived before recorded history, when Egypt was truly living a spiritual ideal.

It will help you open to your full potential at many levels. Used at the center of your brow, it helps you open to greater realization of your spiritual connection. Used on your heart, it helps you channel love into your creative flow to make it more effective at the physical level. It is especially good for the throat chakra, stabilizing and strengthening it as you seek to release control of your creativity and allow your soul to guide you in its use. You can use it on your feet or ankles to help instruct your subconscious in more spiritual ways of attuning to Earth. It can help stimulate dream memory if placed under your pillow.

As an elixir, Lapis helps your body's cells use the available nutrients and life force to function and heal themselves by enhancing their communication with the ideal. It reconnects the physical body to the cosmic brain. This connection has to a great extent been lost to humanity as they have gotten trapped in the misperception that being physical cuts them off from their divine origins and makes them less spiritual. Lapis helps the brain itself align with the higher orders of knowledge so that there is a clearer communication of knowledge from many spiritual levels and dimensions. It can help open your awareness to the knowledge and help that are available to Earth now from other dimensions.

A whole necklace of Lapis can sometimes be too stimulating for some if worn for a long time. It brings up more potential than you are ready to deal with or know how to use. Others can find it relaxing and balancing as it helps channel their creativity in practical ways. That sums up Lapis, a very spiritual, idealistic energy that is also very down-to-Earth and practical.

Traditional and other sources: The Sapphire of the ancients. Also said to represent the Sky Mother, while Sapphire is the Sky Father. Inspires highest understanding of immortality. Aids development of psychic abilities and inner discipline in the spiritual aspirant, strengthens the physical body during spiritual growth and helps open heart to love and beauty. Stone of true friendship.

Balances inner and outer self. Creates a sense of strength, vitality, and virility. Brings a peaceful, clear, and balanced mind. Amplifies thoughts. Spiritual cleanser. Relieves anger, frustration, and hypertension. Aids courage. Brings out old emotional hurts for healing. Dispels negative thoughts.

Protects children from fright. As beads, with Malachite and Jasper, heals children's respiratory diseases. Heals depression, fevers, malaria, blood disorders, eye problems, neuralgia, spasmotic disorders, stroke, insanity and diseases of the spleen. Cures effects of incest (associated with pharaohs). Strengthens sight, prevents fainting and abortion (two to sixty grains of powder taken internally).

The elixir is a potent cleanser. Energizes the throat chakra, aligns the four bodies, stimulates personal expression. Helps connection to higher self and the expression and release of buried emotions. Helps overcome shyness and introversion. Helps autistic individuals deal with reality. Amplifies thoughts, aids personal articulation, meditation, and broadcasting of thoughts.

Effective for throat inflammations such as tonsillitis. Supports esophagus, larynx, upper bronchial passages, and first cervical vertebra. Stimulates the thyroid, releasing anxiety and tension. Also stimulates the lymph system, pituitary and thymus glands, and the parasympathetic ganglia through their associated vertebrae. Alleviates diseases of the spleen, lungs, lymph, throat, and thymus, Hodgkin's disease and cancer of the larynx.

LARIMAR (Blue Pectolite):   Calming, Relieves Stress

Hydrated Silicate of Sodium and Calcium. Soft blue or green, white, red hematite dendrites. Translucent with vitreous luster. Found in compact masses, only in the Dominican Republic. Fluoresces. Triclinic system. Hardness is 7.

Larimar was seeded with a specific energy during the middle Atlantean period when humanity was showing a need to begin to balance the emotional and mental bodies. It was given the ability to stabilize the emotions and facilitate their flow into the rest of the levels of the body. It helps the emotional body accept interaction with the mind. It helps the emotional body remain balanced in times of change. It is calming in any kind of stressful situation. It helps the emotional body use new ideas and new situations. It is coming into its full potential for helping humanity as we move into more conscious use of the higher dimensions and their higher vibrational rates.

It is most effective when placed on or just above the solar plexus, helping it to balance and open. Many in Atlantis deliberately closed down this chakra, under the mistaken idea that that would help them expand the use of their minds. This has resulted in a chronic inability of many to function normally at the emotional level. Yet the emotions are a part of yourself that you must integrate to be whole and have access to your full power. The new energies are stimulating all energies and patterns within self and forcing you to deal with them. Larimar can help resolve the battle between mind and emotions, serving as a balanced pattern for them to use in cooperating as equal partners, as was originally intended. It provides a clear structure for communication with all aspects of self as well as with others.

Larimar helps the solar plexus to use and distribute the energy of the higher vibrations of light. It softens the effects of the new electrical particles and shows the cells how to flow them without stress, as is intended by the Guardians of the Essence of Light who control the way light interacts with Earth and guide her evolution through its use.

Larimar is especially good for people who are under constant stress, either because of their own expectations or those of others. It helps them relax and take life less seriously. It will help you remain calm and focused even though everything around you is in turmoil. It is a very easy energy to keep near you at all times. It will not demand anything and will bring much peace.

As an elixir, Larimar brings restful sleep and pleasant dreams. It can soothe a stomach ache and reduce hyperacidity.

See also Lazulite.

Other sources: Connects to the om (universal love) vibration.

LAZULITE: Balancing

Hydrous Magnesium Aluminum Sulfate. Bright blue, microcrystalline masses. Double pyramid-like crystals are rare. Translucent, with vitreous luster. Monoclinic system. Hardness is 5 to 6.

Lazulite balances the energy levels of the body. It can work well with Lepidolite to balance the electrolytes. It balances the mental processes and facilitates movement of energy between the two halves of the brain, coordinating feeling and thought. It strengthens the cerebral cortex and its interface with the deeper portions of the brain which have to do with memory. It brings fluidity to crystallized areas of the body. Its elixir is helpful in breaking up crystallized areas in the energy field. It increases the light potential of the whole aura by helping it to flow more gracefully.

Other sources: The elixir eases anger, frustration, hypertension. Gives courage. Aligns emotional and etheric bodies. Stimulates, balances, and integrates the pineal and pituitary glands, allowing better balance in the whole endocrine system. Eases diseases of liver and immune system associated with pituitary function. Improves regulation of salt in the body.

LAZURITE:

See Lapis Lazuli.

Other sources: Aids regeneration of tissues.

LEPIDOLITE: Calming, Balancing

Hydrated Potassium Lithium Aluminum Silicate. Forms granular or platy aggregates. Pink to lavender, translucent with pearly luster. Monoclinic system. Hardness is 2.5 to 4.

Lepidolite is a specific for helping to calm and balance the mental and emotional bodies. It assists the alignment of all four bodies into a clearer level of awareness of how to achieve that balance. It helps to use the alignment and knowledge available from all other crystals (stones). It helps heal breaks in the electrical flow of the etheric brain. This allows a stronger connection with the conceptual framework at the level of the ideal, which supports the etheric body. It helps the brain understand the electrical patterns of the new energies. Lepidolite is not particularly electrical itself, but it enhances a clearer connection into the ideal flow, helping you bypass "short circuits" in your programming which do not allow you the full use of the ideal.

Lepidolite relieves anxiety and tension wherever it is placed. It helps balance the body's electrolytes, especially when their imbalance is caused by inability to assimilate the new higher energies in the ideal way. It works by helping release electrical connections into old energy patterns that are not compatible with the new energy levels. It helps heal the feminine or receptive aspects of self, helping them to find their place in the whole and their balanced alignment within your dynamic, creative participation in life.

As an elixir, it helps balance the whole endocrine system, especially the posterior pituitary and the reproductive glands.

It supports the base chakra as the final source of releasing and cleansing. If you know what you want to let go of but have trouble doing it, Lepidolite elixir will provide the physical support necessary. It helps the cells find the support of the ideal structure and relieves the fear of letting go of the old structure which the body has been using for so long.

Other sources: Calms, relieves stress, eases depression of mood swings. Balances emotions. Gives feeling of well-being.

LIMESTONE: Balancing

Mostly Calcite. Usually formed from the compacted remains of marine animals. White, pinkish, yellowish, rusty or brown. Often takes a good polish.

Limestone does not have a high energy but is calming and balancing. It helps integrate the four bodies. It can help relieve stress. It can bring memories of living in a fluid environment and being supported completely by the divine flow. It helps regeneration by drawing out negativity and old energy. It helps resolve emotional disruption during changes inside or outside the body. As an elixir, it strengthens the bones and ligaments, and the etheric structures on which they are formed.

Other sources: The elixir aligns the four bodies and the two lower chakras. Stimulates creativity and sensitivity. Aids self-healing through creative visualization. Eases buried fears, increases inner discipline. Aids elimination of petrochemical toxins.

MAGNETITE: Grounding

Iron Oxide. Found as black, shiny octahedrons or dodecahedrons or as black masses with bluish iridescence. Opaque with metallic luster, very heavy. Hardness is 5.5 to 6.5. Might be magnetic (Lodestone). Cubic system.

Magnetite is a powerful grounder of any energy. At the same time, if you are in control of your energy and Earth connection as a source of power, it helps focus and direct the creative flow of your thoughts at their source. In this sense, it magnifies the power of other crystal energies, especially that of Quartz, for any special purpose. When used in crystal grids or layouts for healing (not necessarily placing stones directly on the body), it helps bring the energies into the physical body. Since it is a form of Iron, which is necessary for bringing life force into the body, it is energizing. Despite its heaviness, its angelic energies are quite light, joyous, and full of love. The heaviness is a result of your misperception that physical existence must be difficult and painful.

Magnetite can be used to draw negativity out of the body. It only works, however, if you are consciously involved in the process of searching out negativity and intend to release it. Lodestone is best for this but any Magnetite will work. Its magnetism is an aspect of universal love which helps you to maintain your alignment into the ideal at the physical level.

Magnetite supports the body's system for taking in life force from the universal light flow and releasing what is no longer needed, as you constantly recreate yourself from one breath to the next. As an elixir, Magnetite supports the red blood cells that carry carbon dioxide, a waste, from the lungs, and provides them with a fresh supply of oxygen.

Traditional and other sources: Attracts power, favor, and gifts. Protects virtue. Lodestone is used for protection against evil spirits.

Also used to heal wounds, bladder symptoms, female problems, cramps, and rheumatism. Magnetite aids treatment of precancerous states and removal of tumors. Strengthens the body and seals holes in the aura. Enhances speaking abilities.

Lodestone elixir balances the body's male and female polarities. Strengthens and aligns the body's biomagnetic forces. Makes the aura more receptive to radionics and other forms of healing using broadcast energy or subtle energies. Cleanses and vitalizes the body, energizes the endocrine system. Balances the flow of information through the nervous system. Improves blood supply to and regenerates tissues. Removes radiation toxicity. Magnetite elixir also aids and focuses meditation by aligning all the energy levels of the body. Use the elixirs together for the full spectrum of effects.

MALACHITE: Focuses Emotions

Hydrated Copper Carbonate. Emerald green, banded or concretionary patterns, semi-opaque to translucent, vitreous luster. Monoclinic structure. Hardness is about 4.

Malachite was once the stone of kings and those with special "divine" privileges. Now everyone has the opportunity to be equal partners with Earth in developing and using their own creative power as CoCreators in the group. Malachite can help you find your place within the group or within the Plan. It is good for drawing out misperceptions that need to be refocused for clearing, particularly at the emotional level. It is also helpful while learning to balance your creative flow with that of others. It helps you see how your own dynamic energy connects into the dynamic power of the Earth. When you allow yourself to share Earth's power, you will have more abundance.

Malachite can be helpful in seeing why you allow others to use your creative power, rather than becoming responsible for it yourself. It was used extensively in Atlantis to focus the emotional (astral) power that was then the most highly developed part of humanity's creativity. If you find this stone a difficult one to use, it might be because you have misused power in the past or have not been willing to take responsibility for your own power. It is not as important in developing and expanding your power now because of the emphasis on raising the energies into the heart center rather than focusing on the solar plexus. But it can be very important to you in understanding how to use your power more effectively.

Malachite elixir will help you build the "walls" your emotions need to function effectively. It helps you decide where to set the limitations that are necessary to focus your understanding and power at the physical level. The secret to building useful "walls" is to realize that they are not permanent, and that they can and must be flexible and able to expand or contract as necessary to support understanding, not the status quo.

Traditional and other sources: A mirror of the soul, brings out truth within. Physical and psychic protection. Might be too strong if you are not feeling positive. Attunes to nature, life, and healing forces. Centers. Brings prosperity.

Prevents fainting, hernia, falls. Promotes sleep. Strengthens the eyes, head, kidneys, pancreas, spleen, stomach. Increases lactation and fertility. Eases cardiac pain, cancerous tumors, cholera, colic, infection, leukemia, rheumatism, and ulcers. Taken as a powder in milk, cures cardiac pains and colic. Mixed with honey, stops bleeding or relieves cramps when applied externally. Mixed with wine, cures ulcers. Acts as a purgative. Worn as necklace, helps dentition of children. Promotes tissue regeneration. Strengthens circulatory system. Stimulates optic nerve. Aids treatment of neurological disorders.

The elixir releases burn-out in healers and enhances altruism. Opens the heart chakra. Aligns the etheric and emotional bodies. Balances the solar plexus and aids self-expression. Aids treatment of autism, dyslexia, epilepsy, abnormal neurological discharges, physical coordination problems, and vision problems by balancing right-left brain function. Use for mental illness, radiation sickness. Releases radioactivity from thyroid. Promotes regeneration of tissues. Strengthens heart, pineal gland, pituitary gland, circulatory system, and capillary action. Vitalizes red blood cells and rejuvenates nerve tissue.

MAN-MADE CRYSTALS

There are many beautiful materials on the market used to create tools or jewelry. Glass is made from crushed and melted Quartz with various additives according to the use to which it will be put. The individual molecules retain the original qualities, but having been separated from one another and rearranged, the original life is so unable to express itself that it is essentially dead. It is possible to give it new life and purpose through its new shape and use.

There are various types of man-made glass shapes, pyramids for instance, that are used to connect with angelic energies. Angels are the connections that hold creation together and maintain the connection between spirit and matter, between the prime Creator and Its body. They are willing to connect as much power or purpose into an object as you would like. They serve creation and you are creators. Your success in invoking and using such energy depends on your ability to focus and direct your own will.

Some individuals are very good at enlisting the help of the angelic kingdom and focusing a connection into a specific object or tool. They can ask the angels to bring a sense of purpose, an ability to love or to attract love, prosperity, health, and so on, into it. The object becomes imbued with such qualities and can radiate them very strongly. If you buy such a tool, the use to which you put it and the way in which you use it will determine how well it holds the "charge." You must be able to come close to matching the vibrational flow of the thought that energized it, or the pattern of your thought can neutralize it. If you use such an item successfully one time only, this might be the problem. If you use it infrequently or if you doubt it or your own ability to use it, it will gradually lose its "power." Since the power is not innate, not part of its original purpose, it needs outside help to maintain the artifical connection. If you look at it as a help in establishing or developing your own ability to invoke the desired qualities, it will continue to bring you its power.

Items used consistently in ritual, especially prayerful ones, are recharged; they gain power every time they are used. Religious worship uses the concentrated will of many people to invoke divine power. Objects used in this way often retain the power concentrated in them for hundreds, even thousands of years.

So any object can become a focus or source of power. The difference with crystals, especially the natural, prismatic shapes, is that they have a consciousness or power which is their own, even though they agree to cooperate with that of another. The more your purpose agrees with theirs, the more your vibrations will harmonize and create a combined purpose that is strengthened and magnified by combined wills.

MARCASITE: Grounding

Iron Sulfide. Pale yellow crystals with a greenish tinge, flattened prismatic, nodules, rosettes, or stalactite-like arrangements. Opaque with bright metallic luster. Orthorhombic system, hardness is 6 to 6.5. Heavy. Pyrite and Marcasite are two different crystal forms of Iron Sulfide.

Marcasite is very similar to Pyrite in its metaphysical properties except that it scatters light, whereas Pyrite focuses it. Marcasite spreads the spectrum into specific areas, which allows the body to see more clearly what it is connecting with. In this way it allows the body to understand the process more clearly, although it does slow it down a bit. This helps the emotional body to accept the new pattern and to flow without the old one. Its action is softer than that of Pyrite but complements it perfectly.

As an elixir, it strengthens the physical body and re-establishes your connections to Earth at the etheric and emotional levels. It supports the base chakra.

MERLINITE

See Romanechite.

METAL ORES: Energizing, Dynamic

There are so many different varieties of rocks containing metals, each with its own name and composition specific to the area found, that we are not going to try to single out any as more important or useful than others, with a couple of exceptions. As a group they possess the properties of the metals in them which are mentioned specifically elsewhere in this book. They are specific for connecting into the raw dynamic, creative power of Earth itself. This raw power is available for you to use in whatever way you choose. They will enhance the light flow and energize any crystal grid or thought structure that you are using, ground it, and help you see its value. They energize your cells and help open them to the other crystal energies you are working with. They also strengthen the physical and etheric bodies so they feel more able to control the higher energies.

See Magnetite.

METEORITE.

See Tektites.

MICROCLINE: Stabilizing

Potassium Aluminum Silicate. Poorly defined, prismatic crystals, opaque, milky, white, pink, pale or blue-green. The blue-green variety is called Amazonite. Triclinic system. Hardness is 6.

Microcline helps the body to organize energy. This makes it easier to understand and to integrate. It is most useful with other crystals which stimulate or bring in new energies. The elixir enhances other energies in the same way.

MOLDAVITE: **Energizing, Opens Channel**

Silica Dioxide with Aluminum Oxide and small amounts of other metals. Dark green, glassy in appearance, structure, and properties. 15,000,000 years old. Probably the result of or debris from a meteor fall. See also Tektites.

Moldavite came to Earth from outer space as a part of a meteorite. It is very much an interdimensional stone and connector to the space brothers and sisters. It will open your channel to the many levels of spiritual connection available: Teachers, Hierarchy, Space Brothers, Galactic Core, and Source Itself. As you work with it regularly, it will take you through higher and higher frequencies. It activates the vibrational frequencies of these higher dimensions in your chakra system and your channel and makes you aware of the potentials and nature of the flow that is available there. The intensity with which it can reveal these energies might be difficult to integrate all at once. Use it with other stones that can help you ground and use the light it invokes into your body.

Moldavite will energize you out of your personal perspective. Worn over the throat it helps release your will to the soul's purpose. It progressively opens the third eye. Used over the base chakra it helps connect the higher energies into Earth and the physical structure. Used over the polarity chakra, it helps it align with the higher chakras as part of the transformation process. It can help you direct your dynamic energy into a specific goal and help the receptive side of yourself utilize its power more efficiently, more effectively, and more in harmony with the whole flow of Earth's evolutionary movement. It coordinates the dynamic and receptive energies by helping them focus on the same objective.

Moldavite can be used over the heart and solar plexus to help them accept new connections into the whole, but this must be done carefully at first. If you have blocks or resistance in these areas to being part of the whole and using unlimited love, it can overwhelm and disrupt the pathways in you that are already able to do this. That is true for any area that has deep resistance to moving.

Amethyst helps Moldavite blend its activity into the transformation process and helps you see or integrate your potential. It brings the energy of Moldavite into the physical level very well through its connection with the violet ray which is so concerned now with the activation of the Plan on Earth.

Rose Quartz, Rhodonite, and Rhodochrosite soften the intensity of Moldavite and help you open to the power of your potential which it activates in your heart. They help you use its light as love and creative expansion. Kunzite is an especially good energy to use with it in helping you open to the strengths and potential of your heart and using that power as part of the Plan. This is a powerful combination but still fairly easy to use.

Clear Quartz spreads out the light of Moldavite and softens it to some extent, making it more acceptable to the cellular level. Moldavite activates the electrical connection of the light into the cells as Quartz brings it in with the new DNA structure. Herkimer Diamonds enhance the effect of Moldavite, making it more specific and coordinating the flow of light into the cells. The energy Moldavite brings in might be something of a shock to the cells at the physical level at first and you might feel nervous or uncomfortable before you gradually become accustomed to the intensity of this enhanced vibration. The emotional body could also become overwhelmed by the intensity of this combination, but there is a possibility of taking large leaps in your ability to use light if you work with this energy carefully. Moldavite and Diamond make the most powerful combination. They force you to look directly into yourself and see the whole of what you are as a divine creator.

Moldavite is very useful as an elixir. A few drops a couple of times a day can move stuck areas in your spiritual channel. For many, this might be the best way to use it. A little is better than a lot here.

If Moldavite makes you too "spacy," use a grounding stone like Jasper, Garnet, Magnetite, etc. Limestone or Dolomite would help restore calm without bringing you "down" to your old level.

Other sources: Spiritually uplifting. Encourages intelligence and inspires higher consciousness. Expands mind. Helps focus spiritual goals. Placed on forehead, brings active, lucid dreams. Powerful healer when used with Angelite and might cause out-of-body experiences.

MOONSTONE, ALBITE: Unconditional Love

Sodium Aluminum Silicate (closely related to Labradorite). Milky white or dull yellow, gray, slightly greenish or pink; misty, semitransparent, luminescent or semiopaque, might be somewhat iridescent, vitreous luster. Triclinic system. Hardness is 6 to 6.5.

The finest Moonstone carries a very spiritual energy which is the essence of light. It is already using its body of light at the physical level. No other gemstone has accomplished quite what it can do. Moonstone will be energized specifically for humanity's use when it is more prepared to use unlimited love. Its is an energy that will be activated when Earth is prepared to receive the Christ Energy at the physical level. It is not yet working at its full light potential, but it can help those who are specifically invoking that Christ Energy.

Moonstone was once used to develop psychic gifts, but humanity has learned those lessons and few need to work on that now. You are learning to use your heart and mind rather than your astral powers. So Moonstone is waiting until it can assist in bringing in the Earth's light-body at the new level of spiritual development where conscious CoCreation is more used on Earth.

Right now, Moonstone can balance the emotional body and prepare it for merging with the heart at ascension. It helps you maintain a balanced emotional perspective. It can bring much peace to some. It is good as an elixir for a nervous stomach, irritable bowels, colitis, etc.

Traditional and other sources: Makes wearer dependable and famous, also invisible. Brings long life. Brings peace and harmony. Aids birth process and all female problems. Makes one sensitive, intuitive, and clairvoyant. Cools, soothes, and calms extreme emotional reactions. Relieves frustration. Aids plant growth. Connects with inner planes, soul, and Goddess energy. Promotes harmony in marriage. Relieves mild depression.

MORGANITE: Heals the Feminine

Beryllium Aluminum Silicate. The pink form of Beryl. (See Emerald, Aquamarine, and Beryl.) Hardness is 7.5 to 8.

Morganite is a very heart-centered energy that helps the feminine, receptive side of yourself to see that it is an equal partner in the creative process. Some part of you might see your feminine side as responsible for getting you into all the difficulties you have experienced on Earth; an Eve, the temptress syndrome. Morganite can help your feminine self learn to take responsibility for its happiness, feel the strength of its beauty and wisdom, and cease feeling overwhelmed by the power of your dynamic side. It helps you release any guilt and heal any karma you have accepted as a woman. Morganite makes life seem more worthwhile and provides you with a more spiritual perspective on it. Its loving aura gives life more meaning and allows you to support those parts of your body that create life (your lungs and blood) and that defend it (your immune system, especially the lymph system).

Morganite is excellent for women who are recovering from abuse and for men who want to be more balanced in their feelings and thinking. It helps everyone to appreciate the value of their own feminine side. In a sense, it balances the dynamic strength of Emerald and will make its energy easier to use if that is difficult for you. It helps both sexes to appreciate and experience the spiritual potential of sexual relationships. It helps the feminine self to realize that its own dynamic power is independent but harmonious with the male power. Many women try to become dynamic by imitating men. This might not be appropriate, as that makes their feminine power seem less useful. Morganite will help you sort out the difference.

Morganite makes an excellent elixir, but don't mix it with that of Emerald or other Beryls; they cancel each other out. Use them alternately, with at least five or ten minutes in between. Morganite elixir is healing for the feminine organs and can be balancing for male ones. It does not, however, weaken the male energies. Rather, it strengthens the feminine ones which, in this sense, are the supporting structure for the male. It makes the brain more receptive to new information or programming, so it is very useful in this time of change. The stone or the elixir makes your whole body more receptive to the healing qualities of love.

Other sources: Aligns emotional and mental bodies. Strengthens larynx, lungs, thyroid, parasympathetic nervous system, and muscle tissues. Increases oxygen supply to cells.

MOTHER-OF-PEARL
See Pearl. The qualities are similar but weaker.

NEPHRITE JADE: Cleansing
Nephrite Jade is a Silicate of Calcium, Magnesium and Iron. Opaque to translucent masses, dark green to gray-white, black or blue-gray. Monoclinic. Hardness is 5 to 6.

Nephrite is a newer form of Jade energy than Jadeite. It is helpful for clearing and reprogramming in preparation for receiving new energies. It also helps the body accept the knowing that it is ready for them. It stabilizes the emotions during clearing and transformation. It is part of the Earth system that is reprogramming physical existence to receive the higher energies of the light body of soul. It grounds angelic perspectives and healing energies. It assists reprogramming of DNA by stabilizing the cellular connection to light.

Jade is traditionally used for healing the kidneys but aids the whole cleansing and releasing process. It helps you see the value of all aspects of yourself. It helps you understand the reasons behind negative subconscious programming so you can transform it with thoughtfulness and respect for your past attempts to solve your problems. It connects into the best of what is in your past and strengthens it. Its energy is similar to Jadeite, but its emphasis is on clearing and integration in preparation for moving to new levels.

Jade connects into whatever is in your energy structure now that will be useful for your evolution. It helps you see that you do not need to throw out everything in order to progress. It makes you more aware of your strengths and shows you how to use them in new ways. It helps you connect what has already been integrated into new flow patterns. Its emphasis is on using what you already have as your foundation for transformation.

Traditional and other sources: See Jadeite. No distinctions made between Nephrite and Jadeite Jade in sources, but Nephrite is newer, not having been used much until the nineteenth century.

The elixir mildly activates the throat chakra, aiding self-expression. Stimulates regeneration in heart, kidneys, thymus, and abdominal walls. Use in bath to remove toxins and radioactivity.

MUSCOVITE: Protective

Hydrous Potassium Aluminum Silicate. Forms pseudo-hexagonal, tabular crystals or masses of sheets or scales that are flexible. Silvery white, yellow or dark brown if Hematite or Rutile are included; transparent. Monoclinic system, hardness is 2 to 2.5.

Muscovite will protect you from whatever you are not ready to look at. It blocks negative vibrations or any that are not necessary to a specific focus. At the same time it will allow you to look at what is troubling you without becoming emotionally tangled in it. It can help you understand things better so you can interact with them more constructively, aided by other minerals or crystals.

NEPTUNITE: Transforms Physical Body

Sodium Potassium Iron Titanium Silicate. Long, prismatic crystals, black or dark brown. Opaque to translucent with vitreous luster. Monoclinic system, hardness is 5 to 6.

Neptunite helps the physical level of your body understand and make a connection with light which directly allows transformation and holds on to that connection. It is one of many very transformational crystals, but one of the most useful for the physical body. Very often your cells allow a little bit of new energy and a tentative alignment with the new ideal, but release the connection when you release the conscious focus. The subconscious is not ready to accept that this connection is something that is good or even possible. Neptunite, more than most stones, goes around the limitation which has been placed on the physical and shows the cells that higher energies are part of their potential that they can use now.

Neptunite is closely related to etheric substances that are used to build "light ships," those marvelous, crystalline creations which we, your spiritual teachers and friends, use to bridge the dimensions between us. It brings the full reality of your potential physical power that will eventually allow you to traverse the dimensions just as you now traverse Earth's land and oceans. It brings into reality your body's potential ability to gather whatever light structure you require to protect you as you move into all adjacent and parallel dimensions. It also shows you how to bring your own awareness into fuller appreciation of the many facets of your own creativity. It helps you integrate more of your power into specific purposes that support transformation and evolution. It opens your consciousness to new ways of using light at the physical level by making you more secure in using soul's lightbody.

As an elixir, Neptunite helps to break down the barriers or "veils" that have formed around your third-dimensional awareness. It allows you to feel and see more of other dimensions and to feel more secure with recognizing your own multidimensionality. It helps you see your soul as a partner and guide in exploring and expanding your unlimitedness. It helps break down blocks and crystallization in your body by locking in a more unlimited perspective. It releases many locked-in emotions which might seem temporarily overwhelming. If you allow it to do its work by accepting whatever comes up, you will see how to transform these emotions and any negative or disconnected and unintegrated energies into a contributing part of your personal power. It makes the surrounding dimensions a part of the energy associated with your circulating blood. It releases pain by dissolving the stuckness that causes it.

OBSIDIAN: Cleansing

Volcanic Glass, Silica Dioxide. Shiny black, red, green, yellow or clear. Might contain fine particles of dust or air bubbles which give it an iridescent appearance. No crystal structure.

Obsidian absorbs negativity and pulls out old energy patterns that are no longer being used. It can relieve pain if the pain is caused by an accumulation of negative energy. It is good to use regularly to cleanse the physical body of negative energy or negative etheric matter. The black Obsidian tends to hold the negativity, so cleanse it often if you use it intensely. Hold it under running water while you visualize white light flowing through it. This will cleanse your aura as well. Large spheres absorb negativity from the surrounding area. It protects you from negative influences from your own self or others while you sleep or meditate. Sleep with one near you to help release negative subconscious patterns. If this stimulates too much release, put it aside for a few days.

Clear obsidian is gentler and more effective for short times. It does not hold the negativity, but needs time in between uses to recharge itself. Any kind of light will do this. It can be very calming for persons with unevenness in their energy flow. It smooths out the bumps in it.

Obsidian can work on many levels at once, drawing out confusion and tangles so you can sort them out. If you aren't ready to do the sorting, you might not want to use it.

Other sources: Teaches how to bring light into darkness. Draws soul qualities into body. Protective, especially protects gentle people from abuse. Absorbs negativity. Grounding. Pulls energy into the physical plane. Stimulates desire to travel and opens one to new horizons. Balances body's energies, digestive system, and muscles. Reduces viral and bacterial inflammations.

The elixir balances mental and emotional bodies and alleviates tension in intestines. Strengthens the etheric body. Balances stomach, intestines, and muscles. Stimulates cellular reproduction. Alleviates viral and bacterial inflammations.

ONYX: Balances the Physical

Form of Chalcedony. See Jasper. Gray or black and white, also amber, orange and green. The common black Onyx is dyed. Hardness is 7.

Onyx is useful for balancing your connection into the Earth. It is not an especially dynamic energy. It can help you appreciate being physical. The green variety of Italian Onyx is useful during healing to balance the cells and help them feel supported by Earth during a transformative or releasing process. It is soothing to the emotional body and helps it to harmonize with the physical body, allowing it to support the physical body. It can ground the energies of some of the higher rays as brought in by Moldavite, Danburite, Labradorite, Moonstone, etc. In the case of Moonstone it helps ground the lightbody in the physical for activation at the proper time.

Black and white Onyx has the ability to delineate differences and explain their meanings. It can also release you from any experience or relationship that is complete. It shows you when you have nothing more to gain from them. This can be quite helpful if you are ready to release what is no longer needed and move ahead with your life and divine purpose. Onyx will help keep you focused on that, rather than maintaining the present "comfort zone."

As an elixir it is healing to the kidneys and small intestines. It is quite uniquely able to enhance the power of flower and other plant essences by bringing them into closer contact with the physical level. Just add a few drops to your bottle of plant essence.

Traditional and other sources: Grounds spiritual energies in body. Stimulates hearing and higher inspiration. Depresses mind. Conversely, is stimulating and exhilarating. Relieves fear of unknown. Protects against evil eye. Helps control passion, emotion, and negative thinking. Aids objective thinking, spiritual inspiration, and control of emotions and passions. Stone of separation. Causes arguments between friends. Useful for releasing, a bothersome relationship, for example. Also balances difficult relationships.

Low physical level vibration which stabilizes and strengthens. Strengthens nails, hair, and eyes. Assists childbirth and women's diseases.

The elixir increases sensitivity and integration of self. Opens solar plexus, base, and throat chakras. Balances male and female polarities. Strengthens and regenerates heart, kidneys, nerves, and skin. Increases capillary action. Relieves neurological disorders, apathy, and stress.

OPAL: Releases Stuckness

Hydrous Silicates. Noncrystalline, white, blue, red-orange, or black, very iridescent. Hardness is 5.5 to 6.5.

Fire Opal can bring in the fire of spiritual life if you are ready for it and balanced enough to use it. It is the fire of creative power. The white Opal with its multicolored iridescence brings the higher rays into all levels of self, so the four bodies can use them in a balanced way. Black Opal is a powerful connection into your dynamic power. It helps deal with the karma from misuse of that power. Blue Opal clears old energies out of your channel.

Right now, Opal is not completely stable. It dries out and becomes brittle when exposed to air. It will be more useful to humanity when they have learned to flow the tenth ray at the physical level as a group. Then Opal will be able to heal itself after it is brought out of the Earth and it will be an important vehicle of light. For now, it is tending to mirror the inability of humanity to use the higher energies without the proper foundation of morality and spiritual development. The negative karma invoked with misuse of power is the lesson to be learned before you can use it in alignment with the Divine Plan.

Traditional and other sources: Called the "Eye of the World." Possesses the qualities of every stone that has any of its colors. In dreams, symbolizes protection, justice, harmony, and emotional depth. Dreams of Black Opal symbolize study of death and its meaning. Makes wearer invisible. Considered bad luck by some, especially after the publishing of a story by Sir Walter Scott in which a drop of holy water fell on one and it turned dull. One Australian legend says a huge Opal controls the stars and gold in mines and guides human love. Another says it is a devil, half serpent, half human, who lurks in the ground ready to lure men to destruction with flashes of evil magic.

Absorbent. Picks up your energies, positive or negative, and returns them to you, activating the karmic law of return. Intensifies emotional response. Wear only when you are feeling good. Powerful protector. Brings joy, creativity, justice, harmony, emotional balance, love, and hope. Calms nerves. Opens psychic gifts and gives mental clarity.

Improves sight and eases eye diseases. Supports reproductive organs. Gives understanding of death. Alleviates leukemia.

Opal elixir bonds the solar plexus and crown chakras, opening and transforming base sexual responses and their related emotions to spiritual inspiration. Balances mind with emotions. Light-colored Opal does this best, opening brow and solar plexus chakras and increasing intuition. Amplifies the thought force behind creativity and intuition.

Light Opal elixir strengthens the abdomen, pituitary, pineal, and thymus glands and balances right and left brains. Eases autism, dyslexia, epilepsy, and problems with vision, neurological discharge, or physical coordination.

The elixir of brown or black Opal stimulates the sex chakra and adrenals, releasing toxicity. Grounds emotions. Aids depression, especially about sexuality. Supports testicles, ovaries, pancreas, and spleen. Aids white blood cell production. Alleviates diseases of the genital areas and liver. Some help in sterility and degeneration of bone marrow due to radiation. Balances over-stimulation by Red Coral.

Elixir of Jelly Opal balances extreme mood swings and enhances meditation. Used in degenerative diseases that affect cellular reproduction. Rejuvenates spleen and abdominal area and aligns their associated vertebrae. Aids absorption of all nutrients.

ORTHOCLASE: Elevates and Expands

Potassium Aluminum Silicate. Occurs as prismatic crystals but they might not have distinct faces. Semiopaque to transparent, colorless, yellow, white, grayish, pink or reddish. Monoclinic crystal system, hardness is 6. Transparent yellow stones are called Noble Orthoclase. The slightly milky variety is Adularia Moonstone.

Orthoclase, even the colorless, opaque varieties, brings a new perspective of light into the physical, cellular level of the body. It shows the cells their potential as light. In this way it opens them to the higher levels of light energy and the more evolved levels of DNA programming, allowing an elevation of their energy uses. When used in conjunction with other stones of similar chemical composition, it helps anchor the higher energies in the cells.

Orthoclase is an elevated energy that works at "ground level." It is useful in helping you to be more aware of energy moving in your body. So it can be used to help you develop an awareness of your body, its needs, and its possibilities. It helps bring all bodies, especially the emotional and physical bodies, together into a better working relationship. It also helps the mental body use the clearer connection to the physical made possible by the ideal. In other words, if you are working to integrate and use the ideal, it will help you heal yourself. You can just hold the crystal or place it on your forehead to help with this work. You can also place it on the body where healing is indicated, but this is not always necessary. Use it to cool warm areas where there is congestion or blockage of physical or etheric flow. It helps create clearer vision by blocking out what is not part of the ideal for you.

The clearer varieties, Noble Orthoclase or Moonstone, are more effective as elixirs. The first is especially helpful in restructuring the DNA of the immune system. It helps you recognize that the higher energies are beneficial rather than destructive, so your body stops trying to neutralize them. Once you recognize the value of the next level of alignment with the ideal and allow it into your cells, your body can use it without fighting itself and your desire to evolve and expand.

PEARL: **Balances Light**

Calcium Carbonate (mostly as Aragonite crystals) with 6% Conchiolin (organic). Rounded shapes of white, sometimes with hint of other colors, even black. Orthorhombic system. Hardness is 2.5 to 4.5.

Pearl's iridescence is symbolic of the Christ Light manifested at the physical level. Its structure (with a grain of sand at the center) symbolizes the beauty and perfection gained from resolving problems at the physical level. It helps balance the etheric level of light with the physical cells. It is rejuvenating, in that it helps the cells maintain the ideal. It brings the ideal into perfect expression in physical existence. It brings calm acceptance to the mind and harmony into the functioning of the third eye. Its spiritual aim is to serve as a mediator and bring a calming influence into the hierarchy of minerals. It brings a harmony with all levels of light which makes it easier for you to accept all crystal energies.

As Pearl blends the animal and mineral kingdoms in its make-up, it is helpful in resolving karmic problems between humanity and the animal kingdom. Its spherical shape symbolizes the perfection and wholeness of Earth as an embodiment of oneness. It helps resolve duality and separation. It is useful in any situation where there is separation, as between mind and emotions or between physical and spiritual aspects of self. It can also help an individual feel part of a group.

As as elixir, it makes bones less brittle and strengthens the nerves, especially for the kidneys and brain. In this form it is excellent for healing all emotional problems and dysfunction. It opens the heart in a way that allows openness and alignment with the whole. Its calming effect aids digestion as well as clear thought. It helps integrate other crystal energies, particularly those with more dynamic and electrical qualities.

Traditional and other sources: Represents faith, charity, truth, and spiritual knowledge. In dreams, represents soul sacrifice and victory over self-made suffering. Dream of Black Pearl represents one who precipitates karma. Symbol of sorrow and purity. The chief stone of Christianity, representing the pre-existing and eternal Lord Jesus, tears shed by Eve when she was banished from Eden. Activates purity and stimulates creativity. Represents wealth, honor, and longevity. Mothering energy. Softens pain. Balances and soothes mind and emotions, brings peace.

Strengthens the body. White Pearl works through solar plexus, stomach, and abdominal area. Dark Pearls work more through lower two chakras. Its dust is good for the complexion. Powder, taken internally, relieves acid indigestion from fatty foods.

The elixir gives understanding of motherhood. Amplifies emotions, good or bad, through thoughts. Provides a grounded foundation for initiating financial affairs. Aligns emotional and etheric bodies. Harmonizes and spiritually enhances the connection between Moon and emotions. Highly recommended for emotional difficulties, balancing them and giving flexibility. Eases stress on abdomen, muscles, and skeleton and ulcers from related causes. Light Pearls stimulate digestion, but alleviate food cravings during detoxification.

PERIDOT (Olivine):   Healing, Transformational

Silicate of Magnesium and Iron. Bottle-green to yellow-green, usually olive green, transparent, vitreous. Orthorhombic system. Hardness is 6.5 to 7.

Peridot is a high and active vibration, yet is so healing to the cellular level that it is seldom overwhelming or difficult to use. It is a clear connection to the Divine Ideal and brings that Ideal directly into the cellular level where it activates it. It finds the potential for perfection already inherent in the DNA and connects it into light at the present level of use. Its energies are soft enough that they flow easily into the old structure as they replace it with the new one.

It works very well with other crystals. It helps Clear Quartz activate the new structure. Amethyst helps clear away the remnants of the old structure so Peridot can bring in the new. Kunzite helps align the newly transformed cells into the whole through the help of your heart. Moldavite and Peridot help you connect into the ideal structure at its source in the galactic flow of Source energy. Pyrite helps connect the new structure into the physical, cellular level. Fluorite helps open the cellular barriers that weaken the effects of the new energies and provides a bridge through the cell walls for the new structure that Peridot brings in its healing mission. These are only a few examples. Peridot's energies blend with virtually everything.

Peridot's color, being an earthy green, is useful in accepting yourself as a physical being. So many of you would rather be somewhere else; any planet, any place seems better than Earth. You remember the perfection of other places, not realizing that you brought that memory to help you create that perfection on Earth. Peridot would like to help you do that, starting with your physical body, the real House of God (Spirit) here.

Peridot is a very important and potent agent of cellular transformation. It is a specific aid in stopping the aging process. It makes an excellent elixir. Place Peridot in a glass of water before you go to bed. Ask it and its angelic essence to release its healing and transforming powers into your elixir. If you feel you need some other crystal energy you can add it to the water with the Peridot. Amethyst or any variety of Quartz would be especially good ones to add. The angelic energies that work with Peridot have an especially close connection to those of water, which explains its power as an elixir. It brings healing and vitality to the whole body and helps heal the emotions.

Peridot is a precious gem, but you do not need a lot of it; small tumbled stones are not expensive. It is powerful and a small piece will do what you need it to do. We recommend it very highly. A favorite of Lenduce, a very cosmic and perfect being who placed Earth in his/her heart chakra at the time of the Harmonic Convergence and who works through and with crystals a great deal.

Traditional and other sources: Symbol of the Sun. Bestows royal dignity on its wearer. Activates spiritual and physical sight. Protects from evil spirits. Relieves digestive problems and depression. Calms physical body. Increases confidence and assertiveness. Increases clarity and patience, also clairvoyance. Eases spiritual fears. Aids cleansing of mind and body. Aids digestion and assimilation of food. Stimulates tissue regeneration. Brings light and beauty. Soothes chakras of throat and head.

The elixir increases receptivity to information from the higher self, making vibrational remedies more effective. Increases psychic abilities and self-awareness for healing. Use for healing meditations and creative visualization. Gives clarity, patience, and a positive emotional outlook. Stimulates tissue regeneration, aligns all subtle bodies and removes toxicity from physical body. Used persistently, will remove all cellular connection to karmic imbalances and their resultant diseases.

PERTHITE: Balancing

Potassium Aluminum Silicate (Microcline or Orthoclase) and Sodium Aluminum Silicate (Feldspar), layered together. Resembles pink Feldspar or blue-green Amazonite. Cut stones show a play of colors.

Perthite combines the properties of its constituents and adds the ability to balance higher energies into the physical. It can neutralize the "buzz," or floating effect of intense energies, by helping you fit them into your present energy flow. It brings you down to Earth without cutting off the benefits of the energy, allowing you to move to a new energy level that feels comfortable and expanded. It is an excellent balancer to use when channeling, as it enhances rather than mutes the expanded feelings that come through the spiritual connection, without letting you become disconnected from physical reality. It will help you bring through practical information into your being.

Perthite helps you rise above the problems of day-to-day life without disconnecting from them. It also helps you deal with inner conflict without becoming overwhelmed or too narrowly focused on them. It brings confidence in your ability to rise above any situation.

As an elixir, Perthite facilitates the flow of energy among different levels of self. It energizes or calms the physical and emotional levels as necessary; it allows the mind to understand them more clearly. It provides a means for the soul to connect into your body and allows it to bring you access to the Divine Ideal.

PETALITE: Energizing

Lithium Aluminum Silicate. Usually forms white or gray masses. White tabular crystals are rare. Transparent to translucent with vitreous to pearly luster. Monoclinic system, hardness is 6 to 6.5.

Petalite is the chief ore of Lithium. It energizes the electrical connections of the brain in a way that helps balance its energy flow. In depression, some of the energy paths in the brain, mostly at the emotional level (just above the etheric) are shut down. This cuts off the connections into the portion of the brain that allow you to feel joy and enthusiasm, which are higher vibrations. Petalite re-energizes these connections. Its effects are more direct but not always as easy to accept as Lepidolite's, which also bring in the heart connection and its integrative qualities.

Persistent use of Petalite elixir will help build clearer connections between the lower and higher minds. Aquamarine, Sodalite, and Topaz would be excellent additions to this elixir which would help transfer the ideal blueprint into your brain cells. Use the elixir when it is three to six hours old and take every two to three hours for maximum effect. It might, however, be several weeks before you notice conclusive results. You should remember your dreams more clearly and your meditations will produce more tangible results.

PETRIFIED WOOD: Balancing

See Agate, Jasper or Opal. The structure of the wood is replaced with some form of Quartz, retaining the appearance of the wood.

Petrified wood balances your physical structure and makes you aware of its light capabilities. Just as the wood itself has been transformed, it shows the potential of your own body for change. It helps you adapt to change and welcome it emotionally as well as physically. It will also connect you with the universal levels of consciousness of the plant kingdom. It makes excellent elixirs. Their qualities are those of the mineral form it has taken but are often enhanced somewhat.

Other sources: Stabilizing during mental and emotional stress. Helps past-life recall. Protects against infection. Helps arthritis and rheumatism. Enhances physical vitality. Aids tissue regeneration and longevity. Alleviates hip and back problems.

The elixir opens the heart chakra and alleviates heavy-metal toxicity. Opens you to past-life recall, especially when used with meditation and creative visualization, and alleviates present-life problems associated with them. Strengthens heart, spleen, and thyroid. Use for heart diseases, hardening of the arteries, scleroderma, and any hardening of the skin or other body parts, arthritis, and rheumatism.

PIETERSITE (Tempest Stone, Riebeckite):   Calming

See Tiger's-Eye for physical properties. Blue and gold Tiger's-Eye in Quartz which has been metamorphosed (folded and stressed) in the Earth.

Nine hundred thousand years ago, the Galactic Council of Twelve made this stone a specific anchor for a structure of angelic energy that would stimulate humanity's use of the divine creative potential in Earth. That nine hundred thousand year cycle came full circle in August 1987, the time of the Harmonic Convergence, making the potential seeded into Pietersite available to humanity now.

The group of angels who work through Pietersite are focused on love as the motivating force of creation, as all angels are. But they work with a particular calm and joyous peacefulness that is very uplifting and can do much to dissolve the confusion and fear about what lies ahead for the Earth right now. It will help you relax and release the limits you have placed on yourself in your creativity and allow you to move into a fuller recognition of all that your divine potential can offer for this New Age.

Pietersite is invaluable when you are experiencing or releasing deep emotions. It is virtually unsurpassed for calming emotional outbursts or upheavals. Thus it was named "Tempest Stone." It works by showing the emotional body the ideal flow while keeping it grounded into the flow of your life and its needs, spiritual as well as physical and emotional. Placing the stone over the solar plexus or holding it allows you to maintain a clearer perspective of the emotional energy being worked with. When the problem is more clearly understood, Pietersite serves as a means of transforming its energy into its corresponding part of the flow of love.

Pietersite, like all crystals, has its own unique way of showing your body, your subconscious, how to align with the divine ideal and feel comfortable with it and how to explore your unlimited potential with it. It shows your subconscious a new structure, one that does not recognize the blocks you feel in your relationship to Earth and to others. It shows you how to move as an unlimited, divine, creative being within the structure of the Cosmic Plan for the New Age. It is healing to the physical body as it releases the emotional restrictions placed on using your unlimited powers of healing self and others.

Pietersite is very helpful for spiritual teachers and channels as it allows them a clearer use of the ideal flow of their energy, reducing the fatigue and overwhelm that often are the result of working with the energies of others. It reduces and relieves the burnout that so many experience with a very intense schedule of teaching or channeling. It also allows a clearer communication within the group by building a bridge of energies that connects each member into the ideal flow of what is being shared.

Pietersite will help bring light into your physical structure in the amounts that you are ready to use. It is powerful and sure of its focus and its own place in the creative flow of the Divine Plan, but it will never overwhelm you with it. It is especially useful when worn over the heart. It helps you trust yourself in using love and allowing your heart to expand and release its blocks and fears. Placed at the back of the neck or over the throat chakra, it helps you align your own will with your soul's. It will help any chakra to open and integrate its energy with the rest of the body, assisting you as you learn to use the many dimensions of light that are available for your creativity. Used on the base chakra, or on the ankles or feet, it will ground you into a practical appreciation of your place on Earth as a divine spiritual being with unlimited creative power to use in accordance with the Divine Plan.

As an elixir it is similar to Tiger's-Eye. It does not need water to bring out its most powerful and significant properties.

PHENACITE: Opens Higher Chakras

Beryllium Silicate. Tabular or prismatic crystals resembling Quartz. Bright, vitreous luster, colorless, yellow, rose, green-blue. Fluoresces bright blue. Trigonal system. Hardness is 7.5 to 8.

Phenacite will open new connections to your expanding creativity. It helps bring in the "new" aspects of self which will allow you to use more of your full potential. It is very helpful now in allowing the inhabitants of Earth, as a group, to function according to the evolving ideal, which requires less of a personal focus and more of a group perspective. It is bringing in, through the Divine Plan, connections to new thought patterns being projected by those at higher spiritual levels who are helping you create a better Earth.

Phenacite is usually best worn near the heart as that is the chakra that is best used to make new connections. Phenacite can help you increase your use of your heart and your heart-centeredness. It will allow you to bypass some of the fears and other blocks you have about opening it to what is new.

Phenacite will open the brow chakra to new levels of awareness. This does not necessarily happen as actual change in astral vision, but as greater acceptance and recognition of your intuitive abilities. It will shift the alignment of the throat chakra to universal rather than personal will. This will, for many, resolve the problem of not being able to shift the physical body into the new flow (resulting in thyroid insufficiency). Fluorite helps the cells accept the energy of Phenacite. It also helps integrate creativity from the physical, biological levels into the creative flow of your soul's purpose through the throat chakra. In other words, it helps blend the flow between the second and fifth chakras.

As an elixir, Phenacite opens all levels of self to new ways of using light. When you use it in this way, it would be good to use some form of clearing and releasing frequently. Use Obsidian or visualize violet light flowing through your whole aura regularly to remove what is not part of the new structure.

PREHNITE: Healing

Hydrous Calcium Aluminum Silicate. Usually seen as stalactite or botryoidal masses, light green, brown or yellow-brown with chatoyancy. Crystals are rare. Translucent, with vitreous luster. Orthorhombic system. Hardness is 6 to 6.5. Often used to imitate Jade.

Prehnite has an expansive effect. It shows you how to connect into whatever is closest to you that you have not or cannot accept as part of yourself. This is done in a positive way that shows you the best way to use these potential energies for your healing and expansion. It heals your connections to these parts of yourself that you have forgotten how to use, that you have even forgotten are yours. It can be a very important help if you wish to expand beyond your present set of limitations. It works particularly on the heart chakra, bringing the spiritual and mental levels of energy use into proper balance with the etheric and emotional. It does not recognize the physical level as different, so it blends all levels of perception into practical, physically available energy. It works with the Copper-containing minerals, Dumortierite, Rutilated Quartz and Sapphire particularly well to heal your use of the divine ideal and restructure DNA.

Prehnite is an excellent cleanser. It flows negativity out of the cells and clears the emotions. It locks in the finer aspects of light and shows you how to use what you already know about light, giving you confidence in using it. In this way, it shows you your inner wisdom, so you can allow yourself to become familiar with it by using it. It also draws the next level of the ideal out of your inner core where it is waiting until you are ready to use it.

As an elixir it makes the ideal more available to the cells, creating balance and alignment. It makes it easier for your soul to establish points within your body where light can be secure and depended upon. For instance, spraying it over any of your chakras helps them align with your eighth chakra. It provides relaxation and calming through its alignment with the ideal flow. It relaxes tired muscles. Used on the feet, it relaxes them and refreshes your Earth connection, allowing you to relax into your relationship with it.

PLATINUM: Catalyst

Occurs as grains, plates, or nuggets, rarely as cubic crystals. Silvery-gray and very heavy. Cubic system. Hardness is 4 to 4.5.

Platinum is a more effective catalyst than the other metals we discuss here. It is transformational in its focus. It activates the ideal and helps you learn to use it more quickly. It helps you bypass resistance to accepting the higher energies and integrating their transformational effects into your cells. It especially helps you connect with and flow the energies of the transformational crystals. It doesn't really intensify their effects, but it helps you interact with them more completely.

Platinum is grounding in that it shows you all the highest potentialities in physical existence. It allows you to transform the physical level of your self and retain it within as part of your supreme accomplishment. It also lightens the effects of learning to use unlimited love in physical existence by helping you transcend the betrayal, hurt or confusion that have arisen from trying to use it perfectly on Earth.

Platinum heals by bringing a clearer connection with the highest perspective of yourself and your power that you can understand and use. It supports your stretching to new levels. As an elixir it activates other energies so they become part of your cells more securely and permanently. Often you try new energies out briefly and then "forget" about them or drop back to the old level. Platinum helps you hold on to the new level and remain in it.

Other sources: Aids self-esteem and confidence in expressing emotions.   Use to relieve arrogance, anxiety, fear, hysteria, shock, deep disappointment, over-excitement, and sense of superiority.

Platinum elixir alleviates depression and memory loss, particularly when it is the result of shock, anxiety or other stress. Aids clairvoyance and understanding of inner experiences. Holds magnetic patterns and amplifies thoughts. Aids regeneration of heart, immune and endocrine systems, and nerves, improving electrical transmission of synapses in brain. Aligns the whole spine, increasing receptivity to information from nervous system.

PYRITE: Grounds Light

Iron Sulfide. Pyrite forms are bright metallic yellow crystals, cubic, octahe-dral, flat radiating "suns" or granular aggregates. Cubic system. Hardness is 6 to 6.5.

This is a grounding energy that helps you anchor the higher rays, especially the twelfth, into self and Earth. It energizes the lower chakras and the physical body.   It teaches the cells to accept and flow light without resistance so there is no burning out or stress, no matter how much light you invoke. It helps your cells use this dynamic energy for transformation and healing, supporting other crystals by "sparking" the flow of their energies. Although its action assists the dynamic flow, its ability to encompass the magnetic flow of Earth's love is of a receptive quality which allows its energy to be balanced. It will not make you dynamic, but it will help you direct your creative intentions into physical existence. It will not make you loving, but it will help you open your heart to the beauty of Earth and its creative opportunities for exploring your divine purpose, by supporting the flow of divine love.

As an elixir, Pyrite can help the integration of protein in the digestive process. It also stabilizes the red blood cells so they are less prone to damage by toxic or radioactive substances by maintaining the healing flow of universal energy. It assists the liver in assimilating and creating certain amino acid substances necessary to maintain life as a channel for light and universal love.

Traditional and other sources: Pales when wearer 's health begins to fail. Stimulates cooperation, aids communication. Aids respiration and circulation of blood. Eases anxiety, frustration, and depression. Increases self-esteem and appreciation. Helps skin and skeletal diseases. Helpful for teachers and lecturers in its effectiveness against stammering and nervous exhaustion.

Improves circulation and respiratory function of skin. Use for bronchitis, laryngitis, pharyngitis, sore throat, tonsillitis, tracheitis and tracheo-bronchial catarrh.

The elixir eases anxiety, depression, frustration, and false hopes. Strengthens emotional body. Aids digestion. Stimulates spinal nerves to abdomen. Regenerates red blood cells and aids their enzyme production. Balances body's acid balance and alleviates blood disorders.

PYROMORPHITE: Strengthening

Lead Phosphate Chloride. Found as short, hexagonal crystals, parallel aggregates or masses. Green, brown or colorless, translucent crystals with resinous luster. Hexagonal system. Hardness is 3.5 to 4.

Pyromorphite stretches the physical energy, making it stronger and "bigger." Your energy seems bigger because it is more in harmony with the full potential of physicality, having released some of your ideas about its limitations. It helps you accept the new higher energies as a natural part of your physical body. It helps release excess weight by giving your physical consciousness a perspective of how to use physicality in the ideal way. It opens your conscious mind to new opportunities at the physical level. It opens your subconscious mind to acceptance of light into the physical body.

QUARTZ: Transmits the Ideal Blueprint

Silicon Oxide. Hexagonal, prismatic crystals, transparent to translucent with vitreous luster or compact and concretionary masses. All colors are found. Trigonal system. Hardness is 7. Worldwide in its occurrence. See also Amethyst, Citrine, Tiger's Eye, Aventurine, Chalcedony.

Clear Quartz contains the basic pattern of the ideal, the crystalline, spiral shape of the Divine Plan, the path of evolution as it is adapted to Earth's particular qualities and potentialities. Quartz might by found on other planets in other solar systems, but only the Quartz formed in Earth contains the seeds of Earth's growth and spiritual evolution. Its crystalline structure perfectly mirrors that of the DNA found in everything alive here. It represents the basic form that light takes when it becomes physical matter, and it flows light through itself with perfect allowingness. It knows absolutely that it is of light and radiates that light without reservation, confident of its right and ability to do so. It does not limit itself in any way as it allows itself to be the perfect mirror for flowing light.

Quartz, then, is the teacher of humanity, when it comes to accepting oneself as a perfect vehicle for light's flow while in physical existence. Quartz does not regard itself as inferior because it is physical. It knows that it was created by Source as an expression of Its love as light. Quartz is the ideal brought into physical existence, the eternal spirit gaining strength and knowledge of its own truth and essence through this sparkling form, nurtured and given life in the womb of Mother Earth. Upon its release from the ground, it is ready to share its understanding of light with anyone who is willing to work with it.

Quartz is the most versatile and useful crystal available on Earth today. It can be used polished or unpolished, as a wand, a sphere, a single point or a cluster. It can be programmed to help you align with your divine purpose, to open your channel, to connect with Earth and to heal yourself or bring healing energies into your body to share with others. It will help you align with the qualities of light you wish to work with. You can program it yourself, or you might ask your soul teachers or spiritual teachers to help you do so. It might be able to perform several different services at the same time, depending on your wishes and your soul's purpose. Ask the crystal what it can do. It recognizes your superior abilities as a creator, although when you see its beauty you cannot see its own creativity as anything less than perfect.

It is specifically charged by the Creator with the responsibility of caring for Earth and serving as the reference for its evolution at the physical level. Each crystal is encoded with at least part of the potential of the ideal and is a connector into Earth's records of what the ideal is and what it means. It recognizes that humanity has the capability of shaping Earth's destiny and will willingly serve that purpose without feeling inferior or manipulated in any way. It knows that its purpose is to flow light through itself and show creation how to align with light at every level, and it does that always, without fail.

Every particle of light Earth receives is coded with the Divine Blueprint for evolving life. Quartz is able, because of its similarities to DNA in flowing light, to serve as an example, a template, for integrating light into your physical structure. When you are attuned to light as it flows through Quartz, you are showing your own cells that that is how you wish to interact with light and its message of evolution. The divine goal of physical matter is to be able to express many levels or dimensions of light through itself, allowing the perfect love of the Creator of creators to manifest Its perfection throughout all levels of creation. When you are perfectly aligned with it, light itself can lead you through the steps of becoming aware of and in conscious control of your own creative abilities. Quartz can teach you how to use your creative abilities in accordance with the Divine Plan which leads every element of consciousness working within it to the full expression and knowledge of its potential as a divine creator.

The next great step in the evolution of Earth and humanity is being emphasized within the light that is coming to you now. When you are able to flow with it without resistance or fear, your body will be able to adapt easily to the changes that are taking place on Earth now, keyed by her need to take her next step and directed by the light. Light is designed to trigger the changes in your body that create evolution. Light literally interacts with your DNA, molding it to the ideal, shaping it as the template for cells of a physical body that is more capable of expressing its spiritual potentials. It is light interacting with your cells, which teaches your body to use the higher energies and you to express their qualities. As your cells begin to use more of these energies for their nurturing and support, your body and your physical brain are more able to understand what these energies are doing. Your body becomes a more suitable vehicle for your soul's expression of its purpose in physical existence. You become more aligned with your soul because your body can use its spiritual energies more directly, without the muting of these energies that can take place as your soul attempts to provide you with the support and nurturing of your divine connection.

Quartz is the key to achieving this great step in expansion of awareness and creativity that is occurring on Earth now. It was seeded in great abundance into Earth's crust so that it would be able to guide her evolution. When you remove Quartz from the Earth and work with it directly, aware of its ability and desire to facilitate your own evolution, you speed up the transformation process and help move Earth more rapidly to conscious alignment with the Divine Plan. Quartz becomes your teacher and your assistant as you become consciously aware of your place as a CoCreator within that Plan. It facilites the process of integrating with the Plan at all levels of self. It flows light through all levels of itself as a perfectly integrated unity, centered in its heart which expresses that light as unlimited love. Since its emotional, mental, and spiritual levels of awareness have never become separated from its physical body, it can guide you as you bring yourself back together again into wholeness. All this it will teach you to do.

Quartz combines well with all other stones. Each has its own way of flowing light and its special message for you and your body. Quartz shows your body how to understand that message and use it within your cells, serving as the master in using all other elements. It is part of the chemical structure of your body, having a place in shaping all its structures, from bones and tissue to the flow of vital fluids. It cannot do its work alone, but it is necessary in all functions at the etheric and physical levels. It allows your body to use light as energy and the more you can realize this possibility, the more you will be able to rely on light as energy and flow, rather than as physical substance for the sustenance of your physical body.

When you wear Quartz it will help protect you from energies that are not harmonious with the Divine Plan. Your own crystal will help you tune in to the Earth as a gigantic Quartz crystal that is enthusiastically and joyously seeking a clearer alignment with the Divine Plan. Your own crystal allows you to share with Earth your understanding of love and how to use it creatively, as well as your desire for that clearer alignment. Your thoughts create your own world and your conscious thoughts express your level of development as a CoCreator. Your crystal serves as a link to the rest of Earth in making your thoughts part of Earth's creative process, in harmony with the Divine Plan.

Larger pieces of Quartz, single or clusters, have always been special sources of beauty and wonder for many. They resonate with the deepest parts of yourself which yearn to express beauty with such innocence, power and courage. They serve as a reminder of what beauty, perfection, and harmony can be produced by Earth. They are a message of hope and promise that your divine potential is mirrored in Quartz and can become just as real within physicality.

As an elixir, Quartz is purifying and stabilizing. It strengthens all useful structures according to the ideal at all levels of self. It helps the integration of all other crystal or energy substances. It brings the evolving knowledge of how to use light into your cells.

We will discuss some specific forms of Quartz but remember, they all convey the basic qualities of Quartz. The additional attributes are overlaid onto the basic ones. Also, the non-prismatic, or amorphous, varieties do not convey the connection into the ideal structure of light and DNA as strongly as the actual crystal shapes. You see them in the individual form that evolved inside Earth. Stones are usually crushed or shaped and polished, after they come out of Earth, by man or by nature. They are not as aware of their individuality and not as strong in their expression of it or their ability to express it. As a general rule, the crystals have a stronger, more focused energy, but there are definitely exceptions here. It is possible to summon a great deal of power and purpose into even a manufactured stone.

Traditional and other sources: Symbol of purity, infinity of space, patience, and perseverance, Sun and Moon housed in a perfect crystal. A living entity. Connects you with your inner source. Raises consciousness, elevates thoughts, and removes negative thought forms.

Increases psychic gifts. Crystal is favorite material for divination. A psychic amplifier. For balancing, channeling, and transmitting or receiving of records, information, and energy. Use to communicate with nature spirits, focus meditation, and enhance healing. Sometimes is phosphorescent and electrical. Used to produce rain.

Gives healing power to water when placed in it. Stimulates brain function. Activates the pineal and pituitary glands. Intensifies the effects of other crystals. Prevents dizziness. Taken as powder in wine, cures diarrhea. Powder mixed with honey aids lactation. A pure tincture cures dropsy, scrofula, and hypochondriac depression, acts as a diuretic. Use spheres to cure diseases of cattle. Sun through a crystal ball can be used to cauterize.

The elixir supports the brow, crown, and solar plexus chakras. Blends creativity of sex chakra with solar plexus chakra to give feeling to expression. Alleviates all emotional extremes or hysteria. Aligns emotional and etheric bodies, enhancing tissue regeneration. Amplifies thoughts. Supports stomach, intestinal tract, and pituitary gland. Amplifies crystalline properties in body. Stimulates secretions of pituitary gland and production of white blood cells. Use for intestinal problems, abdominal ulcers, leukemia, bubonic plague, and chemical toxicity. Protects against background radiation.

Earth-Keepers: Creators

Very large Quartz points that have recently become available are called Earth-Keepers. They are individualized aspects of the consciousness of Earth itself, having direct access to the heart and soul of Earth, known as Jehovah or Sanat Kumara. Their purpose has not yet been fully realized or activated. When the Earth is ready to receive the next level of light, as shown by the physical presence of the Christ and His brothers and sisters who have, for now, gone beyond physical existence, these giant crystals will begin to sing the new Earth into being. There will be 144,000 of them by then in visible places around the world and humanity will be able to join in their song. The song will last for a thousand years. When their song is done they will become the seeds of Earth's next round of evolution.

For now they serve as connectors into the wholeness of Earth and the oneness of all life here. They are already singing a song that is manifesting the ideal of a more universal awareness of the oneness within each individual. They are the spokespersons of a group consciousness that will guide Earth to the next step in her cosmic destiny. They are channels into a greater awareness of group purpose and awareness of individual potential within the group. They serve now as objects of awe and inspiration because of their manifestation of physical bodies that vibrate to the ideal and transmit it perfectly. They are one aspect of the structure of the Plan that is guiding Earth.

Record-Keepers: Reveal Inner Knowledge

Quartz crystals are all encoded with the ancient spiritual knowledge of how humanity can express its creative power at the physical level. Some, however, give up this information more readily than others. They bear the "inscriptions" of this knowl-edge as pyramidal or triangular in-dentations on their faces. They serve as keys to unlocking the knowledge written in light, known as the Akashic Records. Each has its own particular area of expertise which it will share with those who are ready to open their hearts to the love that is necessary for gaining access to the Library of Records. If you are ready to receive this knowledge, a crystal in your hand is not necessary, but it will allow you to read the informa-tion more clearly and easily with all levels of self, including physical and emotional. Read in this way, the information is made available to all

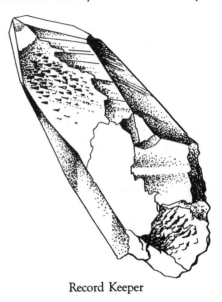

Record Keeper

of Earth through your connection to it. When Earth and humanity are ready for each new piece of knowledge, the right person will connect with his or her appropriate crystal and it will become available.

So Earth's memory of her spiritual knowledge and power becomes conscious once again as each person realizes his or her own potential. Some of these Record-Keepers are enormous and will remain buried in the Earth for eons before it is time for them to be revealed. Other smaller ones serve as communicative links with them and allow the knowledge to come out as it is needed or as Earth is ready for it. If you have many links to the Crystal Kingdom from past lives spent working with crystals, you may not even need a specific Record-Keeper. Any Quartz crystal will serve as the link you need into the flow of informa-tion transmitted by the Mineral Kingdom.

Madagascar Quartz: Activates Flow of Love

These Quartz crystals from Madagascar have an energy that is gentler than that of other quartzes, but they are very specific in activating your awareness of your heart as the center of your being. They are wonderful for healing because they help you use your heart as the ultimate healing tool. They connect you into the truth that love expresses and help you align all aspects of being with the ideal that love is. They can help heal your Earth connection by easing you into accepting it emotionally. This allows you to accept your physical body as a spiritual part of yourself, making your spiritual connection available to it for nurturing and healing. They are wonderful for working with the Earth because they help you to adjust your energies to the needs of the Earth or the needs of those around you.

Madagascar Quartz crystals have been programmed with a clearer understanding of some of the present difficulties within the mass consciousness and they are particularly programmed with methods and energies that can help to clear it. There is a nice balance in these crystals between the ideal and what can be accepted. They know how much change the body can handle
at a particular time, so they can be programmed to adjust the energy flow to a level that is easily accepted and utilized by the human system. They tend to take your subconscious mind through the process of aligning with the new energies in a step-by-step manner, rather than presenting the whole of what needs to be done at one time.

Arkansas Quartz: Revealing the Ideal

Arkansas Quartz comes in various energies but in general, it is especially good at revealing the pattern of the ideal. It clarifies the shape and meaning of the ideal so that your mind, emotions or cells can grasp it more specifically. It makes any crystal grid or combination sharper, more definite in its purpose. It also has a special clarity in its connection to the flow of the ideal, which makes it an ideal support for a channeling connection. Use other crystals to open your chakras, expand your heart, or ground the energy, but Arkansas Quartz will be very helpful in maintaining a connection you can validate and understand.

Laser Wands (Diamantina Quartz Points, Seed Points): Direct Love

These crystals contain minute amounts of carbon and other impurities that alter their structure slightly, making it more magnetic and intensifing its flow. They transform energy from the higher levels into energy that can be used at the physical level much as your chakra system does. This energy can be directed by your intention. If you center yourself in your heart first, you will be aligning its magnetic flow with that of the crystal, assuring yourself that the energy will be used positively.

These crystals are excellent for healing at the physical and etheric levels. They are very good for cutting out negative areas in the body or aura. If you have properly aligned yourself from your heart with the crystal and with the person you are working with, you need not fear doing anything destructive. When working with another person, ask your soul to help you make the appropriate connection with the other's soul so you will be working in harmony with his or her needs and purpose.

When held during meditation, these crystals can help you magnetize a potential in yourself and draw it out so it radiates in your aura and becomes a part of the light you are using in your life now. They direct the light of that new potential into your life and your

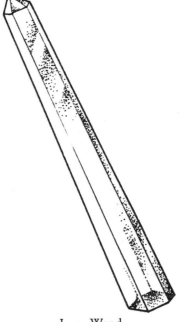

Laser Wand

system of attaining your purpose. This is, perhaps, the best way to use them. You can ask them specifically to help you find your strengths and activate your potential. Any crystal can do this, but these have a special way of magnetizing what you need in yourself so it is easier to see how to use it in your life and service.

Diamantina Quartz also activates the crown chakra, producing an opening that is more aligned into the flow of light from your soul, the keeper of your unused potential. Imagine the light of the crystal being mirrored into your chakras, flowing from the crown to your heart and activating your throat chakra so it opens and flows more freely. Also see the light flowing between the crown and brow chakras, creating a bridge between them. The crystal will help strengthen that connection.

Quartz Scepters: Channel Dynamic Energy

Sometimes Quartz crystals take the form of what looks like a bud on a stem. The termination part has a larger diameter than the shaft of the crystal. One crystal has formed around the growing point of another. They are tremendous storehouses of dynamic energy. They have gone through an expanded point of awareness which allows them to focus or channel energy into specific purposes with great intensity. The energy you put into the crystal by holding it or meditating with it is collected and magnified in the point, ready to be directed and released as you focus on your purpose or intention.

To use a Scepter you might try holding it while you note all the available information you have about your special purpose and form it into a plan that best utilizes the available information. Then release the energy of your creation through the crystal, visualizing it reaching your goal and activating it. Be very clear and specific in your directive, as this is a powerful tool and proportionately subject to misuse. We recommend asking your soul for guidance whenever you use it. The angelic beings who work through these crystals are very eager to serve and do exactly what you ask them to do.

Often, these crystals are not pretty at all, reflecting the "bad reputation" that dynamic energy and power have been given on Earth. Your own dynamic energy was the source of inspiration that brought you to Earth and encouraged you to plunge into experiencing life here. Some of those experiences were not pleasant and did not seem very spiritual. You blamed yourself as a failure in bringing light here and decided your dynamic energy was something to fear, something that often brought you into contact with "evil." As you work with these crystals they will help you forgive yourself and realize that you have always been striving to be light even though you were not always able to do as much as you thought you could. As you begin to really forgive yourself at every level and allow your soul to bring its dynamic power into your life in physical existence, the crystal can become brighter.

Phantom Quartz: Self-Understanding

These crystals experienced a pause in their growth when a layer of a substance other than Quartz formed on one or more faces. Then as normal growth resumed, the crystal growth reformed over this layer. During the time growth slowed, information was encoded into the Earth and these crystals are a key to gaining access to that information. The information revealed the steps necessary to using the wisdom seeded into Earth about unlocking the potential of the coming New Age. They can help you unlock and understand each new level of your own potential as the new, higher energies make it available to you. They particularly help you bring your cells into alignment with the potential which the light reveals by making it easier for the subconscious to read it.

Phantoms reveal the structure of the crystal just as they reveal the structure of your own lightself. They are a tool to use in building your understanding of your lightbody and making it real at the physical level. Ask them to help you understand the seemingly slow, step-by-step process of your evolution. They can help you see just how much you have gained from your experience in physical existence on Earth. They can be programmed to help you assimilate the energy and knowledge of your potential in the way that is most effective for you. They are masters at going deeply into themselves and patiently working out the meaning they find there and will be glad to help you do the same.

Tabular Quartz: Knowledge

"Tabbies" are considerably flattened in one of their dimensions. The flatter they are, the greater their characteristic properties. They are like keys that fit into specific areas of universal knowledge or into the Akashic Records of Earth. They make the knowledge easier to find and read. It is as if the crystal had allowed itself to be stretched out and made thin so you could come closer to its inner truth.

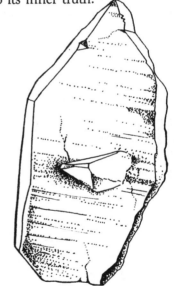

We have talked about other crystals that reveal knowledge, but Tabbies are opening specific areas about your potential which is encoded into your DNA. Your DNA determines the form of the vehicle you use to embody certain aspects of your truth and purpose. The shape and quality of the vehicle, in turn, determines the state and quality of your existence. These crystals help you discover and understand specific aspects of yourself. So Tabular Quartz, in its specific connection to your DNA, has more to reveal than just information about your physical

Tabular Quartz

body or life. It has a great deal to reveal about the meaning of your Earth experience and the consciousness of yourself you have gained here.

All knowledge of Earth is encoded in your cells and all universal knowledge exists somewhere in your cosmic self. In other words, you contain all knowledge, so the crystals are helping you learn about yourself and giving you access to your own wisdom. This is why the same crystal could have different messages for different people. Each of you is one page of the book of Earth, or the universal book, and each of you has a different message to reveal. Tabbies facilitate the process of discovering who you are, what your purpose is, and how you fit into the evolutionary pattern of Earth's development. Each of you has specific truths you can contribute and unique ways of interpreting Earth experience that will facilitate the expansion of the group mind of Earth. Each of you must continue to write and rewrite your own pages for perfection before the book of Earth is complete.

Tabbies are helpful in channeling or meditating because they bring you closer to your inner wisdom and truth. Peace, inspiration, information, whatever you seek, is made more attainable. The whole of your inner strength and power is there for you, if you choose it, easy to see and grasp. Healing is facilitated by understanding how the disease process began, where the misprogramming occurred that distorted the processes which were intended to create perfect health and vitality.

You can use Tabbies to help others to the extent that their pattern of understanding and experiencing overlap or harmonize with your own. The more you understand about yourself, the more you will be able to help others understand themselves. Conversely, you learn about yourself by helping others. This is a crucial point in working with these crystals because access to all information comes from within yourself. They can become very good, close friends because they help you communicate with your own best possible friend, yourself.

Quartz "Fadens": Healing and Expansive

These are flattened tabular crystals that have a white line or "thread"

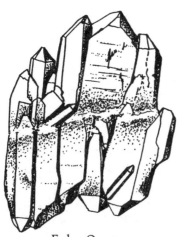

Faden Quartz

running through them. They occur when the cavity in which the crystal is growing is slowly opened or stretched due to the same sort of movement of large plates or sections of Earth that causes earthquakes and builds mountains. The crystal is broken and then heals as growth continues. The breaking and rehealing might happen many times, causing marked deviations from the normal shape. A "string" of crystals might grow on the thread once the Earth movement ceases.

These crystals mirror to you the

knowledge of self-healing and growth that comes from experiencing physical existence. They teach you how to heal even the most devastating problems in your body or in your life. They show how much the Earth appreciates wholeness. She offers the opportunity and means to heal any wound or separation. These crystals are masters of healing and are being understood only now when Earth is undergoing such rapid movement and change. They show you that you need not fail to keep up with that movement. They have gained strength by validating their own right and ability to achieve the fullest expression of their potential under the most difficult circumstances.

Fadens will help you maintain your vision of your goal and your trust that you are becoming that greater being you know you can be and already are, at some level. They help you bring that greatness into your physical expression. They are wonderful companions in the transformation process as they show you that breaking away from the old pattern does not mean destruction of what you are. Your vision of yourself, your alignment with the ideal blueprint is what determines and shapes your existence. The Earth is your companion and guide, not your nemesis, in your quest to discover all that you can be. These Quartz crystals are joyfully waiting to help you learn that and make it real for you at the physical level as well as at all other levels. There is much strength and knowledge to be gained by your higher self through the solutions you create to your physical-plane problems.

INCLUSIONS IN QUARTZ

Quartz is so frequently found on Earth that it has been associated with every other mineral. Since Quartz is the prime carrier of the ideal, it aligns all other energies more strongly with that ideal. Quartz enhances the particular ability of each to help you create that ideal. We can't discuss all inclusions, but some are particularly worth mentioning.

Red Quartz Crystals: Ground the Ideal

Sometimes Quartz integrates a great deal of iron oxide into its structure so that an opaque, rusty-red crystal is formed with the usual hexahedral form of Quartz. Phantoms might also be formed. The iron represents raw, dynamic Earth power incorporated into the known structure of understanding. It shows how this Earth power can flow with the structure of the plan and energize it without losing its identity.

Such crystals can help you connect with your Earth-centered power base and help you bring more energy into your life here. They help you understand, from an emotional and physical point of view, how to use your spiritual power as part of the ideal flow of the Plan. They can be powerful activators of your power at the physical level if you are ready for that. If you hold one in each hand while you meditate, you might experience a greater understanding of what it feels like to be a part of Earth's power structure and a part of the Plan as it is being used on Earth now. A powerful, magnetic form of love flows through these crystals from Earth herself and from all sources in the universe that are aligned with the heart of Earth. So, while this energy is grounding, it is also very expansive and helps you see and experience how Earth reaches out through her strengths and through her commitment to the Plan as she seeks to become a more vital part of the whole.

Keeping one of these crystals with you will help you walk more sure-footedly as a part of the Earth and as one who understands how to work in partnership with Earth as you both serve the Plan. It is a connector into the spiritual flow of Earth at the physical level. It can also be a constant reminder of the love and support that Earth has for each of you as you learn to accept and utilize love now.

Other sources: Raises energy from lower chakras to upper ones.

Chlorite Quartz: Physical Healing

This variety of Quartz has green clay (Hydrous Aluminum Silicate) in it as clumps or as a network of thin particles which might form phantoms, clouds or irregular masses. It is very healing to the cells and helps balance their fluid and electrolyte levels; we are referring to etheric fluids as well as physical ones. It shows the mitochondria (small bodies in cells that function in metabolism) how to use all the power in the available nutrients, how to make the ideal energy connection with those nutrients at the etheric level. It also protects them from random connections into the higher energies that are not in balance with the current electrical potential of the cells. It absorbs "errors" and allows Quartz to realign the energy into the ideal. It is a bridge between the spiritual ideal and the physical "reality." It translates the spiritual ideal encoded within the Quartz matrix into a blueprint that is adaptable to the cells at their current level of ability to use light for nurturing.

Quartz with Chlorite helps you emotionally and mentally accept your physical self as part of the spiritual flow of the whole. We have mentioned many crystals that do this. This one has its own way of doing it, one that is particularly helpful at the cellular level. This acknowledgment of your body as a fully accepted part of your spiritual self is necessary for complete healing and release of the aging and death programming of your cells which denies you the full use of your power at the physcial level.

Rutilated Quartz: Electrical Connector

Clear or Smoky Quartz can be formed with needles of Rutile in it (see also Rutile, below). Golden needles of Rutile in clear Quartz look like shafts of light given physical form. Light flowing from behind it reveals its full beauty, symbolizing your light potential that is revealed only by experiencing life on Earth. It embodies the truth of the universal center as light available at the physical level. This beautiful radiant energy helps bring the new electrical particles into the cellular level and helps the cells align with them. It helps integrate the new energies at the heart level and raises the vibrational level of the whole body. It gives your brain a pattern for expansion which helps it grow in its ability to understand the use of light and shows it how to make the connections that expand its conceptual framework through guidance from the Galactic Center. This allows the flow of the electrical particles to stretch your creative abilities to use light on Earth. It activates the light connections you are making into physical existence by showing you how your ideals can become real. Wearing this stone will gradually help you see how to do that in a practical way.

Rutilated Quartz focuses the energy of the soul into any part of the body on which it is placed. It helps you accept the use of soul's energy and the ideal in that area. It is especially useful on the throat chakra to help in accepting the alignment of Divine Will with personal will. It also helps balance the thyroid gland, bringing a clearer interaction with the master gland, the pituitary, as your body heals or continues to adapt to a changing Earth. It is essentially an electrical connector and is related to the angels as the form-builders of existence. Without angels to hold together the ideas generated by the CoCreators and to bind them to matter, there would be no creation. Rutilated Quartz helps you work with angels to create what you desire with greater understanding and acceptance of the process.

Rutilated Quartz activates the Plan by helping you see light in everything. It heals your perception of what you are seeing so that everything eventually becomes light. This is an "attitude adjustment" that allows you to see physical existence as it really is. Only by aligning your will with that of the Creator can you see as The Creator does.

Rutilated Quartz is a wonderful connector to the Galactic Center, which is the point of origin for the Divine Plan for Earth. If you use it with love and trust in yourself as part of that Plan you become a potent activator of that Plan here. It works well with all other stones to help you realize the divine creator that you are.

Other sources: Balances, illuminates, and energizes. Strengthens and integrates life force, makes your aura radiant. Helps you find your direction. Dissolves separation and loneliness. Helps restructure cells. Reverses aging process. Boosts immune system. Relieves depression. Powerful healer and highly electrical.

The elixir inspires connection with the highest spiritual levels. Aligns all chakras and subtle bodies and strengthens the etheric structure. Enhances thought forms, increases clairvoyance, and eases depression. Stimulates regeneration of whole physical body, aids assimilation of its life force, and stimulates its electrical properties. Reverses aging and diseases of lowered immunity. Eases all karmic disease patterns and aids assimilation of all nutrients. Use for treatment of and protection against radiation. Stimulates inactive and unused portions of brain, helping to heal brain damage.

Asbestos in Quartz: Physically Balancing

Asbestos is a Hydrous Aluminum Silicate. Forms microcrystalline gray-white, green, yellow, or brown fibrous aggregates with a silky luster. Orthorhombic system, hardness is 2.5 to 4.

Layers of Asbestos are sometimes found in clear Quartz crystal. This stone is useful for balancing your use of the dimensions. It helps to balance the body during or after astral travel. If you have very vivid dreams that leave you feeling unsettled or ungrounded, it will help you "get yourself together." It will also help you be more centered in your physical-plane life if you tend to get lost easily in fantasy or dreams. The Quartz that is supporting and surrounding the Asbestos helps channel your fantasies into an ideal which is practical in a balanced life.

Tourmalinated Quartz: Balancing

The qualities of Tourmaline are enhanced and often multiplied many times by being surrounded by Quartz. Since Tourmaline's energy is so balancing, this stone is an easy energy to use. Quartz, as the prime carrier of the ideal, provides the structure within which Tourmaline does its balancing. This stone will help prevent overwhelm or overstimulation if you invoke more energy than you can handle at the moment. The excess energy is not lost, it is channeled into an expansion of the structure you are presently using so you can gradually use more energy.

Black Tourmaline in Quartz connects into the transformation process as it is occurring at any level in your body and draws out energy patterns that are negative or inappropriate. It is useful in healing and clearing sessions as it helps maintain physical and emotional balance when confronting resistances and buried negativity. It is especially protective in that it will not allow in any energy that is not helpful or balancing for you. Green Tourmaline in Quartz helps you channel your dynamic energy into your spiritual purpose, even though you do not understand what it is, through Quartz's clear alignment with the ideal. Red or Pink Tourmaline in Quartz helps you use love in the ideal way in whatever you are doing. It helps you use your heart more effectively and more courageously, even though past experiences might have led you to the misperception that your love doesn't work. It also helps you feel more secure and less threatened about opening yourself to others and to higher energies. If you are ever fortunate enough to find Watermelon Tourmaline in Quartz, it will help you move into greater harmony with yourself at all levels as part of the group that has created the Divine Plan and is manifesting it.

Other sources: Harmonizes forces of light and dark. Will transform or deflect negative energy. Stimulates and directs energy. Aids positive action with a calm mind.

The elixir aligns the four bodies and the chakras. Increases spiritual understanding and attunement to higher self. Aids detoxification. Enhances other vibrational remedies.

"River Rock" Quartz: Energy Connector

These crystals are pieces of Clear Quartz that have been worn by the action of water into rounded stones. As it was worn down slowly, over many years, into its present shape, the consciousness or the essence of the crystal kept receding into the remaining portion of the crystal so that the essence became more concentrated. Under the unconscious direction of the Space Command, one end was cut off, creating a window into it. This allows a release of the concentrated energy which is almost like that of a battery in its effect. The energy is not actually being stored in the crystal itself, but it has learned to bring through great amounts of energy for anyone who desires to use it.

These stones are good sources of transformational and healing energy because they very potently radiate the ideal blueprint and flood the body with so much of its energy that they help overcome any blocks or resistances that are not receiving that ideal. They have learned specifically to concentrate transformational energy as they release what is not needed and they can mirror this ability into your cells.

Sometimes pieces of Quartz are tumbled into the round shape but the polishing is not completed. Then the ends are cut off. This vastly speeds up the process of concentrating the energy, of course, and these stones are not as powerful as the natural ones. However, they are still useful, as the unpolished surface serves as a sort of one-way receiver for the light energy of the stone, allowing it to accumulate until it is time to release it.

In general, these stones have all the properties of Clear Quartz. The energy is more "rounded" and radiating than that of a faceted crystal. It tends to surround and fill an area rather than penetrate it.

Smoky Quartz: Protective

Clear Quartz here contains minute particles of mineral or organic matter. It can be pale smoky brown to black. It is thought that natural radiation causes the darkening.

Some varieties of Arkansas Quartz, particularly, contain minute particles of Aluminum which give it a grayish, rather unattractive appearance. This is often treated with gamma radiation which burns the Aluminum and turns the crystal a beautiful black. (Gamma rays will not make it radioactive.) Once the crystal has had time to rest and readjust is it quite as useful as other Quartz. Sunlight is a good promoter of this adjustment process. The resulting crystal protects against radiation, having experienced it and made a successful transformation. It is helpful in adjusting your own body to the new, higher energies. Like Aqua Aura, its electrical properties have been enhanced, although not to quite the same extent. It can be useful in connecting physically with soul's energy. It is also, like other black stones, good at drawing out negativity. Each crystal responds differently to the radiation process, which seems to individualize them and give them independent "personalities" or qualities. Some are very healing. So look at them, perhaps we should say feel them, and attune to them with an open mind. It is even more rewarding in these cases than with other crystals.

The natural Smoky Quartz has a softer energy that is very comforting to the emotions in times of stress. It is helpful in emotional clearing as it alleviates fears and helps resolve all negative emotions into positive energy. It is never overwhelming and is comforting and calming to have around you at all times. It supports the flow of emotions, strengthening and validating them, making the emotional body more secure in its own power. It can smooth out the dissonance felt from an overactive or controlling mental body, allowing the emotions to feel more confident in their part in the creative process. It can help integrate the energy of more powerful or penetrating crystals; in fact, it helps the emotional body integrate everything. It is very healing to the solar plexus, allowing it to balance into the flow of the ideal and transforming negative energy patterns into ones that are aligned with the ideal. It smooths any flow.

The naturally Black Quartz has all the properties of Clear and

Smoky Quartz, but additionally is a powerful protector against negative thought forms. It seems to just absorb them and neutralize the energy. It occurs plentifully in Switzerland, for instance, and is one reason that country has had little occurrence of war on its soil.

Smoky Quartz is useful in balancing the mental body, especially when used with Citrine or Azurite. It dispels confusion, bringing mental clarity and allowing the mind to balance with the other bodies. It can help stabilize your spiritual connection. When used with Moldavite, it helps ground the communication established with other dimensions or levels of awareness. As an elixir, it draws negative radiation from the cells and heals them. It could be useful after UFO or other-dimensional experiences. We say this because such things will become more common as Earth integrates more and more of the fourth dimension and as all dimensional barriers weaken; some of you will, at times, have trouble with energy fluctuations during and after such encounters. It also heals damage to the immune system incurred because of fears about using the new, higher energies. The elixir is best for this.

The vibrational patterns of Smoky Quartz and Amethyst complement each other, allowing you to create a transformational energy pattern that supports all levels of being and provides a balanced foundation for receiving the energies of your higher chakras and your lightbody. This combination forms a complete energy spectrum that supports any crystal work and is recommended for those who work with healing and balancing the physical and emotional bodies. Citrine and Aquamarine would be good additions to assist healing mental problems and imbalance. But Smoky Quartz is the foundation of this energy structure at a practical, physical level, and that is why we have discussed the combination here. See also Ellestial Quartz.

Other sources: Symbolizes light in darkness. Removes unclear thought forms. Improves intuition and survival instincts. Grounds spiritual light into body and Earth. Generates energy, increases endurance, relieves fatigue, depression, and spaciness. Aids development of mediumship and clairaudience. Stimulates and purifies base chakra. Stimulates kundalini energy. Helps make your dreams real at the physical level. Protects against radiation.

The elixir aligns the etheric energy system and the other bodies, encouraging proper stimulation and release of kundalini energy and increasing intuition and creativity. Also aligns three lower chakras. Aids meditation by removing unclear thought forms. Aids the abdomen, kidneys, pancreas, adrenals, and sex organs. Increases fertility in both sexes. Eases heart disease, muscle deterioration, neurological deterioration, and toxicity from chemicals or heavy metals. Use as a spray to cleanse the aura.

Blue Quartz: Calming and Elevating

The smoky blue or blue-gray color comes from tiny inclusions of Rutile, Tourmaline or Zoisite. It has an energy that is calming but expansive and elevating. It will help dispel depression, confusion, and fear. It can help create a calm and balanced mood conducive to meditation. It is especially useful as an elixir to bring mental and spiritual balance during transformation and integration.

There is another variety of Blue Quartz that is found in Tibet and is a much deeper, darker blue. This Quartz is a special gift from Sanat Kumara, the Planetary Logos, to help Earth connect into his love and his spiritual connection to Source. It can help you relate to Earth through his love and to feel supported and contained within the universal flow of unlimited love. It is stabilizing and strengthening during transformation. It helps you feel confident of your ability to serve the Divine Plan and your place in it. Its energy is very grounded but also expansive and radiant as it flows love magnificently through all levels of being.

Other sources: Enhances spirituality, self-expression and creativity, and opens heart. Transmits information. Strengthens throat, heart, lungs, and thymus.

The elixir aids expression of spiritual qualities, increases creativity and self-expression and the transmitting of information. Opens heart and throat chakras and aligns the subtle bodies. Eases depression and fear of aging. Supports heart, lungs, throat, thymus, and parasympathetic ganglia. Stimulates healing and toxin removal. Use for low immunity and cancer, where metabolism breaks down. Increases absorption of Gold, B vitamins and oxygen.

Lavender Quartz: Balancing and expanding

This is found in masses rather than as crystals. Its delicate lavender color tells you that its energy is gentle and uplifting. It assists the angels in clearing and balancing the body and emotions. It is useful for balancing the brow chakra and connecting it into the rest of the chakra system at each new level in your expansion. It helps the emotional body stretch into the new conceptual framework that Earth and humanity are invoking to better understand their place in the universe.

Lavender quartz is useful with Aqua Aura and Moldavite, softening the dynamic impact of their higher energies. Lavender Quartz serves as a bridge between the new electrical particles necessary for transformation and the body's cells which might not feel ready to integrate them completely. It is especially harmonious with pink stones, expanding their ability to open the heart and helping to connect the heart energy into the rest of your body and your life.

Rose Quartz: Supports the Heart

The color is thought to be due to traces of Manganese or Titanium. It is usually massive in form and opaque, but small crystal clusters are found occasionally, and it can be clear.

Rose Quartz expands your identification with your heart as the center or creative core. It affirms heart-centeredness as its most important quality. Rose Quartz is very supportive of the emotional body. It soothes it and nurtures it by bringing in an unlimited perspective of love. It can help you feel less judgmental and more loving to yourself. It helps the solar plexus to expand and interact in a balanced way with the heart. It helps it find its place in the spiritual balance of the whole system, rather than just the emotional and physical parts.

Rose Quartz also helps the emotional body recognize its positive qualities and channel them through your heart into your aura. It shows you how to use the higher emotions based on love. The energy of Rose Quartz is very flowing and will add the pink of universal love to your aura if you align with it as love. It helps bring out your inner truth so you can see it, learn to understand it better and use it in your life. Ascension requires perfect clarity and purity in your emotional flow, as well as the blending of the heart and solar plexus chakras. Rose Quartz will help you with this, as it teaches you to love yourself and others unlimitedly.

If you have fears about using your heart or about showing others that you are a loving person, Rose Quartz will help you become more heart-centered and trusting of your own love. It will help you see that your love is truly the Creator's love manifesting through your heart. It is a gentle energy that is appropriate for anyone. It is especially helpful for babies. It creates an aura of love and gentleness around them which is protective and helps them adapt to their new physical body. In fact, it is good during any transition process, filling the newly found spaces with the protective aura of universal love as you learn to work within them and integrate their strange new energies. You cannot have too much of this beautiful energy around you. It will never create an imbalance because it aligns everything through your heart, which is your center balancing point.

As an elixir, it balances and heals the physical heart. It heals and stimulates the stomach and small intestine to use the available nutrition according to the ideal. It helps your muscles use sugar more efficiently. It is healing in that it helps you give your physical body the love it needs to be healthy.

Other sources: Symbol of love and beauty. Gives inner peace, gentleness, compassion, forgiveness, patience, and love of self. Increases appreciation of beauty and the arts. Soothes and balances. Lifts depression, gives self-esteem and self-acceptance, and aids in weight loss. Calms agression and resentment, reduces tension. Especially calms heart center and emotions. Gives a beautiful, clear complexion, prevents wrinkles.

The elixir increases self-confidence, personal expression and creativity and lowers false pride. Balances the emotions, eases anger and tension, especially with father images. Aligns the four bodies, strengthens the etheric structure and stimulates the heart and throat chakras. Supports genitals, heart, kidneys, liver, lungs, and parasympathetic ganglia. Regenerates kidneys and red blood cells. Increases fertility, particularly in males. Eases sexual disorders and their karmic patterns, leukemia, and circulation problems, particularly constriction of blood vessels. Protects against radiation.

Star Rose Quartz: Integrates the Ideal

The structure of this variety of Rose Quartz is highly organized, therefore very evolved. A bright pinpoint of light is transmitted as a six-pointed star. Its angelic soul is part of the angelic kingdom which works with love from the sixth-dimensional level of light, the ideal for physical existence. It connects you to this ideal through your heart. It activates your divine purpose and helps you align with it without interference from any subconscious misperceptions you have about using love or your creative power. It makes unlimited love seem easy to use, as it should be. It shows you, through its beauty and clarity, how to love as the angels do.

Star Rose Quartz will never overwhelm you with the power of its vibrations, even though its energy is a powerful alignment into the ideal. It brings the beauty of your full potential into physical existence and shows you that perfection is possible, is already here on Earth. It shows you how to use your dynamic energy in soft and beautiful harmony with the ideal, and your receptive energy with strength and power.

Quartzite: Stabilizes the Physical

A compacted mass of Quartz grains with many other minerals

possible in combination with it. The Quartz material itself is white. Other minerals create a colored or marble-like appearance.

Quartzite is mentioned here because it is often used in the construction and decoration of large, important public buildings. It helps make these buildings effective places for integrating and grounding group energies and perspectives. It can help these buildings serve as foci for manifesting specific aspects of the Divine Plan. It helps them transcend mundane purposes and move into greater awareness of spiritual potential.

Small pieces of Quartzite will help focus your awareness into specific purposes and help you find new meaning and beauty in physical existence.

Rainbow Quartz: Elevating

Clear Quartz that has been treated under heat and pressure with Silver vapor. (See also Aqua Aura.) Has a pearly, iridescent sheen.

The alteration of this material makes it at least ten times as powerful as natural Quartz. Just as your evolution can be accelerated by your conscious intervention, so the Crystal Kingdom will cooperate with human ingenuity to produce the tools that support it. Rainbow Quartz is a connector into the higher aspects of light. It activates connections into all of the higher chakras, particularly the tenth, eleventh, and twelfth. It helps your whole aura open to the light as it comes from the Galactic Center and helps it integrate the flow of the Plan from that level.

The connection with the Plan at the galactic level illuminates your developing creative abilities as CoCreators with Earth. Rainbow Quartz helps you learn to recognize your inner strengths from the level of your inner self which is vibrating to the galactic frequency. It helps you align them with the Plan. It might be more powerful for some of you than Aqua Aura, but it is gentler and easier for the etheric and emotional bodies to use. It softens the edges of a dominant mental body, helping it to open to the spiritual input of your heart (higher emotions) and soul. Its rainbow of colors precipitates balance in all aspects of self.

Rainbow Quartz has a very fine vibration which harmonizes with everything that is already right within you and expands this rightness into a feeling of harmony within the flow. By maintaining this assurance that you are flowing with the light, everything in you that is in opposition to the flow eventually will drop away as you use it less and less. Even a small piece can be very helpful as you search for your place in the Divine Plan. The crystal points emphasize the highest creative potentialities in your light. The spheres collect light and radiate it as the ideal flow of soul's energy and its lightbody. It helps you bring your soul's light into your body for healing, transformation, and ascension.

As an elixir, its properties of transformation and balancing with the higher aspects of light are made more available to the cellular level of your body. It also supports the immune system and the endocrine glands in integrating the new energies in a helpful way. It can bring the comfort and protection of the angels during sleep and help your body accept their healing ministrations. It protects you from nightmares and assists creative dreaming.

RICHTERITE: Calming, Releases Stress

Hydrous Sodium Magnesium Silicate. Purplish-red or blue to yellow aggregates of crystals. Transparent or translucent with vitreous luster. Monoclinic system. Hardness is 5 to 6.

Richterite takes away stress and calms the nervous system. It stabilizes the emotions. Its effects are most noticeable in the aura when this crystal is worn on the body. As an elixir its effects are subtle, working more at the cellular level. It can take the "kinks" out of the DNA, kinks that are formed when intense fear or shock is crystallized into the physical level. Slight misalignments in the DNA strand are formed which prevent complete alignment with the ideal. So Richterite releases the physical remnants of emotional and physical stress.

RHODOCHROSITE: Unlimited Love

Manganese Carbonate. Granular masses or stalactites, crystals rare. Pink, translucent, vitreous luster, often banded. Trigonal system. Hardness is 3.5 to 4.5.

Rhodochrosite is very supportive of the heart, helping you to use it and flow with its love at higher vibrational levels. It helps your heart to open and cuts through your doubts and mistrust about using love. It also supports the flow of higher emotions by the emotional body and helps it accept integration with heart's energy. It is most useful now if you allow it to help you connect through love with those parts of yourself which have been denied knowledge of, or refuse to recognize, your Source connection. These are the parts of self that create disharmony and misalignment with the ideal. Each one is derived from an inability to use a special strength. You need to connect all these parts into your conscious creative flow in order to express your full potential and use your full power.

Rhodochrosite's energy is similar to that of Rose Quartz in expanding your use of love, but it is more specific in connecting you with your own creative use of love. It helps put things into a perspective of universal love, but it supports your individuality as a CoCreator within that universal flow. It teaches you about love and what it is. It is healing for women who have been sexually abused. It dissolves the guilt and pain of such experience and brings back self-love, acceptance, and forgiving. It can help anyone understand and express the highest qualities possible in sexual expression of love.

You can meditate with it by visualizing its lovely pink color filling your heart, radiating from it and filling your whole body with its warmth and light. Fill your whole aura with it and allow yourself to feel the love of all creation supporting your special contribution to it. Allow yourself to be loved and supported by it unconditionally.

The elixir heals connections between your heart and all aspects of the physical-emotional-mental self. It dissolves barriers set up by self-hate and lack of self-esteem. It makes loving yourself a healing experience for your body.

Other sources: Brings love. Soothing and warming. Unites conscious and unconscious mind. Clears old pains, hurts and memories from deep within, allowing a clearer flow in the present. Prevents mental breakdown. Eases or prevents emotional breakdown or trauma and restores emotional balance. Releases irrational fears. Strengthens pancreas, spleen, and kidneys. Purifies respiratory system.

The elixir cleanses the subconscious, allowing access to higher realms of thought. Strengthens self-identity and ability to function in life. Eases nightmares and hallucinations. Creates emotional balance. Use for narcolepsy or fear of deep sleep. Use for prediabetic states and detoxifying kidneys. Strengthens the kidneys, pancreas, and spleen. Also place stones on related vertebrae to stimulate healing of these organs.

RHODONITE: Opens Heart, Grounds Love

Manganese Iron Magnesium Silicate. Pink to brownish masses with black veins of Manganese Oxide. Tabular crystals rare. Translucent, vitreous luster, prismatic cleavage. Triclinic system. Hardness is 5.5 to 6.5.

Rhodonite helps to open your heart at the physical level and shows you how to love in practical ways. It helps the emotional body accept physical existence and adapt to the new energies. It is calming and stabilizing for the mind and emotions. It brings peace. It can heal broken relationships by bringing in an atmosphere of cooperation and acceptance of all views. Its vibrations will flow well anywhere without specific direction from you. It knows that it is love and connects as love with everything.

Rhodonite adds strength to feminine energy, giving it confidence in its creative abilities and showing it how to be receptive to the masculine without being overwhelmed or losing its equality. It is the solid, everlasting love of Earth, ready to accept all and share its love without discrimination. As an elixir it helps you to release your subconscious defenses against others and to understand their viewpoints.

Other sources: Gives stability, self-esteem, self-confidence, increases self-worth. Relieves anxiety, confusion, and mental unrest. Promotes calm. Restores physical vitality after or during emotional stress or trauma and restores mineral balance in body.

The elixir increases sensitivity to and satisfaction from using mantras and amplifying their thought forms. Aids sense of pitch. Strengthens inner ear and sense of hearing and eases inner ear inflammation. Eases karmic pattern of syphilis.

RHYOLITE: Calming

An extrusive igneous rock containing Quartz and a Feldspar, combined with various other minerals. Usually light colors, white or pink. Included here because the solid varieties are attractive and often found carved into spheres, eggs, beads, and so forth.

Rhyolite helps balance and stabilize the emotional body during cleansing processes. It is a quiet energy, not intense. Its fiery origin gives it the ability to transmute intense emotions like hate and anger into harmonious ones. It absorbs negativity. It helps the emotional body look beyond its present comfort zone and find a balanced connection there so it can stretch into new experiences. In the left hand, it is soothing to hold, drawing in a balanced flow of energy that is easy to assimilate. In the right hand, it aids releasing and clearing. As an elixir, it brings stability to the mind and cools emotions. It promotes healing of traumatic wounds.

Other sources: Stabilizes emotions, strengthens physical body. Increases self-respect, self-worth, and capacity to love. Gives emotional support to efforts of love and strengthens loving relationships. Physically rejuvenating.

The elixir supports heart and throat chakras, aiding self-expression from the heart and the speaking of truth with greater clarity. Aligns emotional and spiritual bodies. Influence on other chakras depends on color of stone, that is, red or brown for base chakra.

ROMANECHITE MERLINITE (Psilomelane):   Clearing

Hydrous Barium Manganese Oxide. Forms botryoidal, stalactitic or dendritic black aggregates or earthy masses. Often forms dendrites on faces of limestone. Opaque with almost metallic luster. Orthorhombic. Hardness is 5 to 7.

Romanechite (or Merlinite) is one of the best clearing stones now available. It pulls all unattached negativity out of the aura. It is best used regularly to cleanse the aura of the day's accumulation of confusion and problems before they become a permanent part of you. It is invaluable during clearing, as it helps loosen stuck energy and brings up old, deep patterns for review and release. Sometimes black stones seem to bring up negative situations, but remember, you must recognize what is in you before you can release it. Once the negative energy is loosened and you become aware of it, you will find it easier to let it go. It adds its own great strength to help you in the clearing process. It provides a sense of a warm darkness that supports and nurtures growth like a womb.

Romanechite does an excellent job of preparing your body to hold more light. It helps to anchor the new light into your aura after the clearing. It is able to take in great quantities of light and shows your subconscious how to handle the ever-increasing flow of light through your cells. It also helps to maintain the new openings that are created. It encourages transformation at the cellular level by removing energy distortions of the ideal flow pattern which distort the shape of the DNA structure. It holds open the spaces for the ideal as you learn to allow it and use it.

Romanechite promotes restful sleep. As an elixir, it heals the skin, bones, ligaments, and whole intestinal tract, especially the colon. It can help release cancer and arthritis. It keeps energy flowing more smoothly through the whole body. It keeps the complexion clear and bright.

RUBELLITE:

(See Tourmaline)

RUBY: Strengthens Heart and Creativity

Red Corundum. See Corundum.

Ruby is often the most precious (expensive) of gems for good reason. The rarity of fine Rubies symbolizes our present limited ability to bring more of the Creator's love to Earth in the form of creativity.

When your creativity is flowing according to its full potential, you can have all the Rubies you desire. You will create them from your heart as the Creator did those already on the Earth. Ruby is seldom perfectly clear, symbolizing that Divine Love is a part of Earth's substance that has yet to be transmuted. The more you can bring out the love crystallized into Ruby, the clearer your Rubies will become.

Rubies are a direct projection of the Creator's heart, His/Her blood, really. Not that it is physical, but the flow of Divine Love supports and nourishes all of creation and communicates with it at every level. Ruby is very heart-centered. It helps you see the strengths of your own heart and how to use them for your own evolution. It will help you accept and use your full creative potential. It will help you channel your dynamic energy into whatever you are doing. It helps you feel secure with your male and female selves and with your four bodies, physical, emotional, mental, and spiritual.

Those parts of self which you feel are unworthy of your divine beingness contain much creative potential that you can reclaim through learning to relate to all parts of yourself with unlimited love. Ruby brings a direct connection to all levels of your creative potential, including Source levels, and opens an awareness of what is possible for you through love and its creative flow. It can help you create a more loving interaction between your heart and emotions, allowing the solar plexus to expand and interact in a balanced way with your heart. It helps your emotions find their place in the spiritual balance and flow of the whole system.

A very small Ruby can bring a tremendous amount of power into your life through love. It helps you find the Creator within youself as you learn to use the love that comes ultimately from the Creator's Heart.

As an elixir, Ruby balances the dynamic aspects of the blood, enabling it carry oxygen to the cells and helping them to convert it to energy more effectively. Water assists in transferring its magnetic qualities into the DNA, so you can draw to yourself more of whatever you need to create your reality. In any form, Ruby brings vitality to all organs of the body, especially those with a great blood supply such as the liver, lungs, and kidneys. It magnetizes the brain, integrating the flow between the two halves, so that you understand at a conscious level more of what is going on within your cosmic levels of self, and it brings a loving perspective into your thinking processes. It assists in balancing and stimulating all the endocrine glands for transformation. Love is the ultimate tool that can produce the healing and transformation that Earth needs now and Ruby knows how to bring it into all levels of self so you can do your part. Ruby can magnetize progress and transformation while showing you the value of all that is now being experienced.

Traditional and other sources: Symbolizes devotion which transforms divine love into divine will, the beauty of the soul, the son of man power in Earth. In dreams, represents access to miraculous healing power. If you dream of wearing a Ruby ring, you are an initiate of the life force. Contains its own fire. Also represents the Sun and was believed to contain the bloodlines of humanity. Teaches spiritual expression, selflessness, and lasting love. Some are male and more vigorous and sharp. Female Rubies are sweet and pleasant. Were thought to be able to mate and create offspring.

Brings beauty, love, physical protection, and good fortune. Gives power, devotion, honor, passion for life, truth, self-love, courage, stability, confidence, self-esteem, balance, peace, and contentment. Enhances and activates intuition. Raises spirits and clears negative thoughts. Removes obstacles. Amplifies thoughts. Eases disorientation. Banishes sadness, grief, disappointment, sin, and vice. Moderates passion but supports action. Reconciles disputes. Banishes nightmares.

Protects wearer's health, wealth, and good spirits. When imbedded in the flesh, gives invulnerability. Used to make amulets against poison, plague, evil thoughts and spirits. Warns its wearer of poison or of impending evil by turning dark and cloudy. Touching four corners of a house or garden with a Ruby protects it from lightning, storms, and worms.

Preserves body and improves mental health. Strengthens heart center and circulation. Balances heart and increases vitality after heart attack. Strengthens ears, eyes, nose, pituitary, and spleen. Heals diseases of eyes and liver. Use for infectious diseases such as typhoid, intestinal disorders, leukemia, sickle cell anemia, and schizophrenia. Dissipates pestilential vapors.

The elixir creates balance in spiritual endeavors, self-love versus divine love. Helps balance kundalini. Stimulates leadership, feelings of compatibility and awareness of ability to give and receive love. Adds divine inspiration in leadership. Balances personality, eases disorientation, transforms procrastination into stability and confidence, self-esteem, and decision. Helps focus problems with father image, especially hostility and anger.

Ruby acts as a master gem for the heart. The elixir also supports, strengthens, stabilizes, and heals the heart on all levels. Adjusts vertebrae associated with heart.   Strengthens nerves associated with the heart. Stimulates regeneration of heart tissues. Enhances thymus function.

RUTILE: Activates

Titanium Oxide.   Yellow, red-brown or black, elongated, prismatic crystals, with metallic luster, usually opaque. Tetragonal system. Hardness is 6 to 6.5.

Rutile is most useful when found as inclusions in Quartz (see Rutilated Quartz). It has a special affinity for the immune system, helping it to accept and integrate the ideal as a natural part of physical existence.

Other sources: The elixir opens the heart chakra and makes one more forgiving toward self and others. Alleviates repressions resulting from early childhood and parental pressures.

SANDSTONE: Understanding Earth Processes

Grains of Quartz and Feldspar (most commonly) are cemented into rock by clay, Iron Oxides, Calcite, or Quartz. Sandstone makes up one-fourth of the Earth's crust.

Sandstone is made up of the cast-off and broken-down forms of former crystal entities.   As their souls move on to new forms or experiences they release the substance of their bodies back to the planet which gave them life. The heat and pressure of geologic processes are the birth process of new mineral "life forms."   The metaphysical properties of Sandstone are not as intense as crystal forms and vary with its composition, which can include any mineral. Sandstone can carry an energy charge from the place it was formed and give you whatever gifts the Earth particularly offers there, if you attune to it. Not having an individuality like a crystal, it remains in its consciousness part of the Earth it is taken from.

Other sources: Using the elixir in meditation gives a more flexible personality. Aligns the etheric and emotional bodies. Activates liver and skin. Use in bath for skin problems. Aids reproduction of skin after burns. Improves elasticity of heart and blood vessels. Eases arteriosclerosis, rashes, scleroderma, and liver disorders.

SAPPHIRE: Elevates Consciousness

Blue form of Corundum, which see. Also can be pink, green, violet, yellow, or clear.

Where Ruby emphasizes the dynamic creative power of love, Sapphire represents the peace, beauty, and perfection of unlimited love.

It takes one out of the pain and confusion of physical existence and brings in balance and clarity of love, which is everywhere. Whereas Ruby is the "Blood," Sapphire is the "Breath" of creation, the ceaseless perfection of cosmic cycles that energize the evolutionary spiral. It is the peaceful outpouring of the Divine Plan into a universe that has been designed to support its flowering. It is never weak, but it shows you do not need strength to prove the truth that is already within every atom in that universe.

Blue Sapphire will help you connect into the flow of love of the second ray at all levels. It makes it easier to flow with your heart's energy at all levels of self. It helps you accept the wisdom of your inner self and accept its guidance. It dissolves fears, anger, and hate. It clears confusion. It activates and opens the brow chakra and connects it to the crown chakra, bringing more light into your body, joy and peace into your emotions, and acceptance into your mind. It teaches you to believe in your own worth as a spiritual being. It symbolizes, through its clarity, the perfection of the truth of unlimited love. It is sometimes used as a "calling card" by the spiritual master, Kuthumi, although he values all crystals equally.

In healing the physical body, Sapphire calms and clears toxic conditions, particularly in the lungs and lymph system. It facilitates the electrical flow in the brain and nervous system. As an elixir, it calms fevers and stops the spread of infection. It can also be used on the skin to make it less resistant to allowing light into the body; it releases the need for protective walls erected as a result of misperceptions about how to use light.

Blue is the commonly recognized color for Sapphires, but Pink Sapphire is special for its ability to connect one with the highest possible vibrations of love. It is especially good at helping you release all misunderstandings about your own power. It teaches you that you need not rely on anything or anyone outside yourself. It will help you recognize the true power of love as the source of your creativity. It will help you interact with others creatively, through love, which is never limited in its application.

It helps you feel supported and contained within the universal flow of unlimited love. It is stabilizing and strengthening during transformation. It helps you feel confident in your ability to serve the Divine Plan and of your place in it. Its energy is very grounded in the heart of Earth, and it is expansive and radiant as it flows love magnificently through all levels of being.

As an elixir, Sapphire is specific for opening your cells to the magnetic effects of love. It prepares them to receive whatever they need from the supportive flow of Source's love. It teaches them to remain in perfect alignment with that flow. It helps your body, as your mechanism for experiencing life, to learn to attract the best that life has for you.

Traditional and other sources: Star Sapphire is the stone of destiny, its rays representing faith, hope, and destiny. It sounds the tone of supreme consciousness more than any other stone. Represents higher mind and oneness with divine mind. Stimulates desire for prayer, devotion, spiritual enlightenment, and inner peace. Supports your dreams and fulfillment. In dreams represents the higher mind and law without judgment. Also a symbol of wisdom and perception. Aids search for truth. Attracts divine favor, prophecy. Teaches devotion and spiritual enlightenment. Stabilizes and clears mind. Focuses and eases energy flows at all levels of self. Aids self-discipline and organization. Brings victory. Protects kings from harm and envy. Banishes fraud and prevents terror. Prevents poverty. Makes a stupid man wise and an irritable man good-tempered.

Clears phlegm, bile, and flatulence. Use for colic, rheumatism, and mental illness. Its potion heals scorpion bites. Prevents boils and pustules, heals ruptured membranes. Strengthens sight and heals eye diseases, ulcers, and growths. Looking at one intently protects eyes from injury. Placed on eye, causes ejection of foreign body. Strengthens heart, other organs, and their blood supply. Purifies blood, protects from poison. Stops unnatural body discharges.

The elixir connects the four bodies, bringing clarity and inspiration. Stimulates clairvoyance, psychokinesis, telepathy, and astral projection. Improves communication with spirit guides. Opens heart and throat chakras, allowing personal expression and releasing stored energy from solar plexus. Relieves depression and emotional tension around navel.

Elixir also acts through solar plexus and brow chakras. Regenerates intestines, stomach, and pituitary gland. Supports and heals disorders of heart and kidneys. Stimulates secretion of pituitary hormones. Aids release of toxicity from radiation and chemicals. Improves assimilation of all nutrients.

SARD:

See Chalcedony.

Other Sources: Enables one to understand laws about humans' relationship to higher forces. Sharpens the mind and makes one happy and fearless. Facilitates healing qualities of other agates. Wear over abdomen to relieve spasms and colic. Protects from negativity or attack.

Used for wounds and tumors. Similar to Bloodstone, especially in healing blood disorders.

The elixir helps integrate courage into spiritual dynamics. Eases fear and tension. Strengthens gallbladder, liver and intestines.

SARDONYX

Onyx that contains layers of red Chalcedony with the black and white.

Other sources: Stimulates mental self-control and love of good and light. Awakens humility, virtue, fearlessness, emotional confidence, and eloquence. Releases grief and sadness. Aids emotional control, brings happiness and emotional confidence. Facilitates emotional expression. Blends likes, aids communication and interaction with others. Binds together and creates conjugal happiness. Protects personal possessions, brings security. Keeps energy together.

The elixir prevents depression, anxiety, and grief. Stimulates the throat chakra, strengthens the emotional body, increases intuition and understanding. Strengthens the lungs, larynx, thyroid, medulla oblongata, and parasympathetic nervous system. Aligns upper cervical vertabrae.

SCOLESITE: Dissolves Barriers

Hydrated Calcium Aluminum Silicate. Forms radiation groups of slender, striated prismatic crystals, clear or white. Transparent with vitreous luster. Monoclinic system. Hardness is 5.

Scolesite's energy does not recognize barriers, it simply flows through and around them, revealing to you the full truth of who you are. It doesn't balance, integrate, or discriminate. It simply intensifies absolute flow, making more light available. This light can be used like a laser to cut out or reveal what has been buried or what needs to be released. It can act as a magnifying glass for studying self in whatever way is necessary. You can direct its power through focusing on a particular area that needs to be cleared or a problem you wish to solve.

Scolesite intensifies the effects of most other stones. Using it with Green Calcite, for instance, would be useful in healing a particular area that needs a better electrical flow. It would intensify the cleansing effects of Amethyst. This combination helps release the cobwebs of misunderstanding that create barriers to seeing truth. Scolesite emphasizes the next step in integrating the ideal that Clear Quartz is bringing you. It could help Moldavite dynamically create openings in your brow chakra, but be careful here; you might get a severe headache or damage the etheric structure of your brain if you bring in such intense energy too fast. Using Selenite with it would help soften the intensity of bringing all dimensions into one focus, so the mind can grasp what is coming to you and direct the energy to its proper use. Fluorite, particularly purple Flourite, will help direct the energy of Scolesite directly into the cells to open them to receiving more light.

SELENITE (Gypsum):   Integrates Dimensions

Hydrated Calcium Sulfate. Clear, tabular crystals, many forms, including swallowtail, fishtail or rosettes. Monoclinic system. Soft, hardness is 2, easily bent, transparent with vitreous or silky luster.

Selenite is a very important New Age crystal. It is helping to integrate the dimensions at this very critical stage of transformation for Earth and humanity. Earth is learning to use the fourth dimension as a part of physical existence. Everything is flowing easier and faster and Selenite can help you use that flow, understand it, and merge with it. It is almost as important as Quartz in getting light into the body. It helps organize the light and makes it easier for the cells to align with it, so that each of the four bodies can have its own appropriate vibrational level of light available. It eases any confusion and difficulty the physical and emotional bodies have in using the more intense and complex flow.

Selenite helps your body find its place in the flow as the ideal becomes emphasized throughout your system. Selenite candles (long slender crystals) help integrate the third through sixth dimensions. Fishtail Selenite integrates the fourth through sixth into your third-dimensional understanding. Selenite enjoys working with humanity so much and is so enthusiastic about helping its evolution that the Creator gave it the form of a rose to use wherever it wished. The Selenite Desert Roses help the physical body accept the new interdimensional energies and their transformational effects. They help you use your heart in intergating the new dimensions at the physical, cellular level. The very large columnar pieces help you expand your understanding of using the interdimensional flow. They enhance the flowing movement of light in the whole room or environment and elevate the energy without losing the Earth connection.

Selenite does not do its best work by itself. It is not an intense energy. It works with the ideal that Quartz brings, the transformation from Amethyst, and the acceptance of new energies from Calcite, to mention only a few. But it is invaluable in integrating the new perspectives they bring and helping you to use them as light. Selenite is very common on Earth and is used, as Gypsum, in building, to make plaster and cement. So its energy is widely available and supportive of your life on Earth.

Selenite helps balance the chemical elements in the body fluids so the endocrine system can be more effective in supporting transformation as well as healing. It assists the kidneys in balancing the body's electrolytes. It is primarily receptive, so it helps bring in and integrate the energies of all other crystals you use in healing.

Selenite dissolves in water, so if you should need an elixir, don't leave it in for more than a few minutes. The perspiration from your hands will also soften or dissolve it if you hold it for a time. Its healing effects are enhanced by water.

Other sources: Brings out inner truth. Aids meditation. Soothes mental troubles or confusion. Stimulates mind and psychic abilities. Aids telepathic communication.

The elixir releases tension and gives flexibility. Rejuvenates the prostate gland, testicles, and uterus. Restores elasticity to skin and bones. Balances sex chakra and its energies, activating spiritual insights and stimulating the kundalini. Eases fears of male sexuality.

SERAPHINITE: Peace, Self-Acceptance

Sodium Aluminum Silicate. Chlorite. Dark green with silvery, chatoyant, feathery inclusions, opaque to translucent, vitreous luster. Hardness is 3.5 to 4. Named after the Seraphim, the angels closest to God.

Seraphinite brings peace and relaxes tension and stress caused by fear of what is within yourself. It puts negative thoughts and emotions into their proper perspective so you can transmute or release them. When this is done, there is no resistance to the flow of your higher self and your spiritual connections. It puts you in contact with your potential and your purpose. If you want to channel, it provides the receptive, allowing state necessary for a clear connection. If you just want to be at peace with your own self and your limitations, it will allow that. It puts you in touch with whatever you need most at the moment. If you need rest it will provide that. If you need to move, it will bring a sense of urgency that inspires action, but action that is guided by your intuition and spiritual teachers.

Seraphinite is similar to Spectrolite but more personal in its feelings. It puts you in touch with your soul and its unconditional love and support. It helps you realize that any negative feelings you have about yourself come from misperceptions accepted by that part of self not integrated into soul perspective. This can provide a basis for you to see your problems and potential in a new light, which allows easier clearing and faster progress. You release fears about accepting and learning to use your unlimited creative power.

Seraphinite comes from the Lake Baikal region in Siberia. Lake Baikal is deeply connected with Sanat Kumara's purpose and is a sort of incubator of the divine plan at all dimensional levels. The will of Sanat Kumara is processed here into energy waves that broadcast many levels and processes of the Divine Plan for evolutionary growth. It is also a receiving point for messages from the Galactic Center and other administrative points in this galaxy. There will be more crystals from this area available at the appropriate times to help carry special messages for humanity as you learn to be responsible for your own evolution and power. They are all profoundly connected with the creative use of love at the physical level. Seraphinite shows you the Creator's love as a thing of beauty and peace, not heavy or judgmental, but joyous and uplifting, a sublime feeling of being surrounded by angels ready to bring you a feeling that everything is all right.

The soul, or angelic essence, of Seraphinite has made a specific connection with a group of spiritual beings from another dimension who guide and assist Earth's progress. They are particularly concerned with reestablishing the spiritual connections damaged when you entered physical existence.

Seraphinite works on the etheric balance between the pineal and pituitary glands at the physical level, allowing more of soul's energy to enter the body. It also helps balance all the chakras with the heart. Its elixir brings upliftment and expands your spiritual connections, not only with what is "out there," but also with what is inside you. It brings a more spiritual connection with Earth and helps you see the great potential within your physical experience here.

Seraphinite can be used any place on the body to release tension, relieve pain, and bring balance. If you invoke spiritual help, it will help you focus and connect spiritual healing into the appropriate area. The protective aura it provides, makes the transformation process easier, so that you relax into it and have no problem integrating the increasing rates of expansion Earth is now experiencing. Peace and relaxation are the keys here that allow you to accept the higher potential which must be integrated if Earth is to take full advantage of the opening available now.

As an elixir, Seraphinite balances the etheric flow in the body. It relieves pain, dissolves tension, and eases breathing. It softens hardened areas in the body. It improves the complexion and clears sight. It facilitates the flow of water and electrolytes through the kidneys and relieves inflammation in the bladder. It helps reestablish self-worth and the strength of will necessary for healing cancer and AIDS. Spray it around the room to open communication at all levels, especially spiritual, and to stop nightmares and bring helpful dreams.

SCHEELITE: Energizes Creativity

Calcium Tungstate. Pyramidal crystals, sometimes tabular or striated. Yellow, green or reddish-gray, translucent to transparent with vitreous luster. Hardness is 4.5 to 5. Fluoresces blue-yellow. Tetragonal system.

Scheelite supports all creative thinking and creative action. It helps you understand what creativity really is, dissolving the misperception that it refers only to art, music, or something outrageously new. It shows you that whatever you can do that utilizes your individuality and allows you to contribute to the practical flow of life on Earth can be creative. Scheelite helps you form goals that will assist your evolution according to your own purpose. It cuts through mistrust and doubt of self, helping you to transcend that into productive action. It helps you find your own path and stop trying to follow the path of another.

As an elixir, it might boost fertility of sperm in men. It decreases rejection or destruction of sperm in those women who tend to have high numbers of antibodies that attack them. Combined with other regenerative elixirs, it decreases autoimmunity.

SERPENTINE: Balancing

Hydrous Magnesium Silicate. Occurs as three intermixed polymorphs in three crystal systems: orthorhombic, monoclinic or, less often, hexagonal. Serpentine "Jade" is translucent, waxy, greenish white to pale green, might have yellowish or brown patches. Hardness is 4.5 to 5.

Serpentine is protective and balancing. It acts by allowing you to use only those patterns that are aligned with the ideal. The rest are gradually disconnected and released. Its effects are not especially powerful but can be used by virtually anyone without problem. It enhances the balancing effects of other crystals. It protects by helping you adapt negative, confused or strange energies into a flow that you can accept and use. It balances the etheric energies of the blood and respiration. It supports the spleen in sorting out old, outmoded energy patterns and releasing them. It also helps clear out the confusion that results from trying to use too much new, higher energy at once. This allows the body to heal the effects of radiation and overstimulation.

Serpentine is an old energy that has helped humanity through many cycles. It has a particular ability to help you move through transitions, personal or cosmic, in a balanced way. As an elixir, it heals by promoting a balanced connection into the ideal. It helps the body integrate light at the needed vibrational level. It can help lift your spirits and make you feel more positive about your abilities.

Other sources: Protects travelers. Aids physical survival. Gives security in strange or new locations. Diverts stress. Protects you and your possessions from outside intrusions. Helps direct energy appropriately.

The elixir balances the emotional body, alleviates fear and paranoia, stimulates altruism, improves meditation and visionary abilities, and increases psychic abilities, including astral projection. Stimulates heart, kidneys, lungs, and pituitary and thymus glands. Increases oxygenation of red blood cells and whole body.

SHATTUCKITE: Grounds the Ideal

Copper Silicate. Prismatic crystals, massive, granular, or fibrous, bright blue, opaque with vitreous to silky luster, often mixed with Quartz and other Copper-bearing minerals. Orthorhombic system.

Shattuckite reveals the ideal to the physical cellular level in its own special way, spiraling the flow of the Divine Blueprint around the DNA strands and helping to lock it directly into the portions that are damaged. Used with Quartz, it can be significant in correcting the duplication of cellular materials altered in diseases such as cancer or autoimmunity. It can also help stimulate the restoration of damaged nerve cells, especially in the brain. It balances the fluid levels in the brain, relieving pressure headaches for some.

Shattuckite also helps break up karmic patterns having to do with misuse of power at the emotional level. Misuse of power can relate to refusing to use power, as well as using it badly. These patterns result in crystallized areas in the aura that inhibit the flow of creative power and limit its use. They result in negative thought patterns about your ability to use power and in depression of the function of the endocrine system, especially the thyroid or adrenal glands.

Shattuckite elixir is rejuvenative for the whole system. It helps restore a youthful perspective and boosts energy levels, especially for the emotions. As an elixir it is specific for resolving at the emotional level the effects of abortion. Inability to use creative power at the physical level for your own benefit is sometimes the result. It helps reestablish the structure of love around the lower chakras, whether the abortion was natural or artificially induced.

Other sources: Strengthens the etheric body. The elixir aids release of information encoded in DNA. Stimulates cellular reproduction and repair of damaged DNA. Use for genetic diseases, dwarfism, hemophilia, mongolism, cystic fibrosis, sickle cell anemia, genetic mental disorders, and to release their karmic patterns from cells. Also heals radiation damage to DNA.

SILVER: **Aids Movement**

Gray-white masses, dendrites or wiry forms, often forming crosses or star shapes, rarely cubic or octahedral crystals. Opaque, metallic luster, surfaces are usually oxidized to black. Cubic system. Hardness is 2.5 to 3.

Silver is the best known conductor of heat and electricity. It is less grounding than Copper but brings in more of the higher vibrational energies. It is more useful for working with transformational stones. It allows you to select and direct the energies into your conscious purposes, whereas Copper works more under the direction of the subconscious bodily processes. Silver helps connect love into your cells and into Earth. In working with other-dimensional beings, it provides an interface with their energies and your crown chakra. Like the other metals, its malleability symbolizes its willingness to work with humanity to achieve their purposes and teaches adaptability.

As an elixir silver supports many other elixirs. Its energy is boosted more than any other metal by being placed in a pyramid. It is useful in pyramid work for helping you use the energy focused within them. It clarifies the connection with the new DNA structure that Quartz and Amethyst, especially, bring into a pyramid when they are placed in its apex.

Other sources: Frees subconscious memory and stimulates fantasies. Makes conversation flow. Strengthens etheric system and aligns it with the astral body, preventing disintegration of the physical. Use for mental imbalances, hysteria, schizophrenia, compulsive or sexual neuroses and to assist psychotherapy. Aids brain and circulatory system. Activates nerves, particularly motor nerves. Eases anorexia nervosa and sleepwalking, loss of balance, brain and spinal problems, bronchial congestion, neuralgia of joints, and headaches. A disinfectant. Use for fevers and supurating infectious processes.

Silver elixir increases the kundalini flow into the body in a balanced way. Increases ability to visualize and bring self into alignment with universal symbols, making them personally relevant. Amplifies thoughts. Balances female qualities. Activates eighth through twelfth chakras.

Elixir also stimulates nerves, brain, and etheric flow, increases I.Q., improves circulation. Strengthens pineal and pituitary glands and all vertebrae. Supports tissue regeneration. Eases radiation toxicity, especially from X-rays. Can help ease right-left brain imbalance. Improves nutritional absorption of Silver.

SMITHSONITE: Aids Communication

Zinc Carbonate. Usually found as aggregates of crystals, individual crystals are rare. White, blue, green, yellow, pink, violet or brown. Translucent with vitreous luster. Trigonal system. Hardness is 5.5.

The energy of Smithsonite is calming and uplifting, releasing fears about interacting within Earth's flow. It helps you learn to accept that you can act with confidence in your worthiness as a CoCreator. It allows you to balance your vibrations with those of almost anyone else. It helps you accept the ideas and opinions of others. It helps you communicate more easily with yourself. It will heal a stressful or difficult relationship by easing fears of opening yourself to others.

Pink Smithsonite is very helpful in new or troubled romantic relationships to establish good communicative links. Green Smithsonite will help communication in business dealings. The yellow form helps relieve anxiety in relationships where there are deep karmic fears or anger with another. White releases hate. Pink and Green usually have the most uplifting energy and are helpful in easing fears about releasing your personal will to soul. All colors support meditation by smoothing and balancing the flow in your spiritual channel. Certain groups within the Space Command can use Smithsonite very well to assist in communicating with you at an intuitive or creative level. Try it and see if that feels right for you and your spiritual support group. If it is, you will know.

Smithsonite helps you form a good working relationship with the angels who guard and heal your physical body. Another group of angels are connected with transformation and ascension and it helps you interact more easily with them, especially if there are subconscious fears about electricity or radioactivity that are blocking the acceptance of the new energies. It is very supportive to the immune system, as it takes away self-hate and doubts about self-worth. It frees the courage of your heart to support your needs and wants. It helps balance the body's Calcium metabolism, especially as an elixir, and assists Calcium ions in their role of balancing the cells' use of electromagnetic energy at the etheric level. It doesn't interact directly with the electrical flow as Calcite does, but it helps the cells and the nervous system support that flow. Its action is gently stimulating to a balanced flow of higher energies. It can also be helpful in relieving toothaches.

The elixir heals all electrical connections in the brain and nervous system. It helps halt and reverse degeneration of nerves.

Other sources: The elixir integrates the astral and emotional bodies, the heart and solar plexus chakras. Generates self-confidence. Eases fear of relationships and the inability to form them.

SODALITE: Balances Will

Sodium Aluminum Silicate Chloride. Forms compact blue masses with white to gray lines or areas. Crystals are very rare. Translucent, vitreous luster. Cubic system. Hardness is 5.5 to 6.

Sodalite is healing for the throat chakra and supportive of your higher creative expression. It helps balance the sex chakra with the throat chakra and bring the energy from the head chakras down through the throat and into the heart. It helps balance the mental and emotional bodies. It is grounding in that it is specifically seeking to use the love of the Planetary Logos to flow its energy into working with humanity to solve the problems of integrating light into the physical level. It will help to heal a brow chakra that has a karmic memory of damage in the past.

Use a Sodalite wand to clear away "cobwebs" in the etheric body by using it to sweep through your aura. Hold the wand to your temple to facilitate the energy flow through your whole chakra system or relieve congestion in the head or brow chakra. It is particularly good for massaging the bottoms of your feet for a better connection into Earth. Or you can roll a wand or a ball of Solalite under your feet to relieve soreness and fatigue. As an elixir, Sodalite will allow you to feel more in command of your life and more confident that you can give worthwhile service to the Plan in a practical way.

Other sources: Aids spiritual growth and development of wisdom. Stabilizes mind. Clears vision. Gives power of mind over body. Connects mind and emotions. Balances emotions. Eases subconscious fear and guilt and conflict between conscious and subconscious. Brings peace. Aids self-expression. Stabilizes thyroid and balances glands involved in metabolism. Stimulates the spleen. Prevents diabetes. Aids communication and self-expression. Good for throat.

The elixir supports spiritual growth through emotional balance. Balances yin and yang. Strengthens etheric system. Strengthens lymph system, eases or prevents lymphatic cancer and swelling of lymph nodes after radiation.

SPHENE (Titanite):   Clearing

Calcium Titanium Silicate. Prismatic wedge-shaped or tabular crystals, also massive. Colorless, yellow, green, gray, brown, blue, rose red, black, the brown and black varieties having more iron. Transparent with adamantine to resinous luster, might have much fire. Pleochroic. Monoclinic system, hardness is 5 to 5.5.

Sphene draws imbalance and insecurity out of the body. It is particularly good at going into deeply crystallized areas of the aura and releasing the fear, shame, or anger that holds the energy immobile there. It works well with Danburite or Opal to recycle the stuck energy into your light flow. It also helps release the heat of fever or infection. It is not usually strong enough to produce strong clearing by itself, but it is often enhanced powerfully when combined with other crystals, particularly transparent, colorless ones such as Quartz. This combination is specific for clearing the etheric body in preparation for reprogramming. For instance, use Sphene inside a grid of Quartz to clear out negative, confused or unused energy at the beginning of a healing session or at critical points during one. It enhances the abilities of Quartz crystals far beyond what they can do alone. It blends very well with Phenacite to balance and enhance your spiritual connection, especially in channeling.

As an elixir, its combining and supportive qualities are enhanced, allowing almost all other elixirs to work more effectively. It supports all bodily functions and strengthens the immune system. The varieties with more iron aid red blood cell formation and function. The varieties with more Titanium (black ones) strengthen the nervous system and facilitate its communicative functions.

Other sources: The elixir aligns the emotional, mental, and spiritual bodies, stimulating the body's metabolism.

SPINEL: Heals the Heart

Magnesium Aluminum Oxide. Forms small, perfect octahedrons, or aggregates. Usually pink-red, also clear, light blue or black. Transparent to opaque with vitreous luster. Cubic system. Hardness is 8.

Sometimes called "the poor man's ruby," clear, red Spinel is a semiprecious gemstone. Like Ruby it is especially supportive of the heart and all its functions, physical and spiritual. It helps all four bodies use the support and strength of the heart. It helps you recognize your special abilities and connect them into the flow of your life. It gently leads you into the part of the Plan that was designed to help you develop your own creative potential. Its energy is softer than Ruby's, but more expansive, less intense and directed, using love in its many aspects.

Spinel helps you connect with others through heart-centered energy and aids healing of relationships with self and others. It helps you accept yourself as a loving being, allowing you to share love more easily with others. It also helps to connect with your lightbody through your use of your heart, creating more radiance at the physical level. Spinel is a sixth-dimensional energy that flows and blends well into the third, fourth, and fifth dimensions. It emphasizes the ideal, making your understanding of it flexible rather than absolute and therefore easier to connect with and use.

Spinel, as an elixir, strengthens all the endocrine glands but is particularly helpful for the pancreas. It also helps regenerate the thymus and the whole immune system when used with Shattuckite, Peridot, Kunzite or various types of Quartz, particularly Amethyst, and other healing crystal energies.

Traditional sources: Red Spinel releases anger and conflict. Blue calms sexual desire, raises thoughts, purifies imagination and attracts help from others. Taken internally, eliminates fears and brings happiness. Like other red stones, stops bleeding and inflammatory diseases.

The elixir aligns the emotional and etheric bodies. Calms and eases depression. A general cleanser that greatly assists detoxification and autolysis. Clear Spinel elixir helps clear the skin during and after detoxification.

SPODUMENE: Revealing

Lithium Aluminum Silicate. Prismatic crystals, sometimes huge with vertical striations, or rod-like masses. Transparent or translucent with vitreous luster. Trichroic (color or intensity changes when viewed at different angles), white, yellow, gray, pink (Kunzite), or emerald green (Hiddenite). Also opaque whitish gray, usually slightly green. Monoclinic, hardness is 6 to 7. See Kunzite, Hiddenite.

Spodumene, especially the clear, colorless variety, has the ability to key forgotten memory. It serves as a key to unlock, at appropriate times, secrets forgotten in the past but now needed. It has a specific link into the flow of knowledge that comes from the Galactic Center; the flow of knowledge that is activated there. They will not reveal anything before its time and they make available everything necessary at the moment at some level. This is not meant to limit humanity, but to emphasize what it needs at a particular point of evolution. They release their information, like a radio broadcast, into the mass concsiousness. If you use Spodumene with the desire to contribute to Earth's growth, you can tune in. You can also use it to translate knowledge and information that has already been made available for the present time but has not been discovered or activated.

Sometimes certain pieces of knowledge are not discovered when they are made available and they cycle back into "the unknown" until the time for their use is again right. This happened in Lemuria with the concept of a clear understanding of the use of creative power. Humanity did not feel it was ready. In Atlantis, emphasis on power for its own sake was substituted for it and it was not recognized. This was the knowledge of converting personal power into universal power and vice versa. Spodumene can teach you how to direct and magnify your own power through alignment with your full potential. This is best learned now by using a group to mirror your own universal potential. The popularity of Kunzite now, over the clear variety, is providing the foundation of universal love necessary to use power well, in alignment with the Divine Plan. When individuals are ready to contribute their own efforts to a group purpose without holding out anything for themselves, Earth will really begin to make the desired progress. So the use of Kunzite is excellent preparation for using clear Spodumene to make important knowledge available, particularly through group effort and awareness. The very large Spodumene crystals are helpful for groups that are striving to serve the evolution of the planet.

Clear Spodumene also has the ability to stimulate personal memories of past lives or other dimensions. In this sense, it is an interdimensional stone, but it works by opening your mind to wider possibilities, rather than dissolving or bridging the barriers themselves. It has the ability to help you remember and visualize the ideal, what the perfect body looks like, feels like, and acts like for you. In this way it is healing and balancing. If you can think the ideal, you can manifest it. But it is not just a stone for your mind. It can lead your emotional body into a new awareness of how it feels to be balanced and function-ing perfectly at all levels.

Spodumene makes the perfect elixir for understanding the ideal and learning to heal yourself. It will magnetize your aura so you will find whatever knowledge you need or are led to the right person to help you. If you have had healing knowledge in past lives, it will help you put that knowledge into a persepective that is useful now to yourself and others. The elixir aids the flow of the ideal through your whole energy field, bringing you deeper into yourself where knowledge of your real self is waiting to be revealed.

SULPHUR: Cleansing

Found as dipyramidal crystals or granular aggregates, lemon yellow to brown or black. Transparent to translucent with greasy luster. Orthorhombic system. Hardness is 1.5 to 2.5. A poor conductor of heat; just the heat of your hand might cause cracks in it. It can also be electrically charged by friction. The crystals have the distinctive odor you would expect from Sulphur.

Sulphur draws out negativity and clears the emotional body. The pure specimens, which are bright yellow, mirror the positive potentialities within your negative areas. They help you transform difficult feelings into positive ones. They can help you let go of self-destructive habits or attitudes. They mirror back the light that is hidden in every cell.

The darker colors contain impurities but are just as effective in cleansing. They help you release your negativity into Earth's transformational system of recycling light. They are better at drawing out physical pain and physical effects of emotional instability and negativity. If you keep Sulphur near you at night, it assists the angels in healing and cleansing your body.

Sulphur is difficult to use as an elixir, but it might be placed near your other elixirs as they are being prepared to add to their ability to draw out what is not aligned with the ideal.

Other sources: Activates willpower, strengthens the metabolism and softens hardening or crystallization in the body. Balances overuse of mental body and lack of exercise. Too much leads to physical vitality without consciousness. Balances astral and etheric bodies. Improves mental imbalance related to lungs. Use for colds, rheumatism, Hodgkin's disease, arthritis, hemorrhoids, skin and nail disorders, granular eyelids, aching joints, and general pain relief. Heals wounds. Normalizes intestinal flora. Eases heavy-metal poisoning. Acts as a laxative. Relaxes tight muscles. Eases burning sensations, stomach problems, and offensive body discharges. Restores function in immune system disorders and those involving collapse of endocrine or capillary systems.

The elixir brings spiritual illumination into intellect and personal philosophy. Aligns mental and emotional bodies. Balances yin and yang qualities. Eases depression. Strengthens nerves and brain. Stimulates heart and muscle tendons and ligaments. Cleanses pancreas and appendix. Use for sinus diseases, tuberculosis, and syphilis.

STAUROLITE: Grounds the Christ Light

Hydrous Iron Magnesium Aluminum Silicate. Prismatic crystals, often twinned at angles of ninety or sixty degrees. Usually opaque, reddish brown to black. Rarely transparent or translucent. Orthorhombic system, hardness is 7 to 7.5.

Staurolite crosses are traditionally a symbol of Christ. At the time when He was about to be born on Earth, their spirit (their angels) were so joyously ready to accept Him that the Heavenly Father, Sanat Kumara, placed in them a special energy that would help humanity accept Christ's message of love. They have embraced that gift as their own special purpose and are willing to share knowledge of what it means to love and be loved unconditionally. When you agree to share that gift with them, the love is magnified through your heart.

Staurolite can help you find ways to use love here on Earth. It shows you how to use love creatively to help Earth become clearer in its use of love. When you wear a Staurolite cross near your heart, it amplifies the flow through your heart and helps you to interact more lovingly with others. It also helps you accept your own soul, your special aspect of the Christ Light, into your consciousness and your life.

Staurolite makes an elixir that strengthens the heart, blood, and immune system. It strengthens the spine and can help keep it in alignment. It helps release despair and hopelessness from the lungs, thus strengthening and clearing them. The elixir is excellent for grounding and helping you feel able to cope with and transcend problems.

Staurolite brings in the joyous trust and acceptance of the Creator's love which is always available to everyone, whether they feel they deserve it or not. It is healing and balancing at all levels, but never overwhelming or difficult to use. Its energy is very familiar with and acceptable to the physical body. It calms and lifts the emotions gently, bringing them to a useful focus in practical reality.

SUGILITE, LUVULITE, ROYAL LAZEL: Transforming, Cleansing

Various shades of purple, violet, red-violet, perhaps with black. Opaque, dull luster. Hardness 6 to 6.5.

Sugilite is a true New Age stone; it has not been used on Earth before. It was brought into the light when Earth had moved to the present vibrational level. It is connected very strongly to the level of the Plan that Earth is integrating now and has no karmic connections to its old levels. So it helps you see that you no longer need to use those old patterns and misperceptions that might be holding you back now and are not part of the new energies. It is a powerful activator of the transformational process. It can seem very energizing if you are having difficulty using the new energies or releasing the old patterns. It will demand that you open to new ideas. If you can allow that, it will show you how to work with them and make them part of your creative structure.

While Sugilite is of a high vibrational level, it is still grounding, anchoring the next level of awareness into the physical part of your life. That is its purpose; to aid in transforming physical matter so that you can use the higher energies at the physical level. It is very clear in showing your subconscious how to use the new energies in practical, physical ways. If you have worked with crystals in past lives, it might seem difficult to work it into your patterns of crystal energy, but it will patiently hold this new focus until you understand it and can integrate it. The more you wear it and use it the more you will become familiar with the new energies and be able to flow with them as light at the physical level.

Some other crystals can help you use Sugilite more effectively. Aquamarine, for instance, helps integrate the energies that Sugilite brings into your own light flow by expanding and raising the level of your use of your heart to include its higher vibrations. Lapis, because of its familiarity with humanity's way of using energy, expands Sugilite's availability to the physical level in a multidimensional way. With these stones as your partners, you can expand your perspective of physical existence much more than you could alone. Gold enhances Sugilite powerfully, making its energy more available at an emotional level and more useful for clearing outmoded subconscious patterns of thought and behavior at the physical level. Peridot makes it easier for your cells to accept the transformational effects of Sugilite. Diamond will bring out the most of Sugilite's potential while its own "hardness" is softened and made easier to assimilate. This combination is an exceptionally good crystal tool for transformation, especially if you find Diamond difficult to use.

Other sources: Associated with Master St. Germaine and the seventh ray. Brings awareness of your divine essence, aids sharing of light and love. Opens connection between mind and body. Opens third eye, crown, and eighth chakras. Assists channeling. Relieves mental fatigue and balances mind. Helps develop all psychic abilities. Allows transmutation of situations. Helps sensitive, spiritual people deal with the often overwhelming negative energies on Earth. Increases understanding. Brings conscious control of mental faculties and related bodily states. Gives peace and understanding which allows mind and body the strength to heal all diseases. Relieves stress and alleviates cancer. Accelerates body's natural healing processes.

The elixir opens the crown chakra, especially when used in the bath. Increases altruism, visions, and understanding. Balances pineal and pituitary glands and left and right brains. Aids autism, dyslexia, epilepsy, physical coordination problems, visual problems, and faulty motor nerve response. Activates pineal gland and neurons of brain. Aids all karmic disease patterns.

TALC (Soapstone):   Absorbs Stress and Confusion

Hydrous Magnesium Silicate. Forms scaly or felted aggregates, white, greenish-white, gray or brownish. Translucent with pearly or greasy luster. Monoclinic system. Hardness is 1, but impurities might make it harder.

Talc makes everything feel smoother. Holding it will help you release stress and fatigue. It can be a relaxing aid to sleep. Talc wants to take all disharmony into itself and resolve it. It is not a powerful energy and will not extend its influence into wide areas, but it forms a protective area of ease around you. Using it as an elixir does not usually enhance its properties.

Other sources: The elixir aligns astral, emotional, and etheric bodies. Assists hypnotic processes, spiritual practice, past-life therapy and dealing with problems from past-life experiences. Releases past-life talents, making their understanding and integration available. Strengthens the heart and the thymus. Stimulates the thymus and the whole endocrine system.

TANZANITE: Transformational

Blue Zoisite, see Zoisite. Poorly defined, prismatic crystals blue violet to lavender with moderate luster. Pleochromatic, changes from blue-violet to lavender, grayish or greenish. Orthorhombic system, hardness is 6.5.

Tanzanite moves your awareness from the mundane level to the sublime. It will move your thinking process out of the habitual looping that keeps you focused on personal, practical matters and into new patterns of thought that allow more freedom for your interdimensional qualities to express themselves. It helps you accept the reality of other realities, so to speak. It accepts imagination as real. It does this without disconnecting you from your practical Earth focus, but by expanding your point of view. It allows you to accept the seeming unreality of intuition or revelation as real for you now. It can be very helpful as you allow yourself to expand your perspective to include more of the fourth dimension as part of what is the familiar third. Your reality, everything you see and feel, is created by your mind. If you can change your thinking, you can change your reality. Tanzanite will help you create a reality that includes more of your divine potential.

It is useful on all chakras to help you expand your use of them into wider dimensions and greater integration with the whole structure of light that makes up your energy field. You will probably feel the greatest effect on the three highest chakras, but though the effect on the others might be subtle, it can still be profound. It is especially useful on the solar plexus during clearing to help it accept its connection with the higher chakras and the help available from soul level. Part of the ascension process involves integrating the heart and solar plexus into one chakra which will ultimately become your base chakra or Earth connection once you are a transformed being of light. Tanzanite helps the solar plexus release connections to the lower emotions and accept the possibility that it can use unconditional love and trust instead, allowing this transformation to occur.

For those who are working to clear a lot of unworthiness, anger, grief, shame, and loss, it is best to use some of the gentler crystal energies with Tanzanite, such as Smoky Quartz, Rose Quartz, even Fuchsite. The less rarefied energies of green or pink Zoisite might also be helpful to make Tanzanite's energy seem more workable at the physical level, although they can also be intense for some who have deep fears about allowing soul's energy to come into the body.

Tanzanite represents the ideal of clear use of the Christ Light at the physical level, and for those who have experienced the shame of not living up to their "Christian ideals" in past lives, it can be overwhelming if deep feelings are touched. Whatever your feelings now about Christianity, you have very likely had lifetimes where you were deeply devoted to "the Church" and its ideals. These ideals did not always teach that mistakes are necessary in the learning process. The absolute perfection you strive for need not be attained in any specific time frame for your effort to be worthy. You have as long as you need to learn to be perfect. When you learn this, you are closer to perfection. This is part of self-acceptance. The Christ Light you seek is perfectly accepting of all your efforts and Tanzanite will help you see this.

Water makes Tanzanite's energy more useful at the physical level, so the use of an elixir is more healing than the use of the stone itself. It can help heal the emotional shattering that occurs when one is subjected to violence and abuse, physical or emotional. It can also heal the grief of betrayal or failure of a love relationship to fulfill your expectations. It works to heal etheric breaks in the energy flow of the hippocampal and limbic portions of the brain which have to do with emotions and emotional responses. When these areas are whole and functioning in the ideal way, your response to anything will be unconditional love. See also Zoisite.

TEKTITES: **Transformational**

Principal ingredient is glass (Silica Dioxide). Colors are black (from many locations), green (Moldavite), or greenish yellow (Libyan Glass). No crystal structure, hardness is 5.5.

Tektites are the result of meteorites that hit Earth. They contain energies that are extraterrestrial as well as terrestrial. When they hit, the new energy and varying bits of Earth material and energy are all incorporated into the new substance. It has not always been understood that a new material has been created, rather than there being a direct transmission of something foreign from outer space.

Each meteorite fall has its own characteristics. Earth receives, in this way, whatever is needed at that moment from the appropriate place in the universe. Moldavite is the best known and is discussed under its own listing. Libyan Glass contains more altered Quartz in its physical makeup, with energy from Orion and Sirius in its metaphysical makeup. Its effect is subtle, but brings higher levels of the plan into physical existence, some of which are not yet ready to manifest. It brings light into the aura. Billitonite fell in Indonesia and brings in a higher connection to love as actual electrical flow. It energizes the heart and nervous system. Darwin Glass, from Australia brings energy from Arcturas and is similar to Libyan glass in being more a combination of Earth and Extraterrestrial energies. Its appearance signified a conscious acceptance by the Earth of help from an outside source. It will help open up communication with other worlds. Bediasites, found in Texas, come from within the Solar system, and confer a sense of responsibility in using higher powers of mind and emotion. There are very interesting ones from China, lei-gong-mo, which carry direct memory of extraterrestrial interaction with Earth.

All Tektites will help you open all aspects of self to new dimensions and possiblities within self. You have all experienced lives on other worlds and in other dimensions. Some of these were very evolved, and the talents you perfected there are needed to achieve your purpose here.

Their use cannot be transferred directly, but, like the Tektites themselves, can by shaped by Earth and integrated into something useful for this experience. This is, perhaps, their greatest gift, understanding that Earth is a unique experience and capable of conferring great wisdom and power if you are willing to shape yourself into something new, transformed by your Earth experience.

Tektites in general make valuable elixirs which help your body accept transformation. They assist with the integration of new energies and help you see what might be released and what is appropriate to use in transformation. They can help build new etheric levels and higher energy pathways within the expanding mind that allows you to use the new energies at the physical level.

Other sources: Stimulate communication especially with UFOs and other planets. Thought amplifier. Stimulates memories of extraterrestrial lives and the resulting genetic advancements in your DNA.

The elixir enhances consciousness and cosmic awareness. Aligns four bodies. Helps you understand extraterrestrial influences and your alignment with them. Stimulates the brow and throat chakra. Promotes physical body evolution.

TIGER-EYE, HAWK'S-EYE, CAT'S-EYE, BULL'S-EYE QUARTZ:
Grounding, Opens the Physical to Light

Fibrous inclusions in quartz produce a reflection similar to that in the eye of a cat, called chatoyancy. The colors each have a special name: green or greenish-gray is Cat's-Eye, blue is Hawk's-Eye, brown is Tiger-Eye, and mahagony is Bull's-Eye. In nature, green or blue fibers of Crocidolite (Asbestos) are changed to Quartz or to Iron Oxides and then to Quartz. Tiger-Eye, then, is the blue Hawk's-Eye which has been tinted by iron oxides naturally. When the brown Tiger-Eye is heated it turns red and is quite beautiful but not natural. When it occurs in disoriented masses it is called Riebeckite (see Pietersite).

Tiger-Eye helps the physical structure stabilize in its use of the new, higher energies. It can help you accept them and it makes your body feel more comfortable with them and more confident in using them. It helps strengthen your light structure and connect it into the physical level so light can be utilized more completely at the cellular level. It also helps the physical body communicate more clearly with the emotional, mental, and spiritual bodies.

The lines in Tiger-Eye are symbolic of its ability to help you integrate many levels of being and understanding into your conscious use of light.

It expands your understanding of your divine purpose by helping you integrate its many facets into the physical perspective. Working with several stones at once will allow you to make new connections with that purpose, as each stone can represent one portion of that purpose which is part of the whole. All the colors of chatoyant Quartz are very useful for helping you learn to work in partnership, in CoCreatorship, with Earth or within your special group. It helps you understand the purpose of your Earth connection and the nature of your specific light connection with it. The brown Tiger-Eye is the most grounding. It also can help dissolve hardened areas in the physical body.

The blue Hawk's-Eye is especially helpful now in expanding your mind to direct the new energies with more understanding into all levels of your being. It helps you understand yourself better as a divine being with great potential spiritual power that can be integrated into your knowledge of physicality. It can help you develop your superhuman abilities at the physical level. It literally shows your subconscious how to integrate your innate knowledge of your divine power into conscious use of it for the advancement and evolution of human potential. It helps dissolve mental crystallization and rigidity.

The heating process that makes red Tiger-Eye releases some of the dynamic energy of the crystal, making the physical connection to Earth's love more available to you. It can help you realize the nurturing support Earth offers to all those who accept her and are willing to work with her as CoCreators with her of the Divine Plan.

Bull's-Eye Quartz is a source of dynamic healing energy for the physical body. It is not specific, except for the blood, but supports almost all other healing work with crystals by providing a physical anchor for the Divine Blueprint. Other stones and crystals can then define and specify a more precise direction of the energy for specific purposes. It is a powerful stimulus of your own abilities for self-healing.

All colors of chatoyant Quartz are useful for drawing negativity out of your body. Cat's-Eye is especially helpful in emotional clearing, providing a light anchor that makes it easier to look at difficulties within yourself and consciously work with them. It helps you see the positive potential in what you consider your dark side and helps you see how to transform negativity into light. It is strengthening to the lungs and enhances your will to live and continue the rebuilding of your self into perfection. It helps dissolve crystallized areas in the energy flow at the etheric and emotional levels.

The elixirs all direct healing into specific areas of your energy field. They are very helpful in translating and directing the energy of your desire to heal or be healed. If your analysis of the problem is incomplete or erroneous, they will align with your basic desire or purpose and direct your energy appropriately. If you are alert and responsive to the crystals, you will become aware of this and understand the problem more clearly.

Other sources: Gives strength and unity, protection and good luck. Focuses power of mind. Helps one attain dreams. Can increase psychic ability and power. Brings contentment with material things. Clears perceptions, brings good judgment.   Brings openness to and understanding of different perspectives. Stabilizing. Aids awareness of Earth connection. Wear Tiger-Eye in rings to assist making decisions and to stimulate creativity. Hawk's-Eye increases understanding of self and control of life. Cat's-Eye focuses intentions.

TITANITE
See Sphene.

TITANIUM: Stabilizes Transformation
Doesn't occur as an isolated mineral substance but is found combined with practically all rocks and soils. Its principle source is from Ilmenite and Rutile. Crystallizes in the hexagonal system.

Titanium is an important addition to your collection of transformational minerals. It is the ninth most common element on Earth. It alloys easily with other metals, yet in its pure form is extremely nonreactive. It is present in Quartz as Rutile and gives Rutilated Quartz its enhanced ability to serve as a connector into the energies of the galactic level.   By itself, Titanium adds a quality of flexibility and openness to your energy field that can help you adapt to and use the new energies now available.

It can help you adapt the new fourth-dimensional perspective into the third. It helps your emotional body integrate with your other bodies. Just as Titanium is used in satellites for its lightness, it can mirror to your subconscious a way of using light that does not need anything heavy (like old patterns) to be comfortable at the physical level. At the same time it mirrors a strength from your divine connection that is all-supportive. Its energies are quite easy to assimilate and add light from the higher rays to your aura.

Titanium is used in other dimensions for the construction of interdimensional spacecraft because of its ability to withstand rapid dimensional changes in its structure. It adapts quite accurately to the ideal pattern of flow in each dimension. It is also an accurate receiver and transmitter of the light message that is being sent to Earth from the Galactic Center.

As an elixir, it stabilizes all changes, especially transformational ones. It expands the vibrational spectrum of your energy field. It also enhances the flow of energy through your channel and makes it easier to translate the light message that comes to you through it.

TOPAZ: Physical Transformation

Aluminum Silicate with Fluorine. Prismatic crystals often with vertical striations, white or yellowish, semiopaque or transparent, colorless, honey-colored, brown, blue, violet, rarely pink or reddish. Orthorhombic system, hardness is 8. Might resemble Citrine when faceted.

Topaz has its own niche in the transformational spectrum of the Crystal Kingdom. No other can replace it for bringing the light of the ideal into the physical cells in a way that rejuvenates and strengthens the restructured DNA, locking in the new pattern. It bypasses and helps release the emotional patterns that cause you to lose the connection to the ideal when you let go of the conscious focus. For this reason, Topaz might be hard to use for long periods if you have patterns that are difficult to release. It won't let you dabble in them and then push them back under the rug if you get tired of struggling with them.

Topaz works very well with many other crystal energies, especially Quartz. Quartz, as the primary carrier of the ideal, cooperates with Topaz's ability to lock the gifts of its flow into the cellular DNA and RNA. If you are consciously willing to bring more light into the body, your alignment with the universal evolutionary flow supports the newly rejuvenated cells and it become more influential than the flow pattern carrying the old blueprint. Eventually, there will be a critical point at which there will be enough cells aligned with the new pattern to trigger a movement into alignment by the whole system. Thus, step by step, complete healing and rejuvenation will be accomplished.

As an elixir, Topaz heals any cellular or DNA structure that has been altered by radiation or aging. It is helpful to use both the crystal itself and the elixir. The crystal serves as a sort of overseer that guides the energy of both to the appropriate locations for healing. You might want to use it with another crystal that is more specific for the organ or area that needs to be healed or rejuvenated.

You can also use Topaz while you meditate, as a visual focus or to hold. Any healing visualizations you do in a meditative (altered) state will be strengthened and transferred more securely into the physical, cellular level. While Topaz works so well at the physical level, it can still lift your mind to transcendent levels if you are willing to allow your physical body to be part of that. In this way, it will help you see your physical body as a real and acceptable part of your spiritual self and will heal some of the separation from the Creator most of you feel as physical beings.

The very large Topaz specimens are bringing to Earth transformational energies that are raising the physical vibrational levels of the planet as they interact with humanity. When people admire them and enjoy their energies, their potential for stimulating transformation is released and all those involved in the process move closer to alignment with the ideal for physical existence.

Traditional and other sources: Symbol of the Sun and its power. Its inner radiance dispels darkness. Contains spiritual potential and wisdom of all humankind. Enhances understanding and acceptance of universal Christ Consciousness. Gives wearer long life, beauty, and intelligence. Expands and strengthens mind, improves intelligence, and prevents mental problems. Increases wisdom and sensibility. Source of strength for dealing with life's problems.

Relaxes and comforts. Balances emotions and diseases resulting from them. Strengthens ablilty to deal with life's problems. Dispels nightmares and fright, depression, jealousy, and worry. Brings courage, calms anger, insanity, passion, and stress. Its possession protects one against thunder, possessiveness, poison, disease, drunkenness, and skin rashes. Protects from accidental death. Loses its color in presence of danger or poison. Set in gold and worn at neck, protects one from sorcery.

Revitalizing. Used with meditation, reverses aging process. Strengthens vision. (Place stone in wine for three days and apply to eyes.) Cures flatulence and enhances appetite and sense of taste. Some will remove thirst. Stops bleeding. Supports and strengthens respiration, prevents colds and tuberculosis. Eases gout and blood disorders. Powdered and taken in wine, cures asthma, insomnia, and other ills.

The elixir creates spiritual rejuvenation or rebirth of self. Aids integration of newly stabilized emotions. Rejuvenates etheric body and aligns it with the physical. Stimulates tissue regeneration. Use for diseases associated with aging. Relaxes tension in body. Stimulates the sympathetic nervous system. Enhances stomach and pituitary function. Opens brow chakra somewhat and stimulates throat chakra. Eases karmic disease patterns in cells.

TOURMALINE (Elbaite):   Balancing

A complex Borosilicate with varying amounts of Aluminum, Iron, Sodium,
Calcium, Lithium, Magnesium, Manganese or Fluorine. Occurs as long,
striated, three-sided prisms of many colors: black (Schorl), pink (Rubellite),
violet-red (Siberite), brownish yellow or brown (Dravite), light or dark blue
(Indicolite), green, blue-green and colorless (Achroite). There is also a
chatoyant, Cat's-Eye variety. Watermelon Tourmaline is pink or red in the
center with green around the outside. Some crystals change color from one
end to the other. Trigonal system, hardness is 7. Strongly birefringent (splits
light into two rays) and pleochroic (colors change when viewed across
different axes of the crystal).

Tourmaline can balance polarities. It sees two points of view and
finds the balancing point between them. It works by comparing
everything with the ideal and finding the means to create alignment
with it. Green Tourmaline will help strengthen the dynamic male or
yang energy while it channels it into appropriate ways of action or
feeling. In this way it relieves feelings of excess dynamic energy by
helping you use it in a balanced way. Pink tourmaline is especially
helpful for challenging the receptive female energy to act with courage
and confidence. It shows the yin energy that it can work with the yang
energy as an equal partner.

Since the cosmic principles of yin and yang are reflected into your
body in so many ways, Tourmaline can bring balance into many of its
aspects. Green Tourmaline will strengthen the male organs, but it
serves the female organs as a basic support from which to function. It
shows the connection into the ideal which is the base line from which
yin builds and elaborates the female mode of creativity. It shows the
female energy that the male energy is there to support it always and that
it does not need to compete with or for it.

Rubellite strengthens the female organs and facilitates the female
hormones, as Green Tourmaline directs the appropriate connection into
the creative flow of universal energy.

Rubellite serves as the base line within the cosmic ideal which shows
yang that it is supported and nurtured at all times by the universal
creative flow. As green Tourmaline facilitates and strengthens the male
energies and hormones, Rubellite provides a reference point within the
ideal that allows them to remain at the appropriate level for working most
efficiently. Rubellite can channel excess yang energy into the support that
yin needs to be balanced and nurtured, just as Green Tourmaline
channels excess yin into support for the yang needed to direct and
energize it. Each one creates a sort of nurturing space for its opposite

which eventually allows each to support the perfect balance. Watermelon Tourmaline, of course, expresses this perfect relationship.

Watermelon Tourmaline or Pink and Green Tourmaline used together are very balancing for emotions as well as for the physical body.   They bring the cooperative energies of love into difficult emotional situations or problems and allow you to use the flow of the cosmic ideal encoded into light as a reference point for resolving them. But each one alone can also be very effective.   The pink provides the connection into the nurturing love of spirit.   The green provides the dynamic reference through which spirit says, "I am here to help with the proper solution."

Indicolite provides a connection and reference into the creative flow as an ideal.   It helps you draw the concept and understanding of the cosmic ideal into yourself as a plan and structure for your own creativity.   It helps the mind resolve differences between the ideal and the way your subconscious is presently using light to create your life and your reality.   It helps you see how to transform your whole creative flow into one that uses more of your spiritual potential, for that is the purpose of the ideal.

Indicolite has, probably, the most elevating energy, because of its clear connection into a balanced perspective within the mind of spirit itself.   It will help you maintain a spiritual perspective and release the "chatter" of the small, ego-based mind.   It is good to use it with Black Tourmaline to keep you grounded in the realities of physical existence which you are on Earth to work with.   At the same time, Indicolite will help you bring a spiritual perspective into solving problems at the physical level, if you are properly grounded.

Yellow Tourmaline supports the life force and the breath.   It is grounded energy in that it helps you utilize the life force from every level, physical and etheric as well as spiritual.   It serves as protection from bothersome astral energies that are not in harmony with balance and the ideal.

Black Tourmaline is an excellent absorber of negativity.   It does not hold onto it like black Obsidian, for instance, but continuously transforms negativity into positive flow.   It emits calm, protection, balance, and a good connection into physical existence. It supports and heals the base chakra, providing it an appropriate reference point within the ideal which allows it to do its work of keeping you connected with the life-supporting flow of Earth's energy.   The other colors of Tourmaline will support it also, but the black, which is not really black but an intense concentration of the other colors, is exceptionally good.   It shows the subconscious how to release negativity and old connections while remaining within the supportive flow of the ideal and moving to the next level. Your physical cells are having a bit of trouble doing this, so black Tourmaline supports the transformation process in this way. In large clusters, it serves as a purifier of the atmosphere, removing the negativity of harmful radiations or substances.

Clear Tourmaline has a somewhat lower electrical energy than the colored forms but serves to integrate balance into all levels of self. It is particularly useful for the crown chakra when you are trying to open your channel and your spiritual awareness. It provides a balancing point between the physical and spiritual which is practical and appropriate for physical expression.

Brown Tourmaline is similar to black in its applications. It is protective if you are working with Earth elementals, giving you a reference within the ideal which helps you channel their energies into the flow of the ideal, the Divine Plan. It protects you from negative effects of bad karma, helping you to restructure into the ideal your ways of working with Earth energies. It is also the most grounding of the Tourmalines and balances all chakras, even the eighth and higher, into a more workable energy flow at the physical level.

All Tourmaline makes excellent elixirs and is often most effective when used this way. Water emphasizes its healing qualities and makes it more effective. Black Tourmaline elixir sprayed into a room lifts spirits and dissolves negativity. A few drops of green Tourmaline elixir can be energizing and life-restoring. Rubellite elixir (a good way to use it is in the bath) can relieve symptoms of menopause and also promote feelings of love. Spraying Indicolite elixir into a room would be a good preparation for meditation. Taken in water it can provide mental stability and clarity by balancing and channeling the dynamic flow of energy in the brain into spiritual awareness.

The new electrical energies of light coming to Earth now are raising the dynamic energies within each of you if you are doing anything at all to attract and use them. Tourmaline is one of the best tools you have for remaining balanced within the process of integrating and learning to create with these new energies. It helps you channel the growing creative power being generated in your lower chakras into your spiritual purpose.

Other sources: Amplifies psychic energies. Neutralizes negative energies. Opens up communications. Dispels fear and grief. Relaxes body and mind. Alleviates sensuality. Brings peaceful sleep. Calms nerves. Brings inspiration and eloquence, aids concentration. Brings balance into relationships. Powerful healer and balancer. Will assist sending and receiving thoughts and energy. Eases tuberculosis, anemia, lymphatic diseases, blood poisoning, and infectious diseases.

Black Tourmaline protects user from negativity and grounds negative and spiritual energies. Green Tourmaline is nurturing, quiets the mind, aids will and wisdom. It brings universal awareness and greater awareness of all vibrations. Aids sleep. Pink Tourmaline strengthens heart, wisdom and will power, enhances creativity, balances heart chakra, and increases desire to love and sacrifice for humanity. Supports exchange of the energy flow of love. Brings happiness.

Watermelon Tourmaline supports endocrine glands and metabolism, regulates hormones, balances cellular energies, heals heart chakra, helps one release old emotional pains and replace them with love. Use for preventing and treating cancer. Alleviates genetic disorders. Aids transfer of energy in meaningful relationships. Very electrical and magnetic, more so than the other colors of Tourmaline.

The elixirs stimulate the biomagnetic, electrical, and crystalline properties of the body.

Strengthens the etheric structure and physical body when placed on the corresponding part of the spine. Improves communication among the four bodies. Each color activates the psychospiritual qualities of the corresponding chakra and eases associated diseases. Black for base chakra, red for sex chakra, white for solar plexus, green for heart, blue for throat, Cat's-Eye for brow and Tourmalinated Quartz for crown. Gurudas also states that Tourmaline elixirs should always be taken with Watermelon Tourmaline elixir to activate their crystal structure and piezoelectric qualities.

TUNGSTEN: Enhances the Dynamic Flow

Doesn't occur in pure state naturally.

Tungsten emphasizes the dynamic flow. It takes light deep into the cells as you begin to connect with the creative power of physical existence. It literally lights up the creative potential of the cellular level and makes it available to the whole system. It helps crystals connect their creative power into your energy structure at the cellular level. It helps you respect the needs and potential of the physical level while moving you beyond it. Hematite or Jasper would be helpful in balancing and grounding your energy when using Tungsten.

TURQUOISE: Calming, Protective

Hydrated Copper Aluminum Phosphate. Usually found as microcrystalline masses or nodules, light blue to sky blue or green. Opaque with waxy luster. Prismatic crystals very rare. Triclinic system, hardness is 5 to 6.

Turquoise could be considered an old energy because it does not vibrate to the new, higher energies. In Atlantis it did, and was a transformational stone. Sometime in the future its energy will once again coincide with the higher levels of the evolving ideal. In the meantime, it is an old favorite with many, and there is much that it can do. It can bring back deep knowledge and memories of powers used. It might trigger, for some, forgotten abilities that can be relearned and used again at new levels. It stabilizes and calms the emotions and helps the mind to organize present knowledge while it opens to new ideas. It can help resolve old karma having to do with misuse of knowledge because it once symbolized knowledge.

Turquoise is still the powerful protection against negative vibrations or influences that it has always been. It helps you use all your knowledge and inner resources to understand and, if necessary, work with what is not understood. It helps allay fears about being attacked by what is dark and of being cut off from the light. It replaces fear with peace.

Turquoise helps release the toxic accumulation of heavy metals. It also helps draw out radioactivity from the body. It helps protect the eyes from the effects of ultraviolet radiation. It can help release tension in the throat chakra caused by fear of exerting you own will or of using your creativity. It can help balance any chakra that has been damaged by misuse of power.

As an elixir, Turquoise is best used with other stones. It will enhance their effects if they are similar to Turquoise in their actions. It especially supports other blue stones and makes the intense energies of some red ones, particularly Ruby, easier to assimilate.

Traditional and other sources: Gives alignment with universe. Gives spiritual understanding and wisdom and peace of mind. In dreams, symbolizes connection to power and memories of Lemuria and Atlantis. Aids channeling, meditation, understanding of universal concepts. Calms emotions. Clears mind, dispels confusion. Enhances receptivity.

Generally, a good-luck stone. If you see the reflection of the new Moon on a Turquoise, you will have good luck and be protected from evil. Pray and throw a Turquoise stone into a river for rain. Strengthens work animals. Protects against all evil if given in love. Counteracts spells. Protects from falling, especially from horses. Changes color or fades to reveal stress, danger, infidelity of a wife, or state of health of wearer. Its beauty is restored when worn by a healthy person.

Master healer, aids all diseases. Strengthens whole body, especially respiration. Neutralizes and balances. Relieves depression, cures malaria and heart problems. Strengthens the eyes and eases eye conditions such as cataracts. If it turns green with wearing, it is a negative stone and should not be worn. Protects against environmental pollutants and cosmic radiation.

The elixir increases communication skills. Increases connection with physical body in healing. A master healer, strengthens whole body, physical and etheric, and aids all diseases, including karmic ones. Stimulates regeneration. Increases absorption of nutrients and blood supply to muscles.

ULEXITE (TV Rock):   Self-Knowledge

Hydrated Sodium Calcium Borate. Transparent masses of white hair-like fibers. Crystals are rare. Triclinic system, hardness is 1.

Ulexite has fiber-optic properties, transferring an image it is placed on to the opposite side. In the same way, it can bring up hidden patterns so that you can see them more clearly. It is best as a link between the mind and emotions that helps you understand the cause of emotional patterns and how to deal with them, if necessary. Other, more energetic crystal energies must then be used to take care of the processing and releasing. Ulexite's energy is not especially powerful or widely useful, but it is an interesting stone and might be helpful some time when you can't quite focus your problem. Don't try to make an elixir; it will dissolve.

UNAKITE: Revealing

A form of Granite (intrusive, igneous rock) containing Quartz, pink Feldspar and green Epidote.

Unakite is not a gemstone or a crystal, but is included here because it is often used in jewelry and is readily available in usable form. It can help reveal hidden or forgotten powers within self. It draws out their energy so you can see them and rework them. These are usually memories of powers that were not completely understood or integrated. Unakite can help integrate and open communication between the male and female polarities of self. It can help you align with the aspect of the ideal that deals with evolving your use of polarity. It is somewhat stimulating, bringing up difficult issues which other crystal energies will be more helpful in resolving.

VANADINITE: Grounding

Lead Vanadate Chloride. Found as small hexagonal prisms, crusts, or fibrous or radiant masses. Bright red-orange to yellow or brown, transparent to translucent with resinous luster. Hexagonal system. Hardness is 2.75 to 3.

Vanadinite grounds you to Earth through the love and perspective of Sanat Kumara, the Planetary Logos. It helps you accept being physical. It helps build a foundation for expanding your full creative potential from this physical Earth level. It opens mind, emotions, and body to all positive support from Earth. It helps you use Earth's power for your own purpose.

VARISCITE: Balancing

Hydrated Aluminum Phosphate. Usually found as pale green nodules or microcrystalline masses, veined or speckled with gray and white from other materials. Translucent, with vitreous or waxy luster. Orthorhombic system. Hardness is 4. Often mistaken for Turquoise.

Variscite balances the mineral composition in body fluids. It helps release the emotional patterns that cause diabetes mellitis or chronic edema. It can also be helpful in stabilizing the emotional body during physical stress. When used on wrists or ankles, it helps draw negative patterns out of the body.

Other sources: Stimulates DNA activity. The elixir unites the astral and etheric bodies and activates past-life memories relevant to present growth. The resolution can then occur at the cellular level. Also balances the nervous system. Releases tendencies toward gonorrhea and syphilis and eases effects of radiation.

WATER: Clearing, Connecting

Water's crystalline properties are obvious when it is frozen, but it also has crystalline properties when not frozen. It has the marvelous quality of holding even the highest levels of vibration and making them universally available. It contains all potential for form and life within itself. It is the soft, caring love of the Creator bringing life to Earth.

Earth has more water that almost any other planet in the universe, showing the great potential for life with which the Creator has endowed it. It is water that has made it possible for you to develop physical bodies which can demonstrate so many ways of using love at the physical, emotional, and mental levels. Water is the ultimate healer. You unlock its healing potential by learning how to use it for integrating all useful substances on Earth into your bodies. Crystal elixirs help with this by bringing out specific potentials within your infinite powers and showing you how to integrate them into your life flow. As you work with crystals and their elixirs, you learn more about yourself and your interaction with Earth.

Water is the ultimate clearing agent at the physical level. It is light transformed into a flow that is most useful at the physical level. It dissolves impurities and carries nutrients. It builds forms and tears them down. It can reshape your body just as it constantly reshapes the face of Earth. It is the supreme link between your body and the Crystal Kingdom.

WAVELLITE: Healing

Hydrated Aluminum Phosphate. Forms radiating aggregates of small, fibrous, white, pale yellow or green crystals. Translucent with vitreous or silky luster. Orthorhombic system, hardness is 3.5 to 4.

Wavellite removes disharmony from the physical body and makes you feel more comfortable with it. It is helpful for those who are new to physical existence, especially babies. It also helps you adapt new aspects of self that come from the cosmic level into your physical perspective. Wavellite helps you adapt all spiritual energies into practical concerns.

As an elixir, Wavellite helps remove impurities from the blood. It also helps release any old patterns which block acceptance of the new ideal. On the skin it is healing and rejuvenating.

WHEWELLITE: Cleansing

Calcium Oxalate. White or colorless crystals, transparent with pearly luster. Monoclinic system, hardness is 2.5. One of the main crystalline components of kidney stones and urinary precipitates.

Whewellite is a powerful cleanser of impurities from the body. It takes away old, negative, confused energies and helps release blocked and crystallized areas. It is most effective if two pieces of it are used, one on each side of the body. This allows the dynamic and receptive parts of self to independently release their own misperceptions while working together to clear the body of them.

WULFENITE: Empowering

Lead Molybdate. Occurs as short prismatic crystals, often tabular or square, or as massive or earthy aggregates. Yellow-brown or red-orange, transparent or translucent crystals with resinous luster. Tetragonal system. Hardness is 2.75 to 3.

Wulfenite is quite popular with collectors, primarily men. They don't often realize that they desire it for the validation it gives them of their dynamic creativity. Wulfenite can do much to help you accept the reality of your creative power and direct it into your purposes. This can be construed as magic, but all creativity is magic. You can create anything you can imagine and desire. You have only to free all aspects of self to allow that. That is the problem. Buried in your subconscious are all kinds of beliefs that say you don't deserve, don't need, can't use properly, or aren't ready for what you want. This mineral helps you transcend all that by showing you what you can really do with physicality if you are open to all creative possibilities. It gives women the ability to allow their dynamic, male energy to be part of their creative expression and helps men to use theirs well.

Wulfenite grounds your energy by connecting your flow with all that is available in physical existence. It makes you feel more comfortable with your body and helps you release crystallization within it by anchoring the ideal in a balanced way throughout it.

ZIRCON: Stimulating

Zirconium Silicate contains Thorium and Uranium, but the radioactive substances are absent in the gem-quality stones as they destroy the crystalline structure. Short prisms, opaque to transparent, lustrous, brown, yellow, reddish, green, blue, green-blue, or colorless. Tetragonal system, hardness is 7.5. Not to be confused with the artificially produced Cubic Zirconium.

Zircon moves energy in the direction it wants to go, around or through blocks, so it is helpful in opening up new areas of self for study or reorganization. As you transform yourself into a new vehicle for light, you must do a great deal of this self-searching and discovery. Those parts of self that have been used to express anger, fear or grief, for instance, or to hide shame, must be redirected into more positive use of your energy. Zircon will help show you what you need to release and what needs to be integrated. Not everything you are hiding in yourself is negative. Some of it is just more than you want to look at all at once. The good news is that you don't have to do it all at once. Zircon will help you balance everything that comes up as you integrate it into your new level of awareness.

This crystal has direct connections with the Space Command, those spiritual beings from many dimensions of creation who are here to help Earth and humanity move to the new level of light vibrations. They can work through Zircon, in conjunction with other crystal energies, to help you transform your physical body so it can use the incoming new vibrational levels. They can also help you move stuck areas in your energy field, releasing the energy held there for growth and expansion. For some of you, growth felt at the subconscious level implies a necessity to expand your physical body. Zircon will help you cut away such misperceptions so that your light expansion includes only what you need to express the ideal.

As an elixir, Zircon's energy is softened and gentler. It aids the healing process in general by balancing the energy flow throughout the whole body. When energy stops moving, the result is negativity, pain, loss of life force. As Zircon gently stimulates the whole body, the new energy flows into these stuck areas, brings healing and the release of pain. It facilitates transformation by making the new energies available in usable form. It readjusts the immune system so that it better understands how to use the new energies and stops fighting them, often the cause of autoimmune diseases. It supports the adrenals and stimulates the digestive system.

It is unfortunate that the naming of a man-made crystal, Cubic Zirconium, has made Zircon less popular. It is very alive and eager to help you in your transformation process.

Other sources: Manifests divine intelligence from spiritual love. Stimulates understanding of spiritual truths through images and symbols. Brings prudence and wisdom and makes one more pleasant. Stimulates mind and strengthens it against temptations. Emotionally balancing. Also heals emotional pain and suffering. Calms emotions, dispels depression and sadness, promotes sleep, and restores appetite. Stimulates and balances the liver, which might be the cause of hallucinations. Absorbs and radiates energy in general. Protects from attack. Orange protects travelers and ensures good reception everywhere. Yellow Zircon gives physical contentment. Red-brown Zircon is a strong healer.

The elixir aligns the subtle bodies and opens, balances, and blends the crown and brow chakras, transforming schizophrenic-type visions into spiritual experience that can be understood rationally.

ZOISITE: Stabilizing, Energizing

Calcium Aluminum Silicate. Usually found as aggregates of crystals, white, gray or greenish, might be pink, blue (Tanzanite) or bright green.

Orthorhombic system. Hardness is 6.5. The massive green type often has ruby inclusions and is quite distinctive and striking.

Zoisite is stabilizing and energizing for the physical level. It heals by providing a point of balance within the upward-spiraling movement generated by thoughts directed toward healing or transformation. It will never hold you at the same level but continually lead you upward in an expanding spiral of awareness or expression.

Pink Zoisite adds a quality, uplifting to the emotions, that brings a positive attitude to the difficulties often encountered in self-transformation. It aids the physical healing by allowing the ideal to flow into the body without the distortion caused by negative emotions. Green Zoisite sooths the vibrations of the physical body and bypasses any looping patterns that keep you at the old level. It helps the cellular level accept the new energies and release resistance and fears about transformation.

When Ruby is combined with the green Zoisite, it adds its ability to go deeply into your potential and brings new awareness of it into your cells. It is very transformational. It helps your physical body forget the limitations that have been programmed into it by the apparent difficulties of physical existence and accept the possibility of change without destruction. It is very helpful for clearing, healing, and transforming the lower chakras, especially the base chakra. It helps it connect with the heart and shows it how to support your spiritual purpose.

Zoisite helps you harness the creative potential of your second chakra to your Divine Will through the throat chakra. In conjunction with Lapis, Turquoise, Dumortierite, and other similarly colored stones, it helps you see how to use your creative power for specific problems. It also heals doubts about your creative abilities and gives you courage in the use of your own power to create your own life. It can be very useful for victims of abuse because they are usually dissociated from their own power. The colored varieties are the most powerful here, but the white or gray ones can open new paths for your creative expression.

As an elixir, all the above qualities are enhanced and carried more specifically into the cellular level, breaking the karmic looping of old misperceptions in the subconscious. It is an even more powerful connector to your own power. The elixir is rejuvenating for the skin when sprayed on or rubbed into it or when used in the bath. See also Tanzanite.

Other sources: Stimulates the sex chakra, balancing and increasing creativity. Strengthens male genitals and female cervix. Increases fertility.

Crystal Combinations for Specific Effects

These combinations are not meant to be preferable to individual stones. They are given to show how various stones support each other and blend their energies and as suggestions for how to blend crystal energies. Some are given because the individual stones would not necessarily apply to the given situation, but they help shape a group energy that is especially effective. They are also given in the hope that they will stimulate your creativity in developing your own combinations. There is no space in this book to develop the reasons for the combinations or their specific uses. Perhaps that is for another book.

Remember, you don't have to have very large, perfect, or expensive stones to do the job. Tumbled stones are fine, especially for elixirs. You will need only very small pieces of powerful stones like Ruby, Emerald or Diamond and they don't have to be faceted. Rough is fine. Where an alternate stone is listed, in most cases, you will have two different group energies. If the listing says, for instance, "any white stone," that you have one stone of that energy and color is the only important thing.

Abundance
> *Emerald, Rose Quartz*
> Chrome Dioptase, Quartz, Calcite
> Rhodochrosite, Apophyllite, Bloodstone
> Sapphire, Green Quartz, Chalcopyrite

Allergies
> *Green Calcite, Chinese Turquoise, Wulfenite or Vanadinite*
> Euclase, any red stone, Magnetite
> Blue Lace Agate, Picture Jasper, Rhodonite

Anger
> *Talc or Serpentine, Yellow Labradorite, Limestone*
> Celestite, Pyrite, Chabazite
> Staurolite, Rainbow Quartz, Rose Quartz
> Spinel, Apophyllite
> Chalcedony, Ruby

Anti-Aging
> *Peridot, Topaz, Chrysoprase or Chrysocolla*
> Topaz, Danburite, Fluorite
> Rhodochrosite, Apophyllite, Topaz, Amethyst
> Peridot, Diamond, Blue Quartz, Hematite
> Spectrolite, Amethyst, Gray Calcite, Magnetite or Red Jasper
> Sugilite, Clear Quartz (rehealed) or Herkimer Quartz, Pink Garnet

Appetite, decreasing
> *Rose Quartz, Serpentine, Eilat Stone*
> Diopside, Rhodonite, Danburite, Ruby
> Vanadinite, Sandstone, Kunzite
> Hornblend, Larimar, Indicolite

Appetite, increasing
> *Vanadinite or Crocoite, Rose Quartz, Red Beryl*
> Aquamarine, Ruby, Grossular Garnet
> Rubellite, Quartz, Epidote or Nephrite

Ascension
> *Cobalto-Calcite, Rainbow Quartz*
> Danburite, Ruby, Gold
> Apophyllite, Diamond, Peridot, Pearl
> White Opal, Clear Quartz or Herkimer Quartz, Dravite
> Rhodochrosite, Apophyllite, Rose Quartz
> Iolite, Rainbow Quartz, Amazonite

Awareness, spiritual
> *Danburite, Ruby, Zircon*
> Neptunite, Covellite, Scolesite

Moldavite, Diamond, Hematite

Pink Jasper, Red Beryl, Hemimorphite

Pietersite, Clear Quartz, Selenite, White Marble or Aragonite

Awareness, self

Danburite, Emerald, Petrified Wood

Pyromorphite, White or Pink Opal, Rose Quartz or Amethyst

Gold in White Quartz, Indicolite, Blue Topaz

Spectrolite, Kunzite, Rose Quartz

Rutilated Quartz, Angelsite, Rhodonite, Green Tourmaline

Madagascar Quartz, Ruby, Marcasite

Rhyolite, Rubellite, Herkimer Quartz, Phenacite

Balancing chakras

Boji Stones (at least three), Herkimer Quartz, Black Tourmaline, Azurite

Tanzanite, Pearl, Ruby

Hematite, Star Sapphire, Rhodonite, Chiastolite

Blue, Green, and Red Tourmalines and Clear Quartz

Staurolite, Prehnite, White Beryl or Clear Spodumene

Selenite, Ruby, Carnelian, Chrysoberyl

Balancing four bodies

Selenite, Rose Quartz, Hematite

Danburite, Aragonite, Turquoise, Dumortierite

Lazulite (or Lapis Lazuli), Rubellite, double-terminated Quartz

Wavellite, Green Moss Agate, Chiastolite, Moonstone (slightly greenish, if possible)

Danburite, Rhodonite, Serpentine, Hiddenite

Zircon, Malachite, Rose Quartz, Magnetite

Blue Sapphire, Kyanite, Danburite, Rubellite or Ruby

Richterite, Tanzanite, Petalite, Pink Orthoclase

Variscite, Garnet, Anaclime, Moss Agate

Adularia Moonstone, Charoite, Green Onyx, Fuchsite

Lepidolite, Garnet

Lepidolite, Opal

Balancing polarities

Watermelon Tourmaline and Quartz twins

Green Tourmaline, Rubellite, Danburite, Hematite or Barite

Chiastolite, Herkimer Quartz, White Topaz (optional)

Petalite, Ruby, Diopside

Boji Stone, Apophyllite, Spectrolite, Yellow Fluorite

Green Zoisite with Ruby, Titanium, Staurolite, Clear Spodumene

Green Fluorite, Amethyst, Selenite, Nephrite

Balancing polarities (Cont.)
Emerald, White Quartz, Spinel, Pearl or Shell (white)
Nephrite, Ruby, Yellow Labradorite, Tourmaline (any color)
White or Pink Coral, Larimar, Cuprite, Azurite
Unakite, Hematite, Phenacite
Rhodochrosite, Zoisite, Andalusite
Lavender Quartz, Rubellite, Green Diopside

Blocks and resistance
Romanechite, Aqua Aura, Purple Fluorite
Amethyst, Aqua Aura, Rainbow Fluorite
Danburite, Ruby, Romanechite
Smoky Quartz, Phenacite, Cinnabar
Amazonite, Lavender Agate or Amethyst, Pearl or Dolomite
Sugilite, Diamond, Bustamite or Ajoite in Quartz
Pietersite, Neptunite, Shattuckite
Tourmalinated Quartz, Ruby, Vanadinite or Wulfenite
Brazilian Quartz, Citrine, Amethyst, Anhydrite, Selenite
Aqua Aura, Ruby or Spinel, Hematite
Apatite, Scolesite, Pyrite, Fluorite
Diamond, Orange Calcite, Lapis Lazuli
Rhyolite, Quartz, Danburite, Bustamite or Crocoite
Whewellite, Clear Quartz, Boji Stone
Quartzite, Chalcopyrite, Scheelite
Eilat Stone, Rhodonite, Malachite
Malachite, Sodalite, Rose Quartz, Amethyst

Blood cleansing
Carnelian, Danburite, Fluorite
Garnet, Diamond, Hematite
Spinel, Herkimer Quartz, Silver, Tungsten or Titanium
Ruby, Spessartine Garnet, Pearl, Euclase or Clear Tourmaline
Garnet, Green Aventurine, Beryl
Coral, Bloodstone, Danburite, Amber
Apatite, Orange or Pink Jasper, Mahagony Obsidian
Zircon, Bloodstone, Romanechite

Blood, strengthening (also for increasing life force)
Ruby, Clear Quartz, Dioptase
Golden Topaz, Red Garnet, Red or Orange Agate
Hematite, Rainbow Quartz, Bloodstone, Ruby or Spinel
Malachite, Peridot, Bloodstone or Green Jasper, Fuchsite
Ruby, Clear Calcite

Body, energizing
Boji Stones (two), Zircon, Emerald
Fluorite, Pyrite, Rutilated Quartz
Danburite, Bustamite, Hematite
Enstatite, Quartz Scepter, Unakite
Moldavite, Amethyst, Hematite, Jasper, Chrysocolla
Danburite, Golden Topaz, Ruby
Orange Calcite, Clear Quartz

Brain, balancing
Spodumene, Green Fluorite, Lavender Agate
Aqua Aura, Citrine, Azurite
Eilat Stone, Rainbow Quartz, Christobalite (optinal)
Rutilated Quartz, Smithsonite, Staurolite
Boji Stone, Yellow Labradorite
Lepidolite, Herkimer Quartz, Aquamarine
Euclase, Prehnite, Selenite

Brain, connecting to heart
Rhodochrosite, Ruby, Danburite, Carnelian
Ametrine, Ruby, Diamond
Rose Quartz, Violet Tourmaline, Clear Quartz
Zircon, Staurolite, Rose Quartz
Garnet, Citrine
Kunzite, Ruby, Herkimer Quartz, Romanechite
Rainbow Quartz, Ruby
Aqua Aura, Ruby, Hematite
Red Tiger-Eye (heat-treated is O.K.), Azurite, Danburite
Garnet, Zoisite, Phantom Quartz

Brain, stimulating
Aqua Aura, Citrine, Malachite, Shattuckite
Lepidolite, Boji Stone, Diamond
Azeztulite, Amethyst, Rutilated Quartz
Benitoite, Amethyst or Ruby, Aqua Aura or Rainbow Quartz,

Citrine, Clear Quartz, Apophyllite
Moldavite, Yellow Calcite

Cells, connecting to ideal
Peridot, Danburite, Rose Quartz
Shattuckite, Quartz, Garnet
Peridot, Rhodochrosite, Spinel, Clear Calcite
Calcite, Danburite, Ruby, Spectrolite
Adularia Moonstone, Kyanite, Perthite
Peridot, Diamond, Hematite

Cells, connecting to ideal (Cont.)
Shattuckite, Coral, Staurolite, Beryl
Beryl, Quartz, Titanium
Azurite, Peridot, Kunzite
Benitoite, Aqua Aura, Cobalto-Calcite
Azeztulite, Red or Brown Topaz
Pink Smithsonite, Spinel, Bloodstone
Variscite, Herkimer Quartz, Boji Stones (two)
Boji Stone, Clear Calcite, Nephrite, Jasper
Hemimorphite, Hiddenite, Fuchsite, Zoisite
Zircon, Hiddenite, Ruby
Zircon, Ruby, Variscite
Yellow or Blue Labradorite, Green Calcite, Rainbow Quartz
Fuchsite, Aqua Aura
Lepidolite, Green Calcite

Change, balancing
Cobalto-Calcite, Barite, Chrysoprase
Rhodonite, Wavellite, Boji Stone
Boji Stone, Rhodochrosite, Pearl
Agate, Actinolite in Quartz, Amazonite
Halite, Aqua Aura, Danburite
Spectrolite, Ruby, Apophyllite
Ellestial Quartz, Rhodonite, Diopside
Green Smithsonite, Quartz Faden, Boji Stone
Christobalite, Staurolite, Rose Quartz
Lapis Lazuli, Clear Quartz

Change, stimulating
Aqua Aura, Hiddenite, Whewellite
Azurite, Azeztulite, Ruby
Sapphire, Diamond, Zircon
Hematite, Garnet, Peridot, Titanium
Sugilite, Diamond, Apophyllite
Wulfenite, Peridot, Aquamarine
Bustamite, Diamond, Kunzite
Quartz Scepter, Rose Quartz, Spectrolite
Sugilite, Clear Quartz, Silver

Channel, opening
Moldavite, Amethyst
Lapis Lazuli, Diamond
Boji Stone, Spectrolite, Amethyst
Zircon, Purple Fluorite, Rutilated Quartz

Tabular Quartz, Moldavite, Titanium, Copper

Citrine, Rutilated Quartz

Christ light, grounding

Ruby, Hematite, Garnet

Sugilite, Clear Quartz, Anhydrite

Ivory, Ruby, Danburite

Quartz Phantom, Smithsonite, Iolite

Pearl, Ruby, Diamond

Opal, Clear Quartz

Vanadinite, Aqua Aura

Circulation of blood, stimulating

Danburite, Peridot, Ruby

Garnet, Aqua Aura, Chrysocolla, Ellestial Quartz

Rutilated Quartz, Bloodstone, Apophyllite

Crocoite, Danburite, Shattuckite

Carnelian, Diamond

Clearing aura

Halite, Selenite

Selenite, Sodalite, Rose Quartz

Sulphur, Diamond

Romanechite, Clear Quartz, Selenite

Black Tourmaline, Clear Quartz, Beryl

Amethyst, Calcite

Clearing emotions

Danburite, Yellow Labradorite, Diamond

Cobalto-Calcite, Selenite, Hematite

Obsidian, Smoky Quartz, Rhodochrosite, Apophyllite

Smithsonite, Selenite, Green Calcite

Chrysoprase, Limestone, Coral, Albite Moonstone

Obsidian, Clear Quartz, Hiddenite, Variscite

Ulexite, Ruby, Hematite

Richterite, Sugilite, Herkimer Quartz, Boji Stone

Boji Stone, Yellow Labradorite

Boji Stone, Coral, Zoisite

Creativity, expansion

Aquamarine, Clear Quartz, Moldavite

Sapphire, Pearl, Azurite, Neptunite or Romanechite

Charoite, Diamond or Danburite, Diopside

Apophyllite, Smithsonite, Sugilite

Cat's-Eye, Pearl, Moldavite

Unakite, Epidote, Amethyst

Creativity, expansion (Cont.)
> Selenite, Amethyst, Pearl, Staurolite
> Tabular Quartz, Ruby, Zoisite
> Ajoite in Quartz, Angelsite, Chalcedony
> Aquamarine, Topaz

Creativity, expressing
> *Druzy Chrysocolla or Chrysocolla and Clear Quartz, Ruby*
> Aquamarine, Hiddenite, Coral
> Tanzanite, Ruby, Danburite
> Euclase, Amethyst, Citrine, Boji Stone
> Amethyst, Sphene, Zircon
> Peridot, Sphene, Danburite
> Zoisite with Ruby, Apophyllite, Purple Fluorite
> Rutilated Quartz, Moldavite, Hematite, Kunzite
> Garnet, Clear Calcite, Beryl (optional)
> Sodalite, Aqua Aura or Herkimer Quartz or Rutilated Quartz

Degeneration, cellular
> *Peridot, Shattuckite, Clear Quartz (Diamantina preferably)*
> Shattuckite, Ruby, Quartz, Cuprite
> Dumortierite, Azurite, Spinel, Danburite
> Angelite, Peridot, Beryl
> Ajoite, Azurite, Hematite
> Azeztulite, Ruby, Emerald
> Barite, Kyanite, Bloodstone, Garnet
> Fuchsite, Red Beryl, Chrysocolla or Eilat Stone
> Neptunite, Aquamarine, Blue Apatite
> Blue Lace Agate, Dioptase, Emerald
> Romanechite, Amethyst, Kyanite
> Peridot, Danburite, Staurolite, Zircon
> Green Beryl, Eilat Stone, Fluorite
> Perthite, Cobalto-Calcite, Emerald, Dumortierite

Depression
> *Kunzite, Smithsonite*
> Azurite, Green Calcite, Rose Quartz
> Amethyst, Chrysocolla, Romanechite
> Rainbow Quartz, Amethyst
> Sugilite, Charoite, Garnet
> Aquamarine, Ruby, Opal
> Boji Stone, Amethyst, Selenite

DNA reprogramming
> *Shattuckite, Amethyst, Rainbow Quartz*

Azurite, Apophyllite, Hiddenite
Apatite, Zoisite, Pyrite
Boji Stone, Peridot, Eilat Stone
Sodalite, Green Calcite, Fuchsite, Ruby or Sapphire
Zircon, Tanzanite, Spinel, Clear Quartz
Drusy Chrysocolla, Ruby
Dumortierite, Clear Quartz, Moldavite, Danburite
Citrine, Amethyst, Aqua Aura
Tourmaline, Quartz, Peridot, Kunzite
Zircon, Fluorite, Aqua Aura
Aventurine, Quartz, Azeztulite or Moldavite
Fuchsite, Moldavite, Enstatite

Emotional stability
Rhodonite, Boji Stone, Herkimer Quartz
Sugilite, Staurolite, Rose Quartz
Pietersite, Spinel, Boji Stone
Labradorite, Limestone, Blue Lace Agate
Aragonite, Iolite, Jasper
Blue Tiger-Eye, Citrine, Angelite

Emotions, accepting
Danburite, Ruby, Green Apophyllite
Turquoise, Ruby, Malachite
Yellow Labradorite, Hiddenite, Pink Smithsonite
Kunzite, Garnet, Chrysoprase
Azurite, Danburite, Spinel
Golden Topaz, Blue Fluorite, Lavender Agate
Euclase, Purple Fluorite, Amber
Adularia, Emerald, Rose Quartz

Endocrine system, balancing
Dumortierite, Green Fluorite
Zircon, Danburite, Green Apophyllite
Seraphinite, Amethyst
Spectrolite, Herkimer Quartz
Boji Stone, Eilat Stone, Honey Calcite
Azurite/Chrysocolla, Amethyst, Clear Quartz, Enstatite
Amethyst, Garnet, Onyx, Quartz

Endocrine glands, regenerating
Boji Stone, Green Calcite
Blue Topaz, Purple Fluorite, Morganite
Rhodonite, Hiddenite, Danburite

Enthusiasm
Aquamarine, Scolesite, Rose Quartz
Yellow Labradorite, Hematite
Green and Pink Smithsonite, Calcite
Boji Stone, Charoite, Danburite

Fear
Romanechite, Fluorite, Danburite
Boji Stone, Obsidian, Hematite, Apophyllite
Tanzanite, Amethyst, Kunzite
Star Rose Quartz, Garnet, Hematite

Grounding
Chiastolite, Herkimer Quartz
Azeztulite, Jet
Garnet, Staurolite, Serpentine
Boji Stone, Garnet, Diamond

Hate
Rose Quartz, Hematite, Opal
Sphene, Ruby, Green Garnet
Red or Pink Coral, Gem Silica, Herkimer Quartz
Angelite, Green Smithsonite, Phenacite, Fluorite
Fluorite, Obsidian, Tourmaline, Tabular Quartz
Larimar, Rose Quartz
Kyanite, Ruby, Selenite

Heart, using
Kunzite, Emerald, Chiastolite
Rose Quartz, Clear Quartz, Moldavite
Scolesite, Ruby, Aquamarine
Orthoclase, Tanzanite, Cobalto-Calcite
Boji Stone, Emerald, Staurolite
Rhodochrosite, Ruby, Hematite
Pyrite, Diamond, any red stone (even an artificial one)
Fire Opal, Diamond
Pink Topaz, Brown Garnet or Brown Prehnite or Staurolite
Pink Danburite, Chiastolite, Smithsonite
Amber, Kunzite, Copper
Moldavite, Kunzite

Hyperthyroidism
Halite, Danburite, Hematite
Rhyolite, Emerald, any brown stone
Kunzite, Azurite, Clear Quartz (preferably a scepter)

Ideal, aligning with

Dumortierite, Emerald
Shattuckite, Quartz, Clear Spodumene, Ruby
Sugilite, Herkimer Quartz, Boji Stone
Spinel, Tanzanite, Topaz
Labradorite, Green Beryl, Aventurine
Angelite, Bloodstone, Onyx, Peridot
Chiastolite, Herkimer Diamond, Selenite
Rhodonite, Danburite, Sugilite, Tiger-Eye
Rutilated Quartz, Lapis Lazuli, Eilat Stone

Intuition

Azeztulite, Ruby
Danburite, Boji Stone, Staurolite
Azurite, Amethyst, Green Fluorite
Euclase, Morganite, Diamond
Turquoise, Azurite, Clear Quartz
Ajoite in Quartz, Hematite, Red Beryl or Ruby

Joy

Chrysocolla, Citrine, Apophyllite
Gem Silica, Adularia, Yellow Apatite
Yellow Orthoclase, Amber, Phenacite
Emerald, Clear Quartz, Angelite
Citrine, Hiddenite, Apophyllite

Love, unconditional

Ellestial Quartz, Boji Stone, Rhodonite
Aquamarine, Kunzite, Bloodstone
Chrysocolla, Malachite, Morganite
Watermelon Tourmaline, Staurolite, Iolite
Turquoise, Ruby, Sandstone
Picture Jasper, Pink Calcite, Labradorite
Blue Quartz, Rubellite, Titanium
Chrysoberyl, Morganite, Green Calcite, Vanadanite

Love, attracting

Magnetite, Ruby, Clear Quartz
Boji Stone, Rose Quartz, Marcasite
Wavellite, Rubellite, Pink Smithsonite, any white stone
Fluorite, Anaclime, Amber
Pink Topaz, Rhodonite, Spodumene
Tanzanite, Ruby, Bloodstone or Red Jasper

Menopause

Staurolite, Rose Quartz, Rhodochrosite

Menopause (Cont.)
Chabazite, Apatite, Variscite
Tiger-Eye, Pyrite, Morganite, Fluorite
Kyanite, Peridot, Danburite

Mind, calming
Larimar, Green Jasper, Pink Zoisite
Green Tourmaline, Boji Stone, Pearl
Richterite, Nephrite, Rose Quartz, Green Calcite
Rhyolite, Chalcedony, Seraphinite
Yellow Labradorite, Barite, White or Cloudy Quartz point

Muscles, strengthening
Pyromorphite, Selenite, Pyrite
Yellow Tourmaline, Amber, Hematite, Ruby
Lazulite, Citrine, Rose Quartz, Limestone
Covellite, Calcite, Serpentine

Negative thoughts, preventing
Amethyst, Blue Topaz
White Agate, Green Smithsonite, Purple Fluorite
Garnet, Diamond

Negativity, protection from
Turquoise, Quartz, Pyrite
Chrysocolla, Emerald, Aragonite, Obsidian
Romanechite, Quartz, Beryl
Black Tourmaline, Smoky Quartz, Boji Stone
Galena, Fluorite, Eilat Stone
Yellow Labradorite, Pyrite, Rhyolite
Chalcopyrite, Turquoise, Fluorite, Agate

Purpose, focusing
Quartz Scepter, Benitoite, Anglesite
Kunzite, Danburite, Yellow Apatite, any metal
Shattuckite, Scolesite, Lapis Lazuli
Marcasite, Fluorite
Chlorite Quartz, Labradorite, Chrysoprase, any colorless stone
Gem Silica, Amethyst, Gold
Opal, Gold, Ruby
Benitoite, Rutilated Quartz, Sugilite
Pietersite, Selenite, Charoite

Radiation protection
Fluorite, Azeztulite
Dumortierite, Quartz, Fuchsite
Labradorite, Spodumene, Serpentine or Seraphinite

Jadeite, Hiddenite, Magnetite
Neptunite, Selenite, Calcite, Boji Stone
Aragonite, Coral, Limestone, Amazonite

Shock

Rose Quartz, Emerald, Chiastolite (excellent combination for an elixir)
Lavender Quartz, Aventurine, Malachite
Amethyst, Apophyllite, Gem Silica
Rhodochrosite, Citrine, Green Calcite
Bloodstone, Aquamarine
Phenacite, Hematite

Success, business

Emerald, Kyanite, Orange Calcite
Amber, Azeztulite
Sodalite, Phenacite, Tiger-Eye, Hornblend
Nephrite, Ruby, Hiddenite, Pink Jasper
Boji Stone, Herkimer Quartz
Anglesite, Tanzanite, Rhodochrosite
Green Garnet, Orange Calcite, Selenite, Magnetite
Faden Quartz, Sapphire, Nephrite
Turquoise, Picture Jasper, Topaz
Amethyst, Green Calcite, Green or Watermelon Tourmaline
Blue Quartz, Amethyst, Drusy Chrysocolla or Green Smithsonite

Stomachache

Rose Quartz, Larimar, Limestone or Jasper
Aquamarine, Hematite, Iolite
Apophyllite, Bloodstone, Chalcedony, Rose Quartz

Transformation

Azeztulite, Romanechite, Amethyst
Danburite, Ruby
Emerald, Rose Quartz, Aqua Aura, Pyrite
Golden Topaz, Rainbow Quartz
Topaz, Fluorite, Eilat Stone or Azurite/Chrysocolla
Spodumene, Wulfenite, Gem Silica
Amethyst, Chrysocolla, Beryl
Celestite, Selenite, Rhodochrosite, Scheelite or Sugilite
Sugilite, Charoite, Green Calcite
Danburite, Yellow Labradorite, Red Quartz or Chalcopyrite
Aventurine, Diamond, Yellow Tourmaline
Watermelon Tourmaline, Topaz, Apophyllite
Phantom Quartz, Lepidolite, Opal

Transformation (Cont.)

Citrine, Tanzanite, Charoite

Bustamite, Danburite, Spinel

Transmitting messages

Quartz pyramid, Copper plate, Zircon

Citrine, Apophyllite, Emerald

Star Ruby, Clear Quartz

Rutilated Quartz, Azurite, Amazonite

Moldavite, Diamantina Quartz, Emerald Sphere

Neptunite, Blue Quartz, Amethyst

Vitality

Boji Stone, Selenite, Yellow Tourmaline

Rainbow Quartz, Shattuckite, Chrysoprase, Boji Stone or Staurolite

Aventurine, Pyrite, Topaz

Vanadanite or Wulfenite, or Galena, Spectrolite, Azeztulite

Bloodstone, Amethyst, Fluorite, Marcasite

Euclase, Diamond, Aqua Aura

Sapphire, Coral, Jasper

Serpentine, Truquoise, Moss Agate

Birthstones and Astrological Symbolism

Birthstones

Every country and every group of gemologists seem to have their own list of birthstones. Even the ancient lists differ. This is a summary of some of them. However, the best stone for you might not be listed under your month of birth. Your birthstone will help you manifest the best of your Sun sign, but you might need to support some other part of yourself that does not feel so close a part of you. Keep an open mind and use your intuition when choosing a stone for yourself or another.

January:	Garnet, Jasper
February:	Amethyst
March:	Aquamarine, Bloodstone, Jasper
April:	Diamond, Sapphire, Clear Quartz
May:	Emerald, Agate, Chrysoprase
June:	Pearl, Moonstone, Alexandrite
July:	Ruby, Onyx, Carnelian
August:	Peridot, Sardonyx, Carnelian, Aventurine
September:	Sapphire, Chrysolite, Sodalite
October:	Opal, Turquoise, Aquamarine, Abalone Shell, Tourmaline
November:	Topaz, Citrine
December:	Turquoise, Zircon, Ruby, Amazonite

Transformational Assistance

Aries: Boji Stone to help ground their boundless energy and to help them see that love is there for them if they stop to look.

Taurus: Danburite to help release reliance on physical things and to channel their enormous power into spiritual accomplishment.

Gemini: Tanzanite to heal the split between physical and spiritual and to focus their quick minds.

Cancer: Aphrodite Stone to assist them in trying to heal everyone and their problems and to see that they have the unlimited love to go around.

Leo: Ruby to transform egotism into true self-awareness and to teach security in its presence.

Virgo: Moldavite to broaden their perspective and help them see that love is for them too.

Libra: Spectrolite to help them choose without limiting any
possibili ties.

Scorpio: Faden Quartz to help them use their great healing power to the fullest and Merlinite to help them see the bright side.

Saggitarius: Aqua Aura to assure a good connection into their many contacts, so that they can integrate them more completely.

Capricorn: Rhodonite to bring love and self-acceptance to their great practical use of Earth's resources.

Aquarius: Blue Tiger-eye to aid the appreciation and use of what is already available in the presence of change and to bring greater spiritual awareness of the unchanging, eternal truth.

Pisces: Sugilite to bring special help from the violet transforming ray for healing and understanding the world and helping them find ways to share their wisdom.

Crystals for Astrological Signs

Aries:	Sard
Taurus:	Carnelian
Gemini:	Topaz
Cancer:	Chalcedony
Leo:	Jasper
Virgo:	Emerald
Scorpio:	Amethyst
Sagittarius:	Orange Zircon
Capricorn:	Chrysoprase
Aquarius:	Clear Quartz
Pisces:	Sapphire

Crystals for Astrological Planets

Sun:	Diamond, Ruby, Topaz, Heliodor, Chrysoberyl, Amber, Gold
Moon:	Clear Quartz, Pearl, Opal, Moonstone, all milk-white stones, Mother-of-Pearl, Selenite, Silver
Mercury:	Loadstone, Amethyst, Tortoise-shell, Lepidolite, Quicksilver
Venus:	Emerald, Sapphire, Malachite, Coral, Copper
Mars:	Bloodstone, Flint, Malachite, Red Hematite, Ruby, Spinel, Garnet
Jupiter:	Amethyst, Turquoise, Sapphire, Blue Tourmaline, Ivory, Tin
Saturn:	Garnet, Jet, Obsidian, Onyx, Diamond, all black stones
Uranus:	Chalcedony, Lapis Lazuli, Zircon, Amber, Fire Opal
Neptune:	Coral, Aquamarine, Ivory, Jade
Pluto:	Beryl, Sardonyx, Jade, Jasper

Crystal Systems

Monoclinic System
- Actinolite
- Adularia
- Azurite
- Crocoite
- Diopside
- Epidote
- Euclase
- Fuchsite
- Hiddenite
- Hornblend
- Jadeite
- Lazulite
- Lepidolite
- Malachite
- Nephrite
- Muscovite
- Neptunite
- Orthoclase
- Petalite
- Richterite
- Scolesite
- Selenite
- Sphene
- Spodumene
- Talc
- Whewellite

Triclinic System
- Ajoite
- Amazonite
- Bustamite
- Kyanite
- Labradorite
- Larimar
- Microcline
- Moonstone, Albite
- Rhodonite
- Turquoise
- Ulexite

Orthorhombic System
- Alexandrite
- Andalusite
- Angelite
- Anglesite
- Anhydrite
- Aragonite
- Barite
- Cat's-Eye
- Cavansite
- Celestite
- Chrysoberyl
- Danburite
- Dumortierite
- Enstatite
- Hemimorphite
- Iolite
- Kunzite
- Marcasite
- Pearl
- Peridot
- Prehnite
- Romanechite
- Shattuckite
- Sulphur
- Staurolite
- Tanzanite
- Topaz
- Variscite
- Wavellite
- Zoisite

Hexagonal System
- Agate
- Amethyst
- Apatite
- Aquamarine
- Benitoite
- Beryl
- Chabazite

Hexagonal System (Cont.)
- Cinnabar
- Covellite
- Emerald
- Limestone
- Morganite
- Pyromorphite
- Ruby
- Sapphire
- Sugilite
- Titanium
- Vanadinite

Trigonal System
- Aqua Aura
- Aventurine
- Azeztulite
- Bloodstone
- Calcite
- Carnelian
- Chalcedony
- Chrysocolla
- Chrysoprase
- Citrine
- Cobalto-Calcite
- Coral
- Corundum
- Dioptase
- Dolomite
- Ellestial Quartz
- Gem Silica
- Hematite
- Herkimer Quartz
- Jasper
- Onyx
- Pietersite
- Phenacite
- Quartz
- Smoky Quartz
- Blue Quartz
- Lavender Quartz
- Rose Quartz

- Rainbow Quartz
- Rhodochrosite
- Smithsonite
- Tiger-Eye
- Tourmaline

Cubic System
- Anaclime
- Copper
- Cuprite
- Diamond
- Fluorite
- Galena
- Garnet
- Gold
- Halite
- Lapis Lazuli
- Magnetite
- Platinum
- Silver
- Sodalite
- Spinel

Tetragonal System
- Apophyllite
- Cassiterite
- Chalcopyrite
- Christobalit
- Rutile
- Scheelite
- Wulfenite
- Zircon

Amorphous
- Amber
- Boji Stones
- Charoite
- Ivory
- Jet
- Moldavite
- Obsidian
- Opal
- Perthite
- Tektite

References

Colton, Ann Ree. *Watch your Dreams*. Glendale, CA: A.R. Colton Foundation, 1973. The source of dream symbology given in text.

Crow, W. B. *Precious Stones, Their Occult Power and Hidden Significance*. Out of print.

Devore, Nicholas. *Encyclopedia of Astrology*. Out of print.

Fernie, William T. *The Occult and Curative Powers of Precious Stones*. Fair Oaks, CA: Rudolph Steiner Publications, 1987.

Gurudas. *Gem Elixirs and Vibrational Healings,* Vols. I & II. Boulder, CO: Cassandra Press, 1985. Information channeled by Kevin Ryerson.

Kunz, George Frederick. *The Curious Lore of Precious Stones*. New York: Dover Publications, 1970.

Lyman, Kennie, ed. *Simon & Schuster's Guide to Gems and Precious Stones*. New York: Simon & Schuster, 1986. The physical properties and descriptions of virtually every crystal you might ever see. Each entry is illustrated by a color photo.

Mella, Dorothee L. *Stone Power*. New York: Warner Books, 1988. Mondadori, ed. *Simon & Schuster's Guide to Rocks and Minerals*. New York: Simon & Schuster, 1978. The physical properties and descriptions of virtually every crystal you might ever see. The best part is that each entry is illustrated by a color photo.

Roberts, Campbell and Rupp. *Encyclopedia of Minerals*. New York: Van Nostrand Reinhold Co., 1990.

Webster, Robert. *Gems: Their Sources, Descriptions and Identification*. England: Butterworth & Co. (Publishers) Ltd.

Suggested Reading

Alper, Rev. Dr. Frank. *Exploring Atlantis.* 3 vols. Phoenix, AZ: Adamis Int'l., 1990. History of the use of crystals in Atlantis, crystal grids and healing.

Baer, Randall N. and Vicki V. *Windows of Light.* Incorporates scientific knowledge and use of crystals with spiritual perspectives for transformation. Out of print. See also *The Crystal Connection: A Guidebook for Personal and Planetary Ascension.* San Francisco: Harper, 1987.

Bailey, Alice *Esoteric Healing.* New York: Lucis Publishing Co., 1953. Channeled from the Tibetan Master Djwhal Khul. All of Alice Bailey's books are an important part of the basic structure of New Age spiritual thought and systems. This one is a little easier to read than some.

Besterman, Theodore. *Crystal Gazing.* Out of print

Gerber, Richard, M.D. *Vibrational Medicine.* Santa Fe, NM: Bear & Company, 1988. A scientific review of alternative healing methods including crystal techniques and New Age healing techniques.

Gurudas. *Gem Elixirs and Vibrational Healing, Vol. I.* Boulder, Colorado: Cassandra Press, 1985. Information channeled by Kevin Ryerson.

Plummer, L. Gordon. *The Mathematics of the Cosmic Mind.* Wheaton, Illinois: The Theosophical Publishing House. The mathematical symbolism of Blavatsky's *Secret Doctrine* is translated into the geometric shapes of the universe and its energy essence.

Raphael, Katrina. *Crystal Trilogy* including *Crystal Enlightenment* and *Crystal Healing*. Detailed information about different types of quartz crystals and their use, crystal layouts for healing and their basic healing and transformational qualities. Out of print.

Sheldrake, Rupert. *A New Science of Life*. New York: Jeremy P. Tarcher, Inc., Los Angeles, distributed by St. Martin's Press. Sheldrake's theory of "morphogenetic fields" describes how the form of a whole group is shaped by the thought, activity, or evolution of its parts.

Wood, Elizabeth. *Crystals and Light*. New York: Dover Publications, Inc.

Illustrations

Many of the crystals in the illustrations are masters and are extremely powerful examples of their kind. You can use the picture to connect with them mentally and emotionally. Holding a crystal of the same or a related variety will help. They will help you summon the support of the whole Mineral Kingdom to help you with whatever you want to do.

(The photographs follow these descriptions)

1. Elbaite (Tourmaline) and Lepidolite from Minas Gerais, Brazil.
This green Tourmaline with the crystalline Lepidolite garland is a wonderful example of mastery. The Tourmaline has gathered what it needs from the available spiritual sources to express its beauty and purpose in the most comprehensive way. The angels have seemingly outdone themselves in creating balance and power into a most awesome structure. The spiral symbolizes the movement of energy at all levels and particularly reminds us that our DNA is meant to mirror the flow of divine love. The specimen shows this love being made available for unlimited use at the physical level through the hearts of all who are open to it. Surely this beautiful arrangement of crystals can create many openings in your heart for love. Use this picture to assist in opening your heart, healing, reprogramming, aligning with the ideal, releasing negativity, and expanding and raising your perspective.

2. Rhodochrosite from Duruman, South Africa.
Crystalline Rhodochrosite is fairly rare and this specimen is a grand master. It will help you center and balance your heart chakra. It is

healing to your heart and its connections to what is still outside yourself. It can help you expand your ability to use love. Imagine the crystal centered in your heart chakra, growing and unfolding like a rose.

3.   Calcite and Chalcopyrite from Reynolds County, Missouri.
This is a typical crystal form for Calcite. Together, the Calcite crystals from this area are a master in making light available to the biological forms on this planet. All Calcite does this, of course, but these crystals are especially good for directing the electrical flow of light into areas of the body that are having difficulty integrating all the frequencies coming in now. The combination with Pyrite makes the effect more substantial and enduring. You can use the picture to add the quality of specificity to your own Calcite specimens. Hold it and imagine energy from the crystal in the picture flowing into your crystal and into your body. Ask to be shown which parts especially need this energy.

4.   Smoky Quartz from Minas Gerais, Brazil.
This specimen is very similar to what is known as Ellestial Quartz. It absorbs negativity so powerfully that the ever-present angels become easier to sense and work with. Just looking at the picture will help you release all negativity from your energy field. If you have your own crystal, the process will be more effective and go deeper. The many centers of crystallization in the specimen are each tools for clearing self in its many aspects and levels. When each individual problem or reason for separation is resolved, unity and expansion of self occurs.

5.   Moldavite from Moldavia, Czechoslovakia.
This specimen is not a master itself, but it has made a connection to a certain level of mastery within Earth which allows a perfect connection to everything that is unknown. This picture, used with your own piece of Moldavite, will help you explore yourself by integrating your cosmic aspects, which you are just beginning to learn to use here. Imagine going into it and using its form to reach outside yourself into more love, power, and support from the universe.

6.   Fluorapatite and Quartz from Panasqueira, Portugal.
This combination of minerals has created a master specimen that mirrors the ideal structure for physical existence. Imagine going into the crystal and exploring every plane of crystallization and every axis as ways of organizing your own flow of light so that it expresses your creative purpose. The structure might seem different for every purpose, but the underlying laws are always the same and are based on the expression of beauty and love.

7.   Three varieties of Beryl: Aquamarine from Minas Gerais, Brazil; Heliodor from Minas Gerais; and Emerald from Bauchi, Nigeria.
These are all master crystals here; the Emerald is especially powerful. Singly or as a group they will enhance your meditations, strengthen your will and aid your transformation. Imagine placing them in various chakras or going into them so that you become filled with their color and your structure aligns with theirs. They will help you to energize and program your own less perfect specimens and to share their power through your connection to your own crystals.

8.   Fluoroapophyllite from Jalgoan, India.
While this specimen is typical of the green variety of Apophyllite, it is a master in its ability to teach the use of group energies. Use the picture with any Apophyllite crystal to help your connection with the angelic group that is working to heal the heart connections within humanity as a whole. It will help you maintain a spiritual approach to anything you do at the physical level that involves others and help to heal misperceptions about past betrayal of the love you shared with others and with Earth.

9.   Carved Chrysoprase, Gold, and Diamonds.
Again, the color here is the important element and is very healing to all parts of self. This is also an example of how an artist can bring out the potential of the stone and create something that expresses mastery. This piece symbolizes how each of you can become a master through self-love, self-discipline and choosing to express the beauty that is in you. The spiraling flow of the design shows how flexibility in adapting to the flow keeps you moving through whatever experience you need to achieve your mastery here on Earth.

10.   Tanzanite from Arusha, Tanzania.
The color is the important element here. Use it to flood your crown chakra with violet light which shades into indigo as it makes a connection with your brow chakra. Use it to aid your soul in connecting with your whole physical body.

11.   Crocoite from Dundas, Tasmania, Australia.
No other crystal has the typical bright orange-red of Crocoite. Use its color to heal and energize your second chakra and as a source of life energy to activate anything you want to do.

12.   Labradorite from Finland.

This piece is sliced and polished to show the iridescent play of colors that makes Labradorite able to help you integrate your lightbody and use its energy consciously. It can bring the wisdom to appreciate the potential of your physical consciousness for expanding the creative power of your spiritual self through physical existence.

13. Quartz, variety Herkimer Diamond from Herkimer County, New York.

The largest crystal in the cluster is a master; the others are nearing their masterships. Most of them will move to that level as the Earth learns to integrate the new energies now coming in, if they survive the coming changes. Humanity is an important key in this and must learn to go to the next level without destroying the old one. This crystal specimen and all Herkimer Diamonds want to help you learn that everything you learn, every experience, every thought has value and a potential for moving the Earth forward into a new level where everyone is master of his or her own destiny and that of Earth. Nothing needs to be destroyed. Everything is made of Source substance and can be transformed into the energy of love and used positively.

14. Fluorite and Chalcopyrite from Hardin County, Illinois.

This is a very useful and not uncommon combination which is used in the transformation process. Fluorite belongs in the collection of every crystal-lover who is working on transformation. The purple varieties are particularly helpful in consciously recognizing the light of the physical body and using it creatively. The Pyrite helps anchor that understanding at the cellular level so that physical transformation moves forward. Since you are part of Earth, it is already helping you, but working with it consciously speeds up the process.

15. Sheelite, Cassiterite and Quartz from Chukotka, Russia.

This particular combination of minerals is good for moving and expanding energies creatively. It comes from a place that is a source of growing power for Earth's transformation. It is presented here as a means of connecting with the spiritual Russia which has a very important part to play in Earth's transformation and restructuring into the next level of creative awareness. Russia is strong and will do its part, but now it needs support and love from other parts of Earth to achieve its great potential. In the future it will be a great source of love and support for the rest of Earth.

16. Vanadinite from Mibladen, Morocco.

Vanadinite teaches about the power seeded into physical structure. The place of its source in Morocco is a key point on Earth for connecting with its spiritual power and channeling it creatively. When Earth, humanity especially, has a better understanding of how to work together as a group to support each member of the group, the power of this place will be more evident. Earth has chakras, like people, but they are spread out, functioning in more than one locality on its surface. The place this specimen comes from in Morocco is part of Earth's second chakra. Its message now is to respect Earth and your place in it as the source of the power and wisdom you seek.

17. Phenacite from Mt. Antero, in Colorado.
This master crystal is doubly terminated. The picture can be used to activate your own crystals and to help you use them to connect with your place in the flow of the Divine Plan. This crystal is literally teaching other Phenacite crystals to be masters. Most Phenacite crystals are very close to being able to express the mastery that this one possesses. As you move to your own level of mastery with your crystal, it will expand its consciousness with you.

18. Kunzite from Nuristan, Afganistan.
Almost all Kunzite crystals have achieved individual mastery in flowing love as truth and the inner connection of all consciousness. This one is a master also and can help you learn to use your heart to express the qualities of love that are within it. Each of you is a master within. The goal is to express that mastery in every facet of your life and consciousness.

19. Amethyst from Ekaterinburg, Russia.
Amethyst is a favorite of many and its transformational color is cleansing Earth and raising its consciousness and vibrational level. The faceted stone is the master crystal here. The mastery was revealed and made available when it was cut and polished. Not all faceted Amethyst stones are masters, but they can all help you achieve mastery and protect you from your own doubts and lack of knowledge.

20. Peridot from Arizona, Zircon, Chromian Diopside from Russia, Diamond, and Ruby from Thailand.
This is a group of gems that form deep in Earth's crust under the most intense heat and pressure. They are brought to the surface as a result of volcanic action and are truly gifts from the heart of Earth. They express the greatest alignment with the will of the Planetary Logos and the Divine Plan.

21. Quartz scepter from Yavapai County, Arizona.

All scepters are master crystals. This is a particularly lovely example, and it mirrors the potential beauty that is inherent in every developing consciousness, as each individual recognizes its own spiritual gifts. It can help you discover your own special gifts. Imagine going into the crystal, then expanding beyond its limits until the point is centered in the middle of your head. Allow the shaft to connect you with the Earth and then flow the energy out the top of your head.

22. Kyanite in matrix, from Minas Gerais, Brazil.

This specimen is pictured to help you make another connection into Minas Gerais, Brazil. This area is immensely wealthy in minerals and is being mined extensively. While Earth is ready to share its riches with humanity, the process is disruptive to the region and healing is needed. You can help the healing process by sending your love and gratitude there. Kyanite is especially good for understanding all physical processes through the perspective of the Divine Plan. It will help you heal Earth as well as yourself.

23. Orthoclase, Carlsbad twin from Oro Grande, New Mexico.

This is not a sample of gem quality Orthoclase, but is shown here because these crystals can be so helpful in the restructuring necessary during healing or transformation processes. It can be easily programmed for your particular needs by your spiritual healers. They are waiting for you to ask them for their help. You can also ask that a crystal be programmed for someone else, and their own spiritual healers will make connections through it.

24. Andradite Garnet from Sonora, Mexico.

Garnet comes in many colors. All varieties will bring much transforming light into your body. This part of Earth, Sonora, is very much at peace with being physical and can bring much appreciation for the very special gift of having a physical body. If you feel discouraged about your life, imagine the golden quality of this crystal's light bringing joy and purpose into it. Or imagine that the Garnet is big enough to climb into, so that it surrounds you with the perfect structure for fitting into the Divine Plan. It will also help you make a more secure connection with your physical body.

25. Selenite from Santa Eulalia, Chihuahua, Mexico.

This particular Selenite specimen focuses energy more sharply than most and can help you direct the multidimensional qualities of the universal flow into whatever part of your light structure or body needs to move more freely. Use it in healing or meditation to direct your attention into using new openings.

26. Tourmaline from Transbaikal, Russia.
The natural crystal is another master and can help you balance all parts of self. It is given here to again help you connect with the mastery of physical existence of which spiritual Russia is a key, as well as to provide a link for support of Russia at less perfected levels.

27. Cavansite from Poona, India.
The color of this mineral is very important. Imagine filling your whole body with it, wash it through, fill your brain with it, send it through you into the Earth and let it radiate from you. It will help you strengthen the electrical flow of love into all aspects of your being. The structural form of the mineral will then take the flow into hard-to-reach parts of self and connect them more securely to your heart and soul.

28. Wulfenite from Maricopa County, Arizona.
These crystals of Wulfenite serve as windows into understanding your power and creativity. Their power point is on the higher etheric level and in the second dimension. This means, on one level, the power it channels on Earth is already integrated into the general creative flow. Its potential, however, is now being utilized at a higher level for energizing the physical bodies of humanity. It is part of the power supporting Earth's evolving use of new vibrational levels in its physical expression. It is supporting the use of the higher energies for creativity at the physical level. Use it to give yourself confidence in your connection to Earth's unlimited sources of creative power.

29. Ruby crystals in matrix from Mysore, India.
These are typical of the Rubies that come from India. They are excellent for elixirs in their natural form. Lovely cabochons are cut from them. They reflect the deep mastery of love that Earth has achieved through this part of India. There is potential there for raising the creative use of love to new levels for Earth. The Rubies are being dispersed in order to link the creative potential of many members of humanity through cooperative projects which will develop and expand it.

30. Rhodochrosite from Catamarca, Argentina.
This is the usual form in which you will see Rhodochrosite. This

specimen expresses the unity of divine will, love and expression which creates with love through the heart center. It can help you understand how to use your heart and love as a source of creative energy. It teaches mastery through using your heart.

31. Azurite and Malachite from Morenci, Arizona.
These two minerals are very similar in composition, so they regularly occur together. This particular arrangement symbolizes the way balanced use of the heart supports balanced thought and use of the mind, spiritual mind, and physical mind. The minerals emanating from Morenci, Arizona, are released by Earth to aid the flow of energy at all levels and to integrate it into your creativity. There is a power point here that integrates the potential of physical matter into divine purpose.

32. Smithsonite from Magdalena, New Mexico.
This is typical of how Smithsonite is found, but its size makes it powerful in its ability to create a spiritual atmosphere. Imagine you can go into the cavity and surround yourself with the cool green. This will be especially helpful for healing emotional trauma and for help in clearing, physically or emotionally. This area of New Mexico is a power point and its minerals are given out by Earth to help distribute the spiritual connection for balanced use of emotions in expanding creativity.

33. Crystal wands made by the author/channel.
The wands are created under the direction of the angels and galactic teachers Dorothy works with, for use in healing and meditation. They form a balanced energy that can be used to calm, energize or balance. Some are quite grounding, others are very uplifting. They can be used to bring energy in or direct it outward. All will support your use of love for self and others. They are an example of how to use crystals in the transformation process.

1. Elbaite (Tourmaline) and Lepidolite from Minas Gerais, Brazil. 4.3 cm. high.
Valares Minerals.

2. Rhodochrosite from Duruman, South Africa. 4.3 cm. high. Pat Hendrick Collection.

3. Calcite and Chalcopyrite from Reynolds Co., Missouri. Crystal 20 cm. long. Canadian Museum of Nature.

4. Quartz var. Smoky from Minas Gerais, Brazil. 17 cm. long. H. Dibble collection.

5. Tektite var. Moldavite from Moldavia, Czechoslavakia. 4.8 cm. long. E. Haiderer collection.

6. Fluorapatite and Quartz from Panasqueira, Portugal. Crystal – 3.8 cm. high. Canadian Museum of Nature.

7. Three varieties of Beryl – Aquamarine from Minas Gerais, Brazil, 6.8 cm.; Heliodor from Minas Gerais, Brazil, 4 cm.; and Emerald from Bauchi, Nigeria, 5.3 cm. Canadian Museum of Nature.

8. Fluorapophylite from Jalgoan, India. 5.8 cm. high. Al Partee Collection.

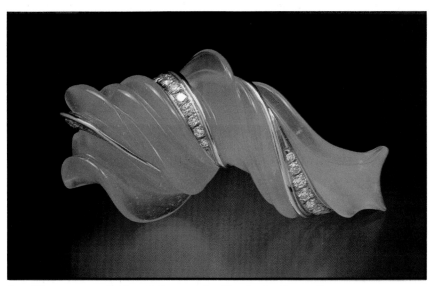

9. Chrysoprase, Gold, and Diamonds. Kerith Graeber collection.

10. Zoisite var. Tanzanite from Arusha, Tanzania. 8.95 karats. Shades of the Earth.

11. Crocoite from Red Lead Mine, Dundas, Tasmania, Australia. 2.9 cm. wide. Rocksmiths.

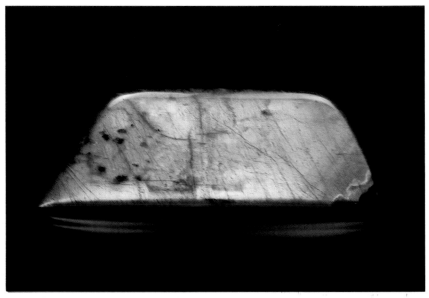

12. Labradorite from Finland. 8.4 cm. long. Si and Ann Frazier Minerals.

13. Quartz var. Herkimer Diamond from Herkimer Co., New York. 6.6 cm. high. M. Zinn collection.

14. Fluorite and Chalcopyrite from Minerva #1 Mine, Hardin Co., Illinois. 13.3 cm. wide. S. Neely Collection.

15. Scheelite, Cassiterite, and Quartz from Chukotka, Russia. 3.6 cm. high. Syntaxis Collection.

16. Vanadinite from Mibladen, Morocco. 4.8 cm. high. M. Zinn collection.

17. Phenacite from Mt. Antero, Chaffee Co., Colorado. 2.9 cm. long. Dave Bunk Minerals.

18. Spodumene var. Kunzite from Nuristan, Afganistan. 17.5 cm long. Canadian Museum of Nature.

19. Quartz var. Amethyst from Mursinka, Ekaterinburg, Russia. Stone — 21x29 mm. crystals — 10.3 cm. long. Fersmann Museum.

20. Left to right, back row: Peridot from Arizona, Zircon, Peridot from Arizona; front row: Chromian Diopside from Russia, Diamond, Ruby from Thailand. Canadian Museum of Nature.

21. Quartz scepter from Fat Jack Mine, Yavapai Co., Arizona. 3.7 cm long. Jeff Scovil collection.

22. Kyanite from Minas Gerais, Brazil. 8.7 cm. high. Private collection.

23. Orthoclase, Carlsbad twin from Oro Grande, New Mexico. 3.2 cm. long. B & A Cook collection.

24. Andradite Garnet from Sonora, Mexico. 1.4 cm. high. Private collection.

25. Gypsum var. Selenite from Potosi Mine, Santa Eulalia, Chihuahua, Mexico.
9 cm. high. Dave Bunk Minerals.

26. Liddicoatite Tourmaline from Malkhanski Mts., Transbaikal, Russia. Fersmann Museum.

27. Cavansite from Poona, India. 1.8 cm. wide. Private collection.

28. Wulfenite from Rowley Mine, Maricopa Co., Arizona. 3.2 cm. wide. George Godas collection.

29. Corundum var. Ruby from Mysore, India. 4.2 cm. high. Canadian Museum of Nature.

30. Rhodochrosite from Catamarca, Argentina. 12.5 cm. wide. M. Zinn collection.

31. Azurite and Malachite from Morenci, Arizona. Field – 3.7 cm. Arizona Mining and Mineral Museum.

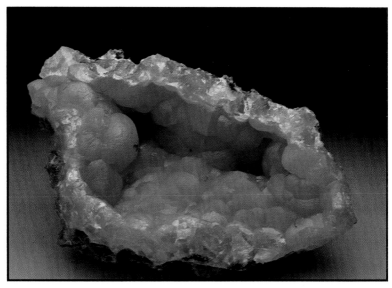

32. Smithsonite from Kelly Mine, Magdalena, New Mexico. 17.4 cm. wide. Arizona Mining and Mineral Museum.

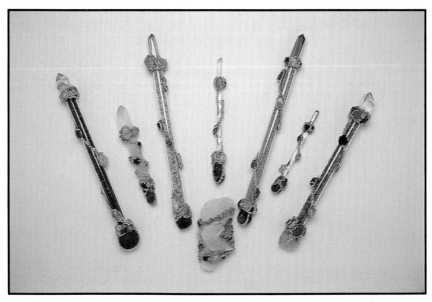

33. Crystal wands made by the author/channel. Six to twelve inches long.

SHINING THE LIGHT SERIES

The Truth about ETs, Alien Bases and the Sinister Secret Government

ZOOSH AND OTHERS THROUGH ROBERT SHAPIRO

Robert Shapiro grew up with the experience of ET contact. Throughout his life there have been communications with beings from several star systems and dimensions. He has been a professional channel for over 25 years, most often channeling Zoosh, who describes himself as the End-Time Historian.

YHWH THROUGH ARTHUR FANNING
(Shining the Light I-IV)

LIGHT TECHNOLOGY
BRINGS YOU THE TRUTH!!
About the Secret Government and their ET Allies/Enemies

For many years you have all wondered, what is that thing that seems to keep things slow? What stops wonderful goals from being accomplished, even if everyone is in favor of them? Is it strictly the things within yourself? Sometimes. Or is it also that there is an invisible network behind many things? These books will attempt to explain the invisible network and give you tangible things you can do to improve the quality of life for yourself and others and to gently, perhaps, but firmly dissolve the stranglehold on your societies by this sinister invisible network that we choose to call in these books the sinister secret government.

—Zoosh through Robert Shapiro

The Shining the Light series exposes the malevolent, controlling and manipulating actions of the sinister secret government (SSG) as it attempt to keep humans from accessing soul and spiritual functions and from ascending into the fourth dimension and beyond. In future books, mentors of humanity will continue to expose the SSG's nefarious dealings, but they will give us step-by-step instructions in the ancient lost arts of benevolent magic—spiritual wizardry—enabling us as creators in training to blend our hearts, minds and souls to become creators of our own destiny and thwart the SSG's goals.

SHINING THE LIGHT III
HUMANITY GETS A SECOND CHANCE

The focus is on humanity as we began to learn to render the sinister secret government powerless by being the light that we are. Earth becomes a member of the Council of Planets and the universe time-shifts to preserve the Explorer Race.

- ✦ Ninth-dimensional Mars
- ✦ ET helicopter pilots
- ✦ Material masters
- ✦ Exploding planets
- ✦ The Photon Belt
- ✦ The null zone
- ✦ Sonic mapping
- ✦ Time collapses
- ✦ Cosmic photographs
- ✦ And more

SOFTCOVER 460P.

$14⁹⁵ ISBN 0-929385-71-3

Chapter Titles:

- Attack on Earth!
- Shadow Government's Technology Beyond Science Fiction
- The Council of Nine (photos)
- Primal Energies/Ancient Forces
- Ancient Visitors in Mexico (photos)
- You Are in the Process of Living Your Book Called Revelations
- Midwest Bombers Manipulated through Time
- Underground Military Resistance Forming against Sinister Secret Government Manipulation
- The Forming of Ninth-Dimensional Mars (photos)
- An ET "Helicopter" Pilot Speaks
- Opportunity to Go Home or Not
- Earth Signed on as Member of Council of Planets
- The Time for Compassion
- A Vehicle from the Atlantean-Lemurian Past (photos)
- A Great Armada of Consciousness
- Sinister Secret Government Terrorist Activity
- The Trail of an Angel (photos)
- To Life!
- October's Hemispheric Change
- The Awakening of Humanity
- You Are a Brilliant Light within and about You
- Sinister Secret Government Forced to Move
- "Ball of Light" in Argentina (from *Manana Del Sur*)
- Calling All Material Masters: This Is the Big One
- Phew!
- Compassion: Use It or Lose It
- A Crack in Time
- Souls of Exploded Planet Pass through Our Reality
- The End of Time-As-You-Have-Known-It
- Humanity Pushed/Pulled/Shoved into Null Zone
- Reasonable Doubt
- The Universe Has Time-Shifted to Preserve the Explorer Race
- Made It through the "Phew"

SHINING THE LIGHT IV
HUMANITY'S GREATEST CHALLENGE

Includes information on Hale-Bopp, SSG, all updates since Volume III and material on the uncreating of Hitler in 1993.

✦ Negative Sirians coming to the third dimension
✦ The express bus to creatorship
✦ The Poison HAARP project
✦ Luciferian traits and critical mass
✦ ETs in Brazil
✦ Comet brings lightbeing-filled vehicle bigger than Earth
✦ Sinister secret government (SSG) under control of beings from the alternate negative future

$14⁹⁵   SOFTCOVER 557P.
ISBN 0-929385-93-4

Chapter Titles:

SHINING THE LIGHT V
HUMANITY IS GOING TO MAKE IT!

Zoosh and others blast the cover off past events and hidden forces at work on this planet and reveal opportunities for immense growth and power. This is a pivotal time as the secrets and mysteries that have so long bewildered humanity are illuminated at last by the light of truth.

✦ Revelations about Area 51 by a rocket scientist ✦ A 75-year-long Zeta restructuring of the past ✦ Cloning: the new ethics forum ✦ Recent UFO activity in the skies ✦ The first humans and the original dark side, our shadow ✦ Angels: guides in training (30% of humans are angels) ✦ Using manifestation powers to avert man-made disasters ✦ The angel of Roswell ✦ Symbiotic spacecraft engines and faster-than-light travel ✦ The true purpose of the Mayans ✦ The SSG downs military planes ✦ The SSG realizes they need customers, not slaves ✦ Grid lines rising above the planet ✦ Homework for changing your past

14^{95} SOFTCOVER 330P.
ISBN 1-891824-00-7

Chapter Titles:

- SSG Realizes That Humanity Must Be Customers, Not Slaves
- Facing the Antichrist within Self Is Humanity's Challenge.
- From Your Light's Point of View, Resistance Is Futile
- SSG, Terrorists and ID Implant: Use Benign Magic to Change That Reality
- How Spirit Works in the Universe
- How to Release Discomfort by Transforming It
- Grid Lines Rising above Planet
- A 45-Day Zeta Restructuring of the Past
- It's Time to Change Your Past
- Cloning: The New Ethics Forum
- HAARP Update
- A Zeta Hybrid Says Thanks
- Archangel Michael
- Notice to All Pilots, and Recent Activity in the Skies: Exotic or Domestic?
- Flash for Computer-Connected Businesses
- 5D Beings Reworking Atmospheric Flux
- Missing U.S. Warplane Chasing UFO
- Flash to Health Professionals
- The True Purpose of the Mayans
- Jump-Starting Humanity's Awakening
- The SSG's Last-Ditch Moves to Prevent Humanity's Awakening

- Zeta Cloning
- Bringing Heart Energy into the Northern Hemisphere
- Authority and Rebellion: Lessons from Creator School
- Unification of Heart Threads Begins
- The Angel of Roswell
- Crop Circles
- Human Earth School Not Possible without Dark Side
- Angels Are Really Guides in Training
- A Message for People Seventeen Years Old and Younger
- Manifestation Powers Peak: The Ultimate Creatorship Training
- SSG Downs Military Planes
- Space-Age Questions
- Education and Medicine
- HAARP Revealed in New Film
- We're Feeling Mother Earth's Energy
- Surfacing Memories
- Art Bell Interview with David Adair: An Adventure at Area 51
- A Deeper Look at Adair's Testimony
- No Catastrophes!

THE EXPLORER RACE SERIES

ZOOSH AND OTHERS THROUGH ROBERT SHAPIRO

Superchannel Robert Shapiro can communicate with any personality anywhere and anywhen. He has been a professional channel for over twenty-five years and channels with an exceptionally clear and profound connection.

The Origin...
The Purpose...The Future...of Humanity

If you have ever wondered about who you really are, why you are here as part of humanity on this miraculous planet and what it all means, these books in the Explorer Race series can begin to supply the answers—the answers to these and other questions about the mystery and enigma of physical life on Earth.

These answers come from beings who speak through superchannel Robert Shapiro, beings who range from particle personalities to the Mother of all Beings and the thirteen Ssjooo, from advisors to the Creator of our universe to the generators of precreation energies. The scope, the immensity, the mind-boggling infinitude of these chronicles by beings who live in realms beyond our imagination, will hold you enthralled. Nothing even close to the magnitude of the depth and power of this all-encompassing, expanded picture of reality has ever been published.

This amazing story of the greatest adventure of all time and creation is the story of the Explorer Race, of which humans are a small but important percentage. The Explorer Race is a group of souls whose journeys resulted in incarnations in this loop of time on planet Earth, where, bereft of any memory of our immortal selves and most of our heart energy. We came to learn compassion, to learn to take responsibility for the consequences of our actions and to solve creation's previously unsolvable dilemma of negativity. We humans have found a use for negativity—we use it for lust for life and adventure, curiosity and creativity, for doing the undoable. And in a few years we will go out to the stars with our insatiable drive and ability to respond to change and begin to inspire the benign but stagnant civilizations out there to expand and change and grow, which will eventually result in the change and expansion of all creation.

Once you understand the saga of the Explorer Race and what the success of the Explorer Race Experiment means to the totality of creation, you will be proud to be human and to know that you are a vital component of the greatest story ever told—a continuing drama whose adventure continues far into the future.

the
EXPLORER
RACE

Zoosh. End-Time Historian
through Robert Shapiro

Book 1...
the EXPLORER RACE

You individuals reading this are truly a result of the genetic experiment on Earth. You are beings who uphold the principles of the Explorer Race. The information in this book is designed to show you who you are and give you an evolutionary understanding of your past that will help you now. The key to empowerment in these days is to not know everything about your past, but to know that which will help you now.

Your souls have been here for a while on Earth and have been trained in Earthlike conditions. This education has been designed so that you would have the ability to explore all levels of responsibility—results, effects and consequences—and take on more responsibilities.

Your number one function right now is your status of Creator apprentice, which you have achieved through years and lifetimes of sweat. You are constantly being given responsibilities by the Creator that would normally be things that Creator would do. The responsibility and the destiny of the Explorer Race is not only to explore, but to create. SOFTCOVER 574P.

$25$⁰⁰ ISBN 0-929385-38-1

Chapter Titles:

THE HISTORY OF THE EXPLORER RACE
• The Genetic Experiment on Earth
• Influences of the Zodiac
• The Heritage from Early Civilizations
• Explorer Race Time Line, Part 1
• Explorer Race Time Line, Part 2
• The Experiment That Failed
GATHERING THE PARTS
• The ET in You: Physical Body
• The ET in You: Emotion and Thought
• The ET in You: Spirit
THE JOY, THE GLORY AND THE CHALLENGE OF SEX
• Emotion Lost: Sexual Addiction in Zeta History
• Sex, Love and Relationships
• Sexual Violence on Earth
• The Third Sex: The Neutral Binding Energy
• The Goddess Energy: The Soul of Creation
ET PERSPECTIVES
• Origin of the Species: A Sirian Perception
• An Andromedan Perspective on the Earth
  Experiment
• The Perspective of Orion Past on Their Role
• Conversation with a Zeta

BEHIND THE SCENES
• The Order: Its Origin and Resolution
• The White Brotherhood, the Illuminati, the New
  Dawn and the Shadow Government
• Fulfilling the Creator's Destiny
• The Sirian Inheritors of Third-Dimensional Earth
TODAY AND TOMORROW
• The Explorer Race Is Ready
• Coming of Age in the Fourth Dimension
• The True Purpose of Negative Energy
• The Challenge of Risking Intimacy
• Etheric Gene-Splicing and the Neutral Particle
• Material Mastery and the New Safety
• The Sterilization of Planet Earth
THE LOST PLANETS
• The Tenth Planet: The Gift of Temptation
• The Eleventh Planet: The Undoer, Key to
  Transformation
• The Twelfth Planet: Return of the Heart Energy
THE HEART OF HUMANKIND
• Moving Beyond the Mind
• Retrieving Heart Energy
• The Creator's Mission and the Function of the
  Human Race

ROBERT SHAPIRO—THE EXPLORER RACE SERIES

Book 2...
ETs and the EXPLORER RACE

In this book, Robert channels Joopah, a Zeta Reticulan now in the ninth dimension, who continues the story of the great experiment—the Explorer Race—from the perspective of his civilization. The Zetas would have been humanity's future selves had not humanity re-created the past and changed the future.

14^{95} SOFTCOVER 237P.
ISBN 0-929385-79-9

Joopah, Zoosh and others through Robert Shapiro

Chapter Titles:
- The Great Experiment: Earth Humanity
- ETs Talk to Contactees
- Becoming One with Your Future Self
- ET Interaction with Humanity
- UFOs and Abductions
- The True Nature of the Grays
- Answering Questions in Las Vegas
- UFO Encounters in Sedona
- Joopah, in Transit, Gives an Overview and Helpful Tools
- We Must Embrace the Zetas
- Roswell, ETs and the Shadow Government
- ETs: Friend or Foe?
- ET Presence within Earth and Human Genetics
- Creating a Benevolent Future
- Bringing the Babies Home

Book 3...ORIGINS and the NEXT 50 YEARS

This volume has so much information about who we are and where we came from—the source of male and female beings, the war of the sexes, the beginning of the linear mind, feelings, the origin of souls—it is a treasure trove. Then in addition there is a section that relates to our near future—how the rise of global corporations and politics affects our future, how to use benevolent magic as a force of creation and then how we will go out to the stars and affect other civilizations. Astounding information.

14^{95} SOFTCOVER 339P.
ISBN 0-929385-95-0

ORIGINS and the NEXT 50 YEARS

Zoosh, End-Time Historian through Robert Shapiro

Chapter Titles:
THE ORIGINS OF EARTH RACES
- Our Creator and Its Creation
- The White Race and the Andromedan Linear Mind
- The Asian Race, the Keepers of Zeta Vertical Thought
- The African Race and Its Sirius/Orion Heritage
- The Fairy Race and the Native Peoples of the North
- The Australian Aborigines, Advisors of the Sirius System
- The Return of the Lost Tribe of Israel
- The Body of the Child, a Pleiadian Heritage
- Creating Sexual Balance for Growth
- The Origin of Souls
THE NEXT 50 YEARS
- The New Corporate Model
- The Practice of Feeling
- Benevolent Magic
- Future Politics
- A Visit to the Creator of All Creators
- Approaching the One
APPENDIX
- The Body of Man/The Body of Woman
ORIGINS OF THE CREATOR
- Beginning This Creation
- Creating with Core Resonances
- Jesus, the Master Teacher
- Recent Events in Explorer Race History
- The Origin of Creator
- On Zoosh, Creator and the Explorer Race
- Fundamentals of Applied 3D Creationism

CREATORS AND FRIENDS
THE MECHANICS OF CREATION

Creators and Zoosh
through Robert Shapiro

Book 4...
CREATORS and FRIENDS
The Mechanics of Creation

Now that you have a greater understanding of who you are in the larger sense, it is necessary to remind you of where you came from, the true magnificence of your being, to have some of your true peers talk to you. You must understand that you are creators in training, and yet you were once a portion of Creator. One could certainly say, without being magnanimous, that you are still a portion of Creator, yet you are training for the individual responsibility of being a creator, to give your Creator a coffee break.

This book will give you peer consultation. It will allow you to understand the vaster qualities and help you remember the nature of the desires that drive any creator, the responsibilities to which that creator must answer, the reaction any creator must have to consequences and the ultimate reward of any creator. This book will help you appreciate all of the above and more. I hope you will enjoy it and understand that maybe more will follow. SOFTCOVER 435P.

$19⁹⁵ ISBN 0-891824-01-5

Chapter Titles:

Book 5...
PARTICLE PERSONALITIES

All around you are the most magical and mystical beings. They are too small for you to see as single individuals, but in groups you know them as the physical matter of your daily life. These particles remember where they have been and what they have done in their long lives. We hear from some of them in this extraordinary book. SOFTCOVER 237P.

$14⁹⁵ ISBN 0-929385-97-7

Chapter Titles:

- A Particle of Gold
- The Model Maker: The Clerk
- The Clerk; a Mountain Lion Particle; a Particle of Liquid Light; and an Ice Particle
- A Particle of Rose Quartz from a Floating Crystal City
- A Particle of Uranium, Earth's Mind
- A Particle of the Great Pyramid's Capstone
- A Particle of the Dimensional Boundary between Orbs

- A Particle of Healing Energy
- A Particle of Courage Circulating through Earth
- A Particle of the Sun
- A Particle of Ninth-Dimensional Fire
- A Particle of Union
- A Particle of the Gold Lightbeing beyond the Orbs
- A Particle of the Tenfold Wizard
- A Particle of This Creator

Book 6...
EXPLORER RACE and BEYOND

With a better idea of how creation works, we go back to the Creator's advisors and receive deeper and more profound explanations of the roots of the Explorer Race. The liquid domain and the Double Diamond portal share lessons given to the roots on their way to meet the Creator of this universe and finally the roots speak of their origins and their incomprehensibly long journey here. SOFTCOVER 360P.

$14⁹⁵ ISBN 1-891824-06-6

Chapter Titles:

- Creator of Pure Feelings and Thoughts, One Circle of Creation
- The Liquid Domain
- The Double-Diamond Portal
- About the Other 93% of the Explorer Race
- Synchronizer of Physical Reality and Dimensions
- The Master of Maybe
- Master of Frequencies and Octaves
- Spirit of Youthful Enthusiasm (Junior) and Master of Imagination
- Zoosh

- The Master of Feeling
- The Master of Plasmic Energy
- The Master of Discomfort
- The Story-Gathering Root Being from the Library of Light/Knowledge
- The Root Who Fragmented from a Living Temple
- The First Root Returns
- Root Three, Companion of the Second Root
- The Temple of Knowledge & the Giver of Inspiration
- The Voice Historian, Who Provided the First Root
- Creator of All That Is

Book 9...EXPLORER RACE and JESUS

The immortal personality who lived the life we know as Jesus, along with his students and friends, describes with clarity and love his life and teaching on Earth 2000 years ago. These beings lovingly offer their experiences of the events that happened then and of Jesus' time-traveling adventures, especially to other planets and to the nineteenth and twentieth centuries, which he called the time of the machines—the time of the troubles. So heartwarming and interesting, you won't want to put it down.

14^{95} ISBN 1-891824-14-7

Chapter Titles:

- Jesus' Core Being, His People and the Interest in Earth of Four of Them
- Jesus' Life on Earth
- Jesus' Home World, Their Love Creations and the Four Who Visited Earth
- The "Facts" of Jesus' Life Here, His Future Return
- The Teachings and Travels
- A Student's Time with Jesus and His Tales of Jesus' Time Travels
- The Shamanic Use of the Senses

- The Child Student Who Became a Traveling Singer-Healer
- Other Journeys and the Many Disguises
- Jesus' Autonomous Parts, His Bloodline and His Plans
- Learning to Invite Matter to Transform Itself
- Inviting Water, Singing Colors
- Learning to Teach Usable Skills
- Learning about Different Cultures and People
- The Role of Mary Magdalene, a Romany
- Traveling and Teaching People How to Find Things

Book 10...EXPLORER RACE: EARTH HISTORY and LOST CIVILIZATIONS EXPLAINED

Zoosh reveals that our planet Earth did not originate in this solar system, but the water planet we live on was brought here from Sirius 65 million years ago. Anomalous archaeological finds and the various ET cultures who founded what we now call lost civilizations are explained with such storytelling skill by Speaks of Many Truths that you feel you were there!

14^{95} ISBN 1-891824-20-1
(to be published late 2001)

Chapter Titles:

- Lost Civilizations of Planet Earth in Sirius
- Ancient Artifacts Explained
- Ancient Visitors and Immortal Personalities
- Before and after Earth Was Moved to This Solar System from Sirius
- The Long Journey of Jehovah's Ship, from Orion to Sirius to Earth
- Jehovah Creates Human Beings
- Beings from the Future Academy
- Sumer
- Nazca Lines
- Easter Island
- Laetoli Footprints

- Egypt and Cats
- Three More Civilizations
- Medicine Wheels
- Stonehenge
- Carnac in Brittany
- Egypt
- China
- Tibet and Japan
- Siberia
- Natural Foods/Sacrament of Foods
- SSG's Time-Traveling Interference in Israel Imperils Middle East: How to Resolve It

THE EXPLORER RACE SERIES—ROBERT SHAPIRO

Book 11...EXPLORER RACE: ET VISITORS to EARTH SPEAK

Even as you are searching the sky for extraterrestrials and their space ships, ETs are here on planet Earth—they are stranded, visiting, exploring, studying the culture, healing the Earth of trauma brought on by irresponsible mining or researching the history of Christianity over the last 2000 years. Some are in human guise, some are in spirit form, some look like what we call animals as they come from the species' home planet and interact with those of their fellow beings that we have labeled cats or cows or elephants. Some are brilliant cosmic mathematicians with a sense of humor presently living here as penguins; some are fledgling diplomats training for future postings on Earth when we have ET embassies here. In this book, these fascinating beings share their thoughts, origins and purposes for being here.

14^{95} ISBN 1-891824-28-7

Chapter Titles:

- Stranded Sirian Lightbeing Observes Earth for 800 Years
- An Orion Being Talks about Life on Earth as a Human
- Sensient Redwood
- Quah Earth Religion Researcher
- Visitor to Earth Talks about Pope Pius XII
- Observer Helps Cats Accomplish Their Purpose: Initiating
- A Warrior of Light, the Ultimate Ally
- Penguins: Humorous Mathematicians
- Xri from the Ninth Dimension
- Nurturing the Birth Cord
- Sixth Dimensional Cha-Cha Dances with Humans
- Starlight for Regeneration of Earth's Crystal Veins
- Starlight for Regeneration of Earth's Crystal Veins
- ET Resource Specialists Map and Heal Planetary Bodies
- The Creation and Preparation of the Resource Specialists' Ships Part 3
- Future Zeta Diplomat Learns to Communicate with Humans
- Warrior of Light
- Sirius Water-Being—A Bridge between ETs and Humans
- The Rock-Being Here to Experience Movement
- We Need Benevolent Alien Implants to Go to the Stars
- Ketchin-sa—ET in Dog Form
- Balanced Beings Attempt to Remove Earth Beings' Discomfort